PRESENTED TO:

———————————————————————————————

By:

———————————————————————————————

EMBRACING
Faith

365 DEVOTIONS®
A Devotional Journal

Standard®
PUBLISHING

Cincinnati, Ohio

Published by Standard Publishing, Cincinnati, Ohio
www.standardpub.com

Copyright © 2010 by Standard Publishing

Printed in: United States of America
Project editor: Margaret Williams
Cover design: FaceOut Studio
Interior design: Andrew Quach

ISBN 978-0-7847-2934-2

15 14 13 12 11 10   1 2 3 4 5 6 7 8 9

January

His name alone is exalted; his splendor is above the earth and the heavens.

—Psalm 148:13

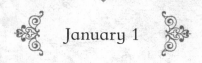

Celebrate!

Have the Israelites celebrate the Passover *(Numbers 9:2).*

Scripture: Numbers 9:1-5

The Israelites were commanded to celebrate the Passover, their deliverance from Egypt. It's crazy, but sometimes—even most of the time—people need to be reminded to celebrate: to appreciate, to be thankful, to remember.

Celebrations are fun but often mean a lot of work. For example, the Passover feast required many preparations. Lambs had to be slaughtered, and other specific rituals precisely followed. Concerning the Passover, verse 3 says to "celebrate it at the appointed time, at twilight on the fourteenth day of this month, in accordance with all its rules and regulations." Most celebrations don't have to be so elaborate, but they still require a concerted effort to make them meaningful.

Surprisingly, celebration comes hard for many Christians. Rather than being party people, we're often seen as sober killjoys. Yet of all people, we have the best reasons to celebrate, for God has come into our world by His Son to bring us new life. And if we are going to celebrate that, then New Year's Day is a great time to start!

> *Lord, throughout the coming year, help me remember who You are and what You have done—and respond in celebration. In Jesus' name, amen.*

_____

_____

_____

_____

_____

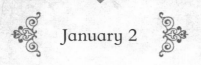

Passed Over

When I see the blood, I will pass over you *(Exodus 12:13)*.

Scripture: Exodus 12:11-14

"Duck, duck, duck, duck, *goose!*" As a child playing Duck Duck Goose, I never liked being the goose. In that situation, I considered being "passed over" a good thing. The Jews celebrated a feast called Passover, commemorating their release from Egyptian bondage. Why that name? The Israelites' release occurred after the final plague, the death of Egypt's firstborn. The firstborn of the Israelites were spared because their families obeyed God and put lamb's blood on the door frames of their homes, a sign for the death angel to "pass over" them.

God's essential character of holiness and justice won't allow Him to merely pass over our sins as if nothing has happened. Christians are indeed forgiven, however, because of the blood of their Passover Lamb, Jesus Christ. Thus, like the Israelites escaping the tyranny of Egyptian slavery, we are freed from the eternal consequences of our sins. By His blood, we escape the impossible tyranny of attempting to earn God's acceptance by good works. As the writer to the Hebrews put it: "He entered the Most Holy Place once for all by his own blood, having obtained eternal redemption" (Hebrews 9:12).

> *God, I breathe a sigh of relief at being passed over, escaping the judgment for sin. Praise You for sending Jesus, my Passover lamb! May I always live gratefully and obediently, in light of His sacrifice. In His name, amen.*

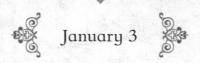

Got Some Growing Up to Do?

The child grew and became strong; he was filled with wisdom, and the grace of God was upon him *(Luke 2:40).*

Scripture: Luke 2:39-45

It was a simple, loving act springing from the innocent heart of a little girl. Without saying a word, she walked over to my father and unlocked the seat belt he was having trouble unfastening from a fun-park ride. It was a gesture of the heart, not done for a sticker or a prize.

A child's tender, trusting heart is often more gracious than our own. For example, young children usually aren't as skeptical as we adults are. When words come from a trusted source, such as a parent or a teacher, children believe what they are told. They haven't yet been scarred by the deceptions of the unscrupulous.

We, as adults, need to regain a simple trust in God and His Word. Jesus himself, in His human nature, had to grow in wisdom and maturity—and respond positively to the grace that came from the Father. We may be adults, but I suspect we each have such growing up to do. The key, for us, is to keep our hearts open to all that God desires to do within us and through us. It's the only way to grow strong in the spiritual life.

> *Dear God, help me recapture the wonder, purity, and innocence of a child-like trust in Your goodness and guidance. I long to be filled with Your wisdom and motivated by Your Kingdom plans. And by Your grace, let me act graciously toward others, as well. Thank You, in Jesus' name. Amen.*

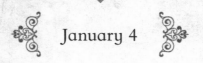

An Amazing God

Everyone who heard him was amazed *(Luke 2:47)*.

Scripture: Luke 2:46-50

Even as a mere boy, Jesus wowed people by what He said and did. These same reactions would follow Jesus throughout His adult life: "The people were amazed at his teaching" (Mark 1:22). "The disciples were amazed at his words" (Mark 10:24). "The men were amazed and asked, 'What kind of man is this?'" (Matthew 8:27).

In a time of cold religion and oppressive rules, Jesus' insights into God's law and character refreshed the weary. Christ's authentic walk with God contrasted with the stagnant lives of many religious leaders of the day. His compassion toward the unpopular and unattractive astonished people who were used to harsh judgment.

Jesus' miracles? Naturally, they produced surprise and elation. And both His crucifixion and resurrection, though unexpected and shocking, resulted in whispers of awe and shouts of freedom.

Today we still stand in awe of the Master. We're astonished at Jesus' ability to transform messed-up lives. We're humbled by His pity and love for us. We're simply amazed by His grace.

Heavenly Father, I'm amazed not only by Your ability to save me from the penalty of my sins but by Your unconditional willingness to do so. By Your Son You have adopted me into Your family and given me Your indwelling Holy Spirit. I will stand amazed forever! Through Christ, amen.

_____

_____

_____

_____

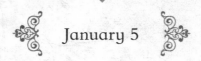

January 5

Perfect Obedience

Then he went down to Nazareth with them and was obedient to them *(Luke 2:51).*

Scripture: Luke 2:51, 52

What are those last words of reminder (or warning) so often uttered by parents before departing from their children? "Be good!"

Whether Mary and Joseph ever said these words to Jesus is unknown. One thing we do know: Our text records that Jesus was an obedient child.

Jesus' perfect childhood obedience, however, isn't just a nice little note in the Gospel text. That obedience was crucial to the plan of salvation. Without His having lived a perfect human life, Jesus would not have been qualified to serve as the unblemished lamb of God who would take away the sins of the world (see John 1:29).

Even at this early period in the life of Christ, the perfection that would be exchanged for the penalty of our sins was in full development. When Jesus died, He took our sins and gave us His righteous standing before God. When our heavenly Father sees us, He sees us as perfectly obedient sons and daughters. His obedience has become our obedience. It's the only way we could ever be good enough for Heaven.

Lord, because You are good I am accounted good, though I know my daily life often shows otherwise. By Your grace may I strive to be in practice what I have already become in position. Through Christ, amen.

_____

_____

_____

_____

_____

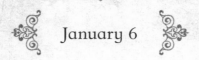

January 6

Why Limit the Praise?

Praise him, sun and moon, praise him, all you shining stars (*Psalm 148:3*).

Scripture: *Psalm 148:1-6*

Mankind walking on the moon, rovers roaming the surface of Mars, and now an unmanned spacecraft on its way to Pluto—these are marvelous feats, but they only reach the outer fringes of one solar system in God's vast universe.

Ever wonder why God created galaxies that no one may ever see? Perhaps it's simply because He can. When we stop to consider the seemingly infinite size of the universe, we realize how awesome and mighty its Creator must be. In Psalm 8:3, 4, King David says, "When I consider your heavens, the work of your fingers, the moon and the stars, which you have set in place, what is man that you are mindful of him?" A big universe proclaims a big God.

The enormous size of the universe also serves as a reminder of the limitlessness of God's attributes: His unlimited love, unlimited grace, and unlimited forgiveness for those who believe. Such infinite attributes remind us that God deserves . . . our unlimited praise.

> ***Lord God of Creation,*** *when I see the stars I am reminded of how big You are and how small I am in comparison. I acknowledge that You alone are the King of the Universe, and I invite You to make my soul, more and more, a territory fully conquered by Your loving reign. In the name of the Father, the Son, and the Holy Spirit, I pray. Amen.*

_____

_____

_____

_____

_____

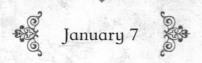

No Fair?

Be still before the Lord and wait patiently for him; do not fret when men succeed in their ways, when they carry out their wicked schemes *(Psalm 37:7).*

Scripture: Psalm 37:1-11

A big-rig truck driver was lying in his hospital bed, worried not about his recovery from a rollover but about how he would pay the hospital bill. His company refused to pay for his treatment. He was being held at fault for the accident caused by a load shift—even though he hadn't loaded the flatbed. More fines to pay and more points on his license. "It's not fair!" he shouted, startling the nurse working at his side. Here was the end of a career.

We all face an unfair life, in which ruthless and unprincipled people may well prosper while honest folk will suffer. Yet God's counsel to us is patience. Just be still and wait.

How hard to do! We want to "get back at them, and make them pay." But God says, "Wait." This approach will pay off—eventually—as a glimpse at the final verse of today's reading clearly reveals: "The meek will inherit the land and enjoy great peace." Let us trust God to right the wrongs, in His way, in His time.

O God, You are so gracious in the midst of an ungracious world. Thank You that judgment does not rest on our shoulders. In Jesus' name, amen.

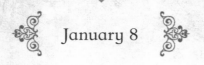

January 8

Stop That!

Do not hate your brother in your heart. Rebuke your neighbor frankly so you will not share in his guilt *(Leviticus 19:17).*

Scripture: Leviticus 19:17, 18

Her 18-year-old stepbrother was headed for her younger brother with hatred in his eyes. Ten-year-old Jana stepped between them. "Don't hit him; he's little." Jason took another step closer, with Jana the first in line for a punch.

Hearing the ruckus, Jason's father rushed into the room. "Stop that!"

Jason halted, then whirled around and left the room. Jana was shaking. "Jana, you should have called me. You can't stop Jason by yourself," her stepfather said as he hugged both of the younger children.

The scene moved me to reflect: While trying to right the wrongs of the world, don't we often neglect to call upon the one who can save both us and our brothers from abuse? We may be called to rebuke the raging hater, but we must allow only our Father to chasten him. What a fine line between protecting the weak and usurping God's role! Thankfully, we can learn to let go of grudges and allow Him to fulfill—in His way and time—His promise: "It is mine to avenge; I will repay" (Romans 12:19).

Dear Father, how like a child I act, rushing into Your role! Help me distinguish between standing up for the right and overstepping Your authority. For You alone are the only perfect judge. In Christ's name, amen.

_____

_____

_____

_____

_____

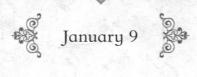

Good for Evil?

I tell you who hear me: Love your enemies, do good to those who hate you *(Luke 6:27).*

Scripture: *Luke 6:27, 28*

Cindy questioned every decision I made. She clothed it as "constructive criticism," but it felt like insubordination. It was hard for me to lead a group of 12 support staff in our office, providing motivation, training, and encouragement to them. Cindy's constant carping undermined my confidence and leadership. I often heard secondhand complaints about her grumbling.

It was time for salary reviews. Our support staff was woefully underpaid, so I went to the CEO on their behalf. He asked whether I thought all of my staff people were working up to their potential. Here was my chance to let him know of Cindy's uncooperative spirit! Somehow, though, God stilled my voice, and I was able to recommend raises for all of them. Cindy never knew that her raise came because I went to bat for her.

It's hard to bless those who curse us. It's even more difficult to pray for them. I do pray for Cindy, since her work habits will no doubt land her in trouble some day. I also pray for myself, that I can love her in spite of my own hurt. After all, Jesus loves and blesses me, even when I fail Him.

Father, it is because of Your Son's intercession for me that I am right with You. Help me learn to love as You love. Through Christ my Lord, amen.

_____

_____

_____

_____

_____

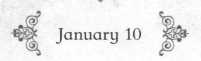

Above and Beyond

If someone strikes you on one cheek, turn to him the other also. If someone takes your cloak, do not stop him from taking your tunic *(Luke 6:29).*

Scripture: *Luke 6:29, 30*

Have you ever been honored for going "above and beyond"? One company I worked for gave unexpected monetary awards to employees who performed well beyond their job descriptions. Of course, those extra tasks were usually done voluntarily and willingly. Still, it was nice to be recognized. And it was exciting to have senior management troop into one's office, smiling—and bearing an envelope with cash inside.

Jesus deals with a different situation: the times when we're coerced and mistreated. Even under duress we are to go above and beyond what is required of us. Under these circumstances, we will not be rewarded or even recognized—at least not by our tormentors! In fact, we may be ridiculed for being easy prey.

However, we are to yield willingly, offering more than is required. The reward comes not from those around us but from Jesus himself. He understands the stress we endure, and He recognizes our sacrifice. He too was coerced but willingly acquiesced for our benefit.

Father, *life often requires more of me than I expect. Help me to look beyond my own "rights." May I willingly lay down my possessions to be generous, in Your name, even to those who exploit me. Through Jesus, amen.*

_____

_____

_____

_____

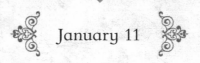

Treat Them Right

Do to others as you would have them do to you *(Luke 6:31).*

Scripture: Luke 6:31

Yesterday my husband came home irritated at the day's events. My child was angry with an apparently unfair world, and my mother complained about her arthritis acting up again.

Why don't they just get over it? I thought. Everybody has troubles, but I wish they wouldn't take it out on me.

Today I'm the one irritated, angry, and complaining. Without a word, my husband gives me a hug. My daughter offers to clean up the kitchen. My mother smiles and pats my cheek. All this kindness bothers me a bit. Why? Because they are treating me the way they wanted me to treat them the day before.

Often I would like to rewind the tape of life a couple of days. I would offer my husband a glass of iced tea and a quiet moment in his recliner. I would allow my child to vent his understandable frustrations in a safe environment. I would offer my mother a cup of hot cocoa and a gentle back rub.

But life doesn't rewind! I need to respond to opportunities as they arise— the privilege of simply treating others as I would like to be treated.

God, forgive my impatience with family members. Help me feel their pain and respond in the same way I want them to respond to me. In this small way, let me be a servant in Your name. Through Christ I pray. Amen.

_____

_____

_____

_____

_____

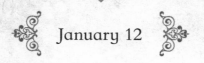

Generosity

Love your enemies, do good to them, and lend to them without expecting to get anything back. Then your reward will be great, and you will be sons of the Most High, because he is kind to the ungrateful and wicked *(Luke 6:35)*.

Scripture: Luke 6:34-36

We tend to think of generosity in connection with our friends or family. As usual, Jesus turns our thinking upside down: He expects us to be generous to our enemies.

First, then, we must identify whom we consider to be an enemy. Is it a coworker, a neighbor, a government agent, a foreigner, a wealthy oppressor? Then we must ask, "How can I be generous to this person?"

One way is simply to be liberal with forgiveness. What greater or more costly gift can we offer someone than our complete forgiveness, whether or not they request it? Another way is to supply what is lacking. If my adversary needs anything I can offer, Jesus tells me to provide it without expecting repayment. And how about imparting an unexpected kindness—a helping hand, a meal, a smile, or an encouraging word?

The supreme gift, though, is love. Can I sincerely love my enemy as I love my family or myself? If I can do that, I am truly reflecting the character of God. As His child, I have "inherited" His traits of kindness and mercy.

Dear Giver of Everything, I want to emulate Your unconditional love. Help me see every enemy as a potential friend. In Jesus' name, amen.

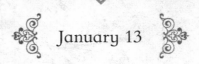
Ultimate Safety Net

The salvation of the righteous comes from the LORD; he is their stronghold in time of trouble *(Psalm 37:39).*

Scripture: Psalm 37:35-40

In 1989 a powerful earthquake shook San Francisco. Highways collapsed in tiers, sandwiching vehicles and drivers between layers of concrete. Buildings erupted in flames, sending firework-like embers skyward. Humanity poured out of downtown buildings, fleeing destruction.

It wasn't a good time for us to be visiting the city! Engulfed in a throng of commuters trying to get home, we didn't know the area well enough to navigate the interruptions in public transportation so we could return to our hotel many miles away. We were vulnerable to physical danger and to opportunists who might see a chance to exploit some naive out-of-towners.

After several hours of wandering the streets, we came upon a hotel employee who offered us a place to spend the night in the reinforced basement of his brand new hotel. We were safe once again.

Earthquake-like trials of life can assault us to the point that we become extremely vulnerable. The ruthless seem to flourish during these times, but we flounder. Yet God promises us a refuge during both physical and emotional upheavals. He alone is our place of ultimate safety.

Dear Father, thank You for being my refuge in the time of trial. Help me let go of my self-sufficiency and turn only to You. In Jesus' name, amen.

_____

_____

_____

_____

_____

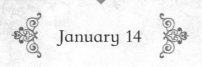

Shields Up!

The LORD is my strength and my shield; my heart trusts in him, and I am helped *(Psalm 28:7).*

Scripture: *Psalm 28:6-9*

A starship glides gracefully through the eternal night of outer space. It passes through fields of stars, smearing streaks of light against the velvety blackness. All is serene. Without warning, an unseen enemy dives to the attack, pummeling the spacecraft with powerful lasers that could rip the ship in half. The seasoned crew reacts instantly, raising an invisible force field as thunderous explosions rock the craft.

It might be a scene from any science fiction movie. In reality, Christians are much like that starship crew sailing through the black night. Our unseen enemy lurks, watching for a vulnerable moment, seeking to exploit our weaknesses. He targets our lives, minds, and emotions. Yet an invisible force field surrounds believers with an impenetrable protection that also fortifies from within. Nothing can pass through the shield except that which our Father allows. He is stronger than every enemy and will see us through our dark night.

O Lord, You are El Shaddai, Almighty God, and there is no other like You. My heart sings for joy, knowing that no plan of Yours can be thwarted. Thank You for shielding me on every side. In Jesus' name, amen.

_____

_____

_____

_____

_____

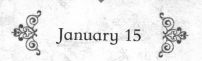
Prodigal to Prayer

One day Jesus was praying in a certain place. When he finished, one of his disciples said to him, "Lord, teach us to pray, just as John taught his disciples" *(Luke 11:1).*

Scripture: Luke 11:1-4

"Lying, stealing, gambling, novel-reading, licentiousness, extravagance, and almost every form of sin was indulged in by him," wrote biographer J. Gilchrist Lawson. "No one would have imagined that the sinful youth would ever become eminent for his faith in God and for his power in prayer."

Who was this miserable sinner? None other than the great nineteenth-century "prayer warrior" George Mueller—and that was before he went to jail for cheating an innkeeper out of a week's rent! In his own words, Mueller says of his youthful days: "I cared nothing for the Word of God."

Eventually, though, Mueller became known for never mentioning his needs to others; he laid everything before God with constant, patient intercession. And he kept precise records of his requests, to prove to the world that there is a God who hears His people.

Jesus had taught Mueller to pray. He will do the same for us, if we come to Him with an open heart, no matter the current state of our lives.

Lord, teach me to pray with a humble and contrite spirit, that those around me will see Your faithfulness when You answer. In Jesus' name, amen.

_____

_____

_____

_____

_____

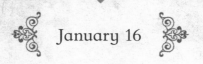

January 16

Be Bold

I tell you, though he will not get up and give him the bread because he is his friend, yet because of the man's boldness he will get up and give him as much as he needs *(Luke 11:8).*

Scripture: Luke 11:5-8

Two girls wanted to go to the local mall one Saturday. "Let's ask my father," said one.

"Oh, no! He'll be angry," the second girl replied. The first girl was puzzled. "Why would he be angry with us, just for asking?"

"Well . . . what if he says no?" The second girl's voice quavered a little. Her friend shrugged her shoulders. "Then he says no. He does sometimes. So what? He'll say yes if he can."

We sometimes fear to ask our heavenly Father for the desires of our hearts, as if we're suspicious of His reaction. Will He strike us down if we ask with wrong motives? Will He be angry if we request something we don't really need? Will He answer no? (We don't always ask wisely, and sometimes the answer *ought* to be no.) But God invites us to ask boldly. He knows our motives are less than pure. Still He loves us. And can't we trust this wonderful Father to sort our imperfect prayers and do whatever is best?

My Abba, even the finest earthly father can't approach Your wisdom, patience, kindness, and love. Help me to keep my needs and desires before You, that our relationship might grow ever deeper. Through Christ, amen.

_____

_____

_____

_____

_____

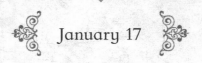

January 17

Too Easy?

Everyone who asks receives; he who seeks finds; and to him who knocks, the door will be opened *(Luke 11:10).*

Scripture: Luke 11:9-12

A woman stood in the darkness before the large, well-lit house. Snow encrusted the toes of her costly leather boots. She had been making her unsteady way home when someone told her about a great party at this house.

She was told, though, that she had to change her clothes to join this gathering. "I paid a lot of money for my outfit," she mumbled, watching a straggly teenaged girl knock and then boldly step over the threshold into the bright interior. She folded her arms around herself, indignant, and kicked the snow from her boots.

Laughter and music flooded into the street each time the door swung wide to admit another. She watched a white-robed woman gently assist a grimy man still reeling with drink. "They'll let *anybody* in there!" It was dark, and growing colder. The hour was late. She should go home and forget about these freaks. Still, those leaving the house looked so peaceful. It seemed too easy—knock, walk in, join the party. The woman frowned, and the worry lines marring her brow deepened.

> *Gracious Lord, may I never cease to wonder at Your wholehearted invitation to me—filthy rags and all. Thank You for clothing me in your righteousness through Your matchless grace. Please keep me alert to assist those still standing in the darkness. Through Christ I pray. Amen.*

_____

_____

_____

_____

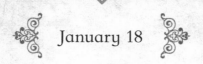
Someone's Daughter

I tell you the truth, anyone who will not receive the kingdom of God like a little child will never enter it (*Luke 18:17*).

Scripture: Luke 18:1-17

Her world is crashing around her, but Rachel hardly notices. She is three years old, and she's known only deep love and protection. Blissfully unaware of the trauma rocking her mother, Rachel spins and twirls in a joyful dance choreographed by her trusting heart. The weary mother watches her daughter. "Like a child," she thinks.

Rachel has no worries. All will be well because Mommy is here. Mommy guards her from monsters in the night, comforts her when she's sad, and gives her everything she needs. Mommy is always there, and somehow she always knows just what to do.

If only that were true! The young woman's shoulders sag with the weight of it all. Bewildering fears and dire possibilities clutch her mind and drag her down into a swamp of confusion. "I can't do this," she thinks. Rachel twirls up to her mother, plants a warm kiss on her cheek, and then leaps away again, laughing. For a moment, the ache eases, and the young woman remembers that she, too, is Someone's daughter.

Father, help me remember that I am Your child. You love me with an everlasting love. You are always here, and always know what to do. I will dance with joy for such a Father. I will curl into Your strong arms and trust. I love You, my good Papa. In the name of Your Son, my Savior, I pray. Amen.

_____

_____

_____

_____

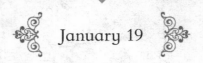

January 19

What a Great Day!

When the day of Pentecost came, they were all together in one place *(Acts 2:1).*

Scripture: Luke 11:13; Acts 2:1-4

Behind a wall of shimmering heat, the lioness patiently stalks her prey—a large herd of antelope. There is strength in the unity of the herd, so she cannot attack them all at once. She might be trampled to death if she tried. She lurks until a single antelope strays from the safety of the herd. Only then does the lioness purr in anticipation of her feast. She crouches, gathering her strength for the chase, and launches her brutal attack.

The enemy of our souls also knows the power of unity. He seeks to divide in order to destroy us, one by one. Though each of us walks through life seemingly alone, no believer is ever truly alone. Our spirits gather at the Lord's table, and as we kneel before His glorious throne. Believers across the entire earth sing His praise as if from one throat.

Every follower of Jesus is part of a mighty fellowship that will never be broken. As our hearts gather in worship, His Spirit flows through us, and each of us is strengthened. All because of Pentecost, a great day indeed!

Dear Lord, thank You for sending Your Spirit to strengthen and encourage us until we all go Home. Help the family of believers always be all together in one place spiritually, so that You may work Your perfect plan through us. In the holy name of Jesus, my Lord and Savior, I pray. Amen.

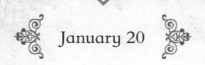

January 20

Authentic Life

Blessed are they who maintain justice, who constantly do what is right *(Psalm 106:3).*

Scripture: Psalm 106:1-3

Once there lived an influential man. At first glance, no one would think him a person of importance. He possessed only modest means, dressing neatly but with no great style. He lived quietly in a humble home with a sweet-tempered wife, and he never did anything extraordinary. Yet when the man passed away, people came by the hundreds to pay their respects to his widow.

"Your husband was a good man," someone said. "I was in trouble once, and he was the only one to help me."

"I respected your husband more than anyone I've ever met," said another. "I don't remember ever hearing him speak an unkind word about anyone."

Another commented with a puzzled look, "He always seemed so peaceful, even when I knew he had troubles of his own." And one woman approached the widow with tears pooling in her eyes. "I always wanted to ask . . . what made your husband so different?"

To all these the widow smiled and replied, "My husband had a wise and faithful Friend. Come to our home this Sunday. I'll introduce you." And she did.

__Dear Lord,__ I ask that Your sweet fragrance saturate my life and draw seekers closer to You. Help me love You above all and live authentically for the sake of those who are watching. Thank You, in Jesus' name. Amen.

_____

_____

_____

_____

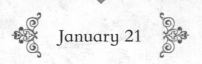

Supposed Friends

Free me from the trap that is set for me, for you are my refuge. Into your hands I commit my spirit; redeem me, O LORD, the God of truth *(Psalm 31:4, 5).*

Scripture: Psalm 31:1-5

It seems strange now, but many years ago I found myself under surveillance as a scientist in a large company. The secret observation wasn't for something I had done but because of someone who worked in the laboratory with me. The young man had a family, a job, and was going to school at night to do even better. I often wondered how he had enough energy to do everything. One day the police came and took him away.

A comment he made a few days earlier struck me: "I shouldn't have trusted my supposed friends; they just used me." I later discovered that his friends were making and selling illegal drugs.

Psalm 31 is a study in contrasts. There is evil around us in the world and in people's hearts; we can get trapped. In contrast, there is the Lord, God of truth and love. Jesus entered this world of lies and deceit, but in dying He preached the message of a father He could trust—"Father, into your hands I commit my spirit" (Luke 23:46).

Lord, I am so thankful that in You there is no deception. I commit my whole life into Your hands. All praise to You, in Christ's name. Amen.

_____

_____

_____

_____

_____

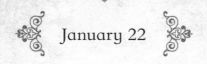

Of Great Worth

Consider the ravens: They do not sow or reap, they have no storeroom or barn; yet God feeds them. And how much more valuable you are than birds! *(Luke 12:24).*

Scripture: Luke 12:22-24

My children love our young cat. They feed, hug, and spoil him constantly. So when he was about to die this past year, we had a very sad household. My wife and I spent a fairly large amount of money to save him. He was worth it—because he was loved.

Jesus told His disciples not to worry. Yet I still find that at times my mind is weighed down. Worries sneak in on me from all kinds of insecurities—like when I'm approaching my yearly performance appraisal at work.

Jesus started His teaching on worry with the key to breaking free. The key is our worth, our value, in God's eyes. Each and every one of us is a great and precious joy to God. If I provided an operation for a family cat, how much more will my heavenly Father take care of me?

And, of course, worry is mostly just a pure waste of emotional energy. As one anonymous quipster once put it: "Don't tell me that worry doesn't do any good. I know better; the things I worry about *never* happen."

Heavenly Father, I accept the truth of Your Word that You love and care for me deeply. Let my burdens fall from my shoulders this day. Let my anxious thoughts be replaced by thoughts of Your care. Thank You, Lord, for Your great and awesome love. I pray through my deliverer, Jesus. Amen.

_____

_____

_____

_____

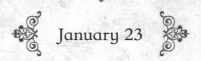

Always a Majority

Who of you by worrying can add a single hour to his life? Since you cannot do this very little thing, why do you worry about the rest? *(Luke 12:25, 26).*

Scripture: Luke 12:25, 26

I read the other day that the word *worry* comes from an old Anglo-Saxon word meaning "to strangle or choke." In my teens I woke one night unable to breathe because my sinuses and lungs were congested. After several minutes of gasping for air, I came through those scary moments, with the help of my parents. However, a deep worry filled my mind for years.

And, recently, after pushing myself and taking on too many commitments, I started having panic attacks. My throat would tighten up, and I worried about breathing. Apparently the old fear was still there.

Jesus taught that worry can't add anything to our lives, not even an hour. Yet, for God to add an hour is a simple thing. And for God to help us move through any tough circumstance—could that ever be too hard for Him?

As I have meditated upon the truths in these Scriptures about worry, I have felt my worries disappear. As the old saying goes: "Me plus God always equals a majority."

Dear Heavenly Father, I praise You for Your awesome power. Since nothing is too hard for You, let me not be anxious but at peace, knowing that my life is in Your infinitely capable hands. I pray this prayer in the name of Jesus, my merciful Savior and Lord. Amen.

_____

_____

_____

_____

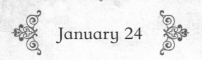

January 24

Growing Beautiful

Consider the lilies, how they grow: they neither toil nor spin; and yet I say to you, even Solomon in all his glory was not arrayed like one of these *(Luke 12:27, New King James Version).*

Scripture: Luke 12:27, 28

Every year I plant flower seeds, and they turn into beautiful, blossoming plants. It amazes me—all of that beauty lies within every tiny seed. The seeds had no say about how they'd be planted, nor the soil they would inhabit, nor how well (or not!) I might care for them. Nor did the seeds produce their own beauty from scratch. God had already placed that potential within them.

What of us? Jesus said we must fall to the ground and die spiritually (John 12:24), be born again of the Spirit (John 3:3), and grow into the image of Jesus Christ (Ephesians 4:15). These things don't arise from our natural humanity or come about by self-effort; they are all of God, all of His grace.

It's true that we are made in the image of God, thus we have intelligence, personality, and will inherent within us. But the ability to save ourselves by "toiling" always escapes us. Like the lilies, if we are to grow beautiful in God's sight, it must be His work alone.

Father, You are at work conforming me to the beautiful likeness of Your Son, Jesus. Day by day, let me rely upon Your grace, being confident of this very thing, that He who has begun a good work in me will complete it until the day of Jesus Christ. In His name, amen.

_____

_____

_____

_____

_____

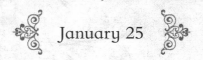
God Gave Favor

Seek the kingdom of God, and all these things shall be added to you *(Luke 12:31, New King James Version).*

Scripture: Luke 12:29-31

There just wasn't enough time each week in my schedule to do all I wanted for God, so I decided to try to work three days as a scientist instead of five. I fasted and prayed. My wife agreed. Then doors opened, I found favor where there usually was none, and my request was approved. My pay and pension were cut accordingly.

The following year, the company I worked for announced that there would be no raises. God then extended more grace. You see, even though I was only working part time in a competitive field, I was given a promotion. It included a raise. Even better, with the promotion to a higher position I was considered *underpaid*—and was therefore exempt from the ban on raises! I received a second raise. As far as I can tell, God wonderfully made up a large part of what I gave up for Him. And I was able to keep blessing others in His name.

During those days, I learned a lot about seeking God's kingdom and His will for my life. As the writer of Hebrews wrote, "He is a rewarder of those who diligently seek Him" (11:6).

*O, **Wondrous God**, thank You for blessing Your servant. You have given me great joy in serving You. Help me remember Your goodness as I reach out to others in Your name. Through Christ, I pray. Amen.*

_____

_____

_____

_____

_____

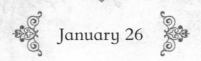

God Said a Thousand

Do not be afraid, little flock, for your Father has been pleased to give you the kingdom *(Luke 12:32)*.

Scripture: Luke 12:32-34

Not long after I truly trusted my life to Jesus, a visiting missions organizer came to our church. He began speaking in general about missions and then, surprisingly, talked at great length about the needs in one of the former states of the Soviet Union. Two members of the church volunteered to go and preach the gospel there. The only thing that remained was the money to send them. God impressed on my heart to give a thousand dollars towards the trip.

Never had I conceived of giving such a large amount to anything! I was reluctant to tell my dear wife. On the way home, though, I tentatively suggested we give substantially to the trip—"maybe several hundred dollars."

Oh, how foolish I was! My wife replied, "I felt God would have us give a thousand dollars."

I learned a lesson, and I'm still learning. We shouldn't be afraid of giving what God asks for, or of talking about it with our spouses. After all, God has already given us the kingdom.

Heavenly Father, how great is Your wisdom and how generous You are toward me. I know I am not very wise about using the resources You have provided, but I pray that in the days ahead You will lead me to treasure Your kingdom deeply and give more generously. In Jesus' name, amen.

_____

_____

_____

_____

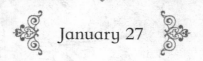

January 27

Which Airline?

Do not put your trust in princes, in mortal men, who cannot save. When their spirit departs, they return to the ground; on that very day their plans come to nothing *(Psalm 146:3, 4)*.

Scripture: Psalm 146:1-7

At the airport, Billy was surprised to have a choice of airlines. The first airline had a sleek plane, offered champagne, hundreds of movies, and good-looking attendants. Royalty, too, was traveling on the flight.

The other airline offered just basic amenities with a smile. They did say the owner and maker of the plane would be with them. And Billy noted their guarantee to get him to his destination safely and on time. Surely, Billy thought, the other plane would do the same. "Hurry up. This is the fun flight," said the man at the fancy airline. Billy quickly got on board.

The rich food left him sick. The movies became annoying. His seat was unreasonably small. Then Billy felt strange. They were losing altitude. He saw the pilot shoot past as his parachute opened. His heart sank. In the distance he saw the other plane. Everyone was smiling. A confident man sat in their midst.

Yes, a fictional scenario. But I am glad my destination is eternal and wonderful. Jacob's God, the God of truth, is also my God. May each person choose wisely his path!

Heavenly Father, today, let my focus be on You and not the things and troubles of this world. I pray this prayer in Jesus' name. Amen.

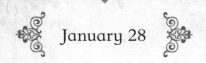
Family Faith

We will not hide them from their children; we will tell the next generation the praiseworthy deeds of the Lord *(Psalm 78:4).*

Scripture: *Psalm 78:1-4*

I knew that my mother's family had been Christians for several generations. When I began to explore the history of her family, though, I discovered the true extent.

In 1662, John Argor, one of my mother's ancestors and a Cambridge educated vicar, refused to sign the Uniformity Act. The Act required all ministers to approve the Book of Common Prayer and to acknowledge the unlawfulness of taking up arms against the king.

Argor lost his pulpit, and friends asked him how he thought he would provide for his large family. To this he answered, "God is my housekeeper, and I believe He will provide for us."

Mom never told me this story, but she lived a faithful life herself. When she developed cancer, her life and writings were an inspiration to many. After her death, one of her articles was published. She wrote that she thanked God for allowing her to have cancer because of the lessons she had learned from the experience.

Father, thank You for our children and grandchildren. Help us to share Jesus and our faith stories with the next generation. In Jesus' name, amen.

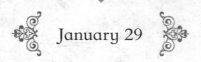

On a Quest

He said to them, "Take nothing for your journey, neither a staff, nor a bag, nor bread, nor money; and do not even have two tunics apiece" *(Luke 9:3, New American Standard Bible).*

Scripture: Luke 9:1-10

My husband, Bill, was nearing graduation from college. I was the current breadwinner, teaching elementary school. As I came in from school, Bill met me. "We're going to Findlay," he said. "They just posted a job opening for assistant city engineer."

We jumped into our old car and drove the 50 miles. Two blocks from the city engineer's office our car stalled and refused to restart. A mechanic from a nearby garage jump-started the engine, but it cost $5, all the money we had between us.

The vehicle quit again. A kind stranger pushed our disabled auto for several blocks, and then into a service station. The verdict was a bad fuel pump.

We walked five blocks to the local minister's house. His wife fed us, and then they took us back to the station, where they paid for the repairs (money we repaid later).

Bill left a note on the closed engineer's office door. But a few weeks later Bill was appointed Assistant City Engineer of Findlay, Ohio.

Dear Father in Heaven, *thank You for providing what I need as I journey through life intent upon bringing glory to Your name. In the name of the Father, the Son, and the Holy Spirit, amen.*

_____

_____

_____

_____

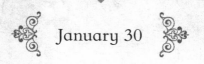

January 30

Postal Moment

Go your ways; behold, I send you out as lambs in the midst of wolves *(Luke 10:3, New American Standard Bible).*

Scripture: Luke 10:1-3

I was going postal. An acquaintance had hired me to teach workshops for her company. My job was to instruct attendees on how to obtain a high score on the postal exam. I had no experience with such tests, but had been trained . . . over the phone.

Preparing for the first class, because I felt insecure, I typed out everything I was to say. Before the first session, I placed the notes on the podium and went to the hallway to greet the participants.

As I collected money from the students, a competitor slipped into the classroom, stole my notes, and left. When I discovered the loss, I was terrified. However, in spite of my panic, I managed to teach the first class successfully. In fact, my presentation from memory was perhaps more effective than a rote reading from notes. It was a learning experience for me as well as the students.

I learned Jesus not only sends His little lambs among wolves. He protects them while they are there.

Dear Father, thank You for protecting me as I go about my days. I am sometimes tempted to think that parts of my life are too small for Your attention. But remind me that You are with me in the midst of every moment. Help me to rest in Your unchanging care this day and every day. In the name of Your precious Son, my Savior, I pray. Amen.

_____

_____

_____

_____

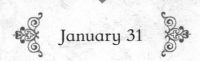

January 31

Peace for Troubled Households

Whatever house you enter, first say, "Peace be to this house" *(Luke 10:5, New American Standard Bible).*

Scripture: Luke 10:4-7

Westin, one of my first graders, was the picture of health, stocky, with dark eyes and hair. But at the beginning of the school year his mother recounted his history. Westin had developed leukemia at age three. He must go to a clinic for periodic tests.

Tearfully, she reported at mid-year: the leukemia had returned. Westin would undergo chemotherapy and be unable to attend school.

In order to continue his educational progress, I agreed to tutor the boy in his home. Once a week, after teaching a full day, I went to Westin's small white house. Before exiting the car each week, I prayed for his strength and peace.

His treatment was lengthy, lasting well into his second year. His second-grade teacher took over the tutoring until he was able to rejoin his class.

Ten years later, both teachers were invited to an anniversary party to rejoice over Westin's prolonged remission from disease. We were thrilled to celebrate with the joyful family. And I was reminded: Christian service, with compassion, brings peace to troubled households.

Dear Father, I pray for the peace of my friends and neighbors. May I serve them with Your compassion. In Jesus' name. Amen.

_____

_____

_____

_____

February

*O my people, hear my teaching . . . tell the next
generation the praiseworthy deeds of the LORD.*
—Psalm 78:1a, 4b

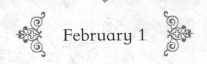

Welcome Food

Whatever city you enter, and they receive you, eat what is set before you *(Luke 10:8, New American Standard Bible).*

Scripture: Luke 10:8-12

In Rostov, Russia, we met a woman who said she knew it was possible to live on just bread and salt. She had done so for a period of time during WW II. The same woman thanked my husband and me for the care packages she had received from America following the war. She credited the food contained in those packages for her survival.

Have you noticed how sharing a meal produces an atmosphere where intimate fellowship can develop? Our conversation took place in 1992 in the elderly woman's house, one of the few buildings in her neighborhood to endure the battle that once raged in her city. As we sat at her dining room table, her story was interpreted by her daughter, Lydia, an English teacher.

The events the Russian lady recalled had taken place many years before, but she had lacked the opportunity to show her gratitude. She now eagerly served a meal to the first Americans she had met since that time.

The borscht soup was delicious. And how our gracious host smiled when my husband asked for seconds!

Father, thank You for blessing me with memories of hospitality, times when I have shared food, and Your love, with others. In Jesus' name. Amen.

_____

_____

_____

_____

_____

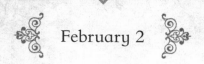

The Heavenly Register

Do not rejoice in this, that the spirits are subject to you, but rejoice that your names are recorded in heaven (*Luke 10:20, New American Standard Bible*).

Scripture: Luke 10:17-20

My college diploma sits proudly on the shelf above my computer. It is precious to me because it took me 25 years to earn it. After high school, I completed two years of college and then dropped out of the academic scene. I married, had three daughters, and thought I would never be able to finish my education.

The Lord had other plans. When a Christian school was established in our congregation, the director asked whether I could renew my teaching license. I contacted a local college and found it was possible. Wilmington College accepted my previous credits and worked out a plan for the completion of my course of study.

Today, my name is listed as a recipient of the Bachelor of Arts degree. What a great day of celebration when I graduated! My dream had finally come true.

We will all "graduate" from this earth some day, entering an existence beyond the grave. If we're recorded on the heavenly register, what a far greater event than any other commencement day!

Dear Father, thank You for loving me, forgiving me, and enrolling me for a heavenly eternity in fellowship with You. I am so grateful to be Your child. In the name of Jesus, Lord and Savior of all, I pray. Amen.

_____

_____

_____

_____

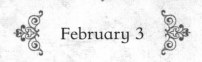

Awesome Deeds

Come and see the works of God, Who is awesome in His deeds toward the sons of men *(Psalm 66:5, New American Standard Bible).*

Scripture: Psalm 66:5-12

Charity Lynch was a Quaker woman who moved with her husband and children to Ohio from South Carolina in the early 1800s. They settled in the town of Waynesville and were very happy there— until tragedy struck in 1813. Their newborn son died. The husband's death soon followed. Then Charity herself fell ill and was not expected to live. The Lynchs' seven surviving children were distributed to six different homes in four towns.

When Charity was told that her children were gone, she could only accept it as a temporary arrangement. She was determined to get them back. Slowly her health returned, and she was able to write about how she dealt with this time of intense tribulation:

"At that time I often retired to my room, shut the door, took my Bible, walked my room, and read some consoling promise of the gospel. I often was able to rejoice in the midst of grief, those days when I lived only for my dear children. For them my daily prayer was offered up to the throne of grace."

She eventually regained all her children.

*Thank You, **Father,** for Your awesome love and care. In the midst of the most difficult times, keep me close! In Jesus' name I pray. Amen.*

_____

_____

_____

_____

_____

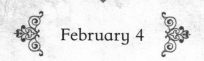

February 4

The Night Meditation

On my bed I remember you; I think of you through the watches of the night *(Psalm 63:6)*.

Scripture: Psalm 63:1-6

Unlike my seatmate who was asleep before the plane left the runway, I couldn't get comfortable. Whenever I closed my eyes, all I could think about was the reason I was making this trip.

The night before, I'd been surrounded by friends traveling behind a horse-drawn sleigh, listening to the sleigh bells and the sounds of horses' hoofs as they crunched through the crusty snow. Now, one night later, my thoughts were troubled as I took the overnight flight to be with my daughter who was facing a lengthy surgical procedure to eradicate cancer. Alone, with no one to talk with, I felt tears threatening to spill down my cheeks. But in the silence I also recalled a hymn I'd learned as a child, "Anywhere with Jesus I can safely go."

Whether we're facing illness, difficult times, or searing loneliness, we are invited to meditate on God's love. In the long night hours He reaches through the darkness to remind us we are never alone.

O God, thank You for reminding me that I am never alone in this life. Help me to recollect Your abiding presence regularly, especially in the times when I'm most tempted to worry. Thank You, in Jesus' name. Amen.

_____

_____

_____

_____

_____

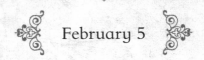

He Went First

This is he that was spoken of by the prophet Esaias, saying, The voice of one crying in the wilderness, Prepare ye the way of the Lord, make his paths straight *(Matthew 3:3, King James Version).*

Scripture: Matthew 3:1-6

"I'm scared."

I'm not exactly sure how old I was when I first uttered those words, but I do remember the circumstances with certainty. I wanted to go with my dad, but the tide was out, and his boat looked so low in the water. And I'd never climbed down a ladder before.

"I'll go first," Dad said. "I'll guide where to put your feet. All you have to do is take one step at a time and hang on." So Dad stood on the ladder, and I backed onto the first rung. Now, instead of seeing the distance to the bobbing boat below, all I saw was my father's arms around me, surrounding me, protecting me from falling, directing my footsteps onto each successive rung.

As John prepared the way for Jesus, so Jesus has gone ahead of us to prepare the way to Heaven. Why look into the distance to see all the obstacles on our journey? Instead, we can visualize His protecting arms around us and hear His gentle voice directing our way. "I'll go first," He says. And He did—at the cross.

***Lord,** thank You for sending Jesus ahead of me to the grave, eternally defeating Death for all who follow Him. Praise to You, in His name! Amen.*

_____

_____

_____

_____

_____

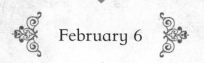

February 6

Bringing Good News

After John was put in prison, Jesus went into Galilee, proclaiming the good news of God *(Mark 1:14).*

Scripture: Mark 1:14, 15

Shortly after my daughter finished her treatments for cancer, she ran a marathon. The act of simply completing the run symbolized a great personal victory.

Historians tell us the first marathon run took place in 490 BC, when a soldier named Pheidippides ran with news from a battlefield on the plain of Marathon to the city of Athens. After a three-hour run of more than 25 miles, Pheidippides died of exhaustion—but not before he delivered this momentous message to his country's citizens: "Nike! (We conquer!)"

Pheidippides was so excited about the Greeks' victory over the Persians that he gave everything he had to tell others the good news. We too have news to share: "Jesus Christ brings victory!"

Christ died on the cross and rose again, defeating Satan and conquering death. As Christians, we have been given good news—no, better than good news. We've been given the best news of all time. Jesus Christ has paid the penalty for our sin. When we tell others of this marvelous victory, should we give less than our all?

Dear God, impress upon me the magnitude of the news Your Son, Jesus, brought to our world. Help me to give my all so that others will know of this great victory. In the precious name of Jesus, I pray. Amen.

_____

_____

_____

_____

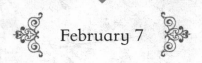

Staying in Tune?

I tell you, no! But unless you repent, you too will all perish *(Luke 13:5).*

Scripture: Luke 13:1-5

When I was taking piano lessons, my teacher always tried to make the instruction more appealing by telling me facts about the composers I was studying. One day we were working through a piece by Handel, and she told me of a time when Handel became impatient with one of the singers in his choir. Apparently, the chorister continued to sing his own unusual interpretations instead of following the maestro's instructions. Handel supposedly took the offending member by the legs and hung him by the heels out of a third-story window! Finally, the chorister repented and agreed to sing in the maestro's way.

Unlike Handel, God doesn't take us by the heels and hold us upside down until we agree to follow Him. Nonetheless, if we are to find peace and harmony in our lives, we will surely be led to times of repentance. This means not only saying we are sorry and asking God to forgive us for our sin. It also calls for making a 180-degree turn away from sin. Thereafter, we will intend to walk in a different direction, relying on the Spirit to keep us steady, strong, and in tune with the Maestro of our days.

Dear God, as I look back through the days of my life, I can see where I have been guilty of rebelling against Your will and Your ways. I'm sorry. From now on, I want to do things Your way. Through Christ, amen.

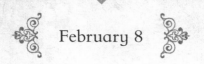

One More Chance!

"Sir," the man replied, "leave it alone for one more year, and I'll dig around it and fertilize it. If it bears fruit next year, fine! If not, then cut it down" *(Luke 13:8, 9).*

Scripture: Luke 13:6-9

There's nothing like watching a living thing grow, even as the cold blasts of winter close in all around us. A few years ago I bought an amaryllis bulb to plant. According to the instructions, I needed to give the bulb a good soaking and then water it only once a week until a green shoot would appear.

All through the month of February I watered and watched. "This thing is never going to grow!" I exclaimed after watering it for the fourth week in a row and finding no sign of life. "I should throw it out."

In the end I decided to water and fertilize it one more time, thus giving it a last chance to show some sign of life. Although slow starting, with the right amount of moisture and fertilizer, the plant grew and produced a beautiful flower.

When we allow the Master to care for us in all His loving ways, we can grow and bring forth fruit. He doesn't give up on us. He patiently lets us make our mistakes or just lie dormant until we've had enough of our lonely living apart from Him. Then, watch us grow!

__God,__ bring forth the kind of fruits in me that demonstrate my roots go deep in Your love. Be the master gardener of my life, in Christ's name. Amen.

_____

_____

_____

_____

_____

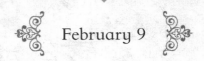

February 9

Turn from Danger

I preached that they should repent and turn to God and prove their repentance by their deeds *(Acts 26:20).*

Scripture: Acts 26:19-23

Nineteen-year-old Jeff was part of a work team that went out from our church to help the victims of Hurricane Katrina in 2005. Upon his return, he told of his experiences.

Fighting back tears, he said, "When I met Don in a church parking lot, he was volunteering to help the flood victims. Although a young man like me, he'd already served jail time and had lost touch with his family.

"During the hurricane he'd found shelter in one of the few churches not already flooded. In the early morning hours, staring at the cross at the front of the church, he repented of his sins and turned to God. So complete was the change in his life that he called his family, asking for their forgiveness and reconciliation. Now, instead of being guarded in a prison cell, he was acting as a security guard at the distribution center."

Don's deeds—helping others, being trustworthy—proved his true repentance. Thankfully, God saves us while we are still *un*worthy. But He doesn't leave us in our sad state. He invites us into a brand new lifestyle.

Dear God, I know others see You through how I conduct my life. Help me to proclaim Your matchless mercy by my life of gratefulness and good works. Through Christ my Savior, I pray. Amen.

_____

_____

_____

_____

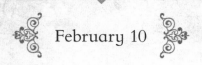

Can't Earn Heaven

For the LORD watches over the way of the righteous, but the way of the wicked will perish *(Psalm 1:6).*

Scripture: Psalm 1

The peace of a beautiful summer afternoon was shattered by the unmistakable sound of a man's voice crying out, *"Help!"* Someone was in danger. My heart raced as I ran to dial 9-1-1. "There's a man in the lake," I said. "He's calling for help."

"Can you tell me where you live?" the voice on the other end of the line asked. Struggling to stay calm so I could give clear directions, I said, "West Bay. Please hurry!" I went on to explain, "When you get to Cleveland there's a fork in the road. Be sure to take the road on the right because the sign marked West Bay Road doesn't actually lead to West Bay." I explained further . . .

If the emergency crew had gone the wrong way, someone could have perished. Today's psalm speaks of the moral decisions we need to make during our lifetimes. Ultimately, they are matters of life and death. Should we choose the path of our own righteousness, we will fall short of eternal life. If we choose God alone as our righteousness, we will enjoy wonderful fellowship with His Son in this life—and enjoy Heaven with Him thereafter. What a loving and gracious Lord is ours!

Dear God, help me to listen closely to Your instructions that I might stay on the path of righteousness this day. Through my Lord Christ. Amen.

_____

_____

_____

_____

_____

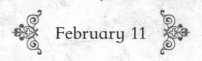

February 11

Egg on My Face

He guides the humble in what is right and teaches them his way *(Psalm 25:9).*

Scripture: Psalm 25:1-10

I was wrestling with a computer problem, but the computer was winning. "Let me show you how this works," said my husband, who seemed to be getting a little frustrated with me. He made a number of suggestions, some of which I'd already tried without success; others, I just didn't think would work. In desperation, though, I finally swallowed my pride and listened carefully to his instructions.

Click. Click. Click. Problem solved.

This is known as "egg on my face time."

I'm sure God must shake His head when we insist on doing things our own way. We think we know the best way to handle a situation, but He can see the whole picture from beginning to end. After making a mess of things, we end up crying out for Him to rescue us. He graciously steps in, guiding us and teaching us His ways when we're finally ready to accept His direction.

Our pride can be the biggest barrier to our relationship with the Lord. It takes a humble attitude to receive truth.

Father, thank You for Your patience when I'm in an I-can-do-it-myself mode. You whisper to my heart through Your Word until I get the message. Praise to You, in the name of Jesus! Amen.

_____

_____

_____

_____

_____

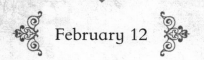

February 12

Watching for a Mistake

One Sabbath, when Jesus went to eat in the house of a prominent Pharisee, he was being carefully watched *(Luke 14:1)*.

Scripture: Luke 14:1-6

In sixth grade, one of my classmates, Judy, was a top-notch student. I wanted to be the best, but the result was always the same: Judy came out number one, while I was the runner-up. The green-eyed monster of jealousy grabbed my heart. I avoided her like the plague.

Did I seize the opportunity to be challenged, learn from her successes, and develop a friendship with her? No. I became upset with her and swirled down into self-pity.

The Pharisees had Jesus right there with them, eating a meal with Him. He spoke to them, encouraging them to look at life through the lens of God's love and concern for a sick man. Yet they allowed pride, jealousy, and a know-it-all attitude to rob them of blessing. Instead of seeing what they could learn, they secretly watched to find some fault or weakness.

It takes a humble heart to rejoice with others. On the other hand, the Germans have a word, *schadenfreude,* meaning to "rejoice in the misfortunes of others." We have that option too. But why not choose to learn from others' mistakes—and celebrate with them in their successes?

Lord, may I recognize You as the source of my strength and ability. Therefore, let me be thankful for the successes in my own life and in the lives of others. All the glory goes to You alone. In Jesus' name, amen.

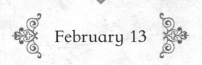

February 13

SPS!

When someone invites you to a wedding feast, do not take the place of honor, for a person more distinguished than you may have been invited *(Luke 14:8).*

Scripture: Luke 14:7-9

When I was growing up, Mom tried to instill certain strong values in me. For example, she wouldn't allow bragging. Whenever I showed any signs of self-aggrandizement, she would comment, "SPS," which stood for "self-praise stinks." While she was lavish with her praise of my accomplishments and abilities, she didn't hesitate to correct me if I was becoming obnoxious.

Jesus' words usually fly in the face of human wisdom. We're told it's a dog-eat-dog world, so we have to compete aggressively and push ourselves into the limelight. But Jesus spoke of handling the everyday experiences of life with humility and grace. He told people not to grab the best seats for themselves but to take a lower place. He pointed out how embarrassing it would be if someone told them to give up their hard-won place of privilege for an even more favored guest.

Giving ourselves honor leaves us unfulfilled—and constantly vulnerable to being "taken down a peg." How much sweeter our reward when it comes by pure grace!

Father, when I'm tempted to grab position or honor, help me to remember that self-praise ends in meager satisfaction. Let me find my joy in honoring You with a servant heart. In the precious name of Jesus I pray. Amen.

_____

_____

_____

_____

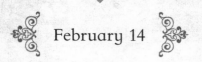

Parade for ... Whom?

Everyone who exalts himself will be humbled, and he who humbles himself will be exalted *(Luke 14:11)*.

Scripture: Luke 14:10, 11

In the book of Esther, Haman enjoyed great power in the king's court. Instead of being thankful, though, he longed for honor and praise. Therefore, when godly Mordecai refused to "bow and scrape" before him, Haman raged.

One day, Mordecai discovered a plot against the king, notified the authorities, and thereby saved the king's life. Mordecai didn't demand any recognition; he just went about his business. Later, however, when the king came across the account of Mordecai's good deed, he was disturbed to find this courageous whistle-blower hadn't been properly rewarded.

The king called Haman and asked him what he would do for a great man. Haman assumed the king was talking about him and suggested the equivalent of our ticker-tape parade. You can imagine Haman's shock and humiliation when the king commanded him to do all these things for Mordecai!

Someone once said, "The way up is down." If you try to set up your own ticker-tape parade, you'll likely find you've prepared it for someone else.

Father, thank You for Your many blessings. Help me to remember that true promotion and favor come only from You. In Jesus' name, amen.

_____

_____

_____

_____

_____

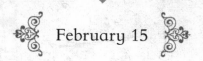

No Strings Attached

When you give a banquet, invite the poor, the crippled, the lame, the blind, and you will be blessed. Although they cannot repay you, you will be repaid at the resurrection of the righteous *(Luke 14:13, 14).*

Scripture: Luke 14:12-14

A mom smiles as a server puts a scoop of mashed potatoes on her child's plate. An elderly man happily chats with people at his table, glad for the company. A woman in a wheelchair is thankful she can get out of the house.

The server's back aches from hours of preparation. Her family has sacrificed their own traditions to be here. None of these people will ever invite her for dinner at their homes. Yet, her heart overflows with joy as their faces radiate hope for the future.

Jesus told His hosts not to invite their friends, relatives, or rich neighbors in hopes that they'd reciprocate in turn. Instead, He instructed them to extend hospitality to those who had no way of repaying. Such hosts would be blessed and honored by God on the day when He puts all things right.

Giving "with no strings attached" can produce great joy in our hearts. Whatever it costs us in time, money, and effort to serve the poor is far outweighed by the delight it brings to God's heart.

Heavenly Father, give me a heart filled with compassion and love for those who can't repay the kindness You call me to share. In Jesus' name, amen.

_____

_____

_____

_____

_____

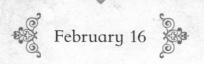

Credit Where It's Due

Whereof I was made a minister, according to the gift of the grace of God given unto me by the effectual working of his power. Unto me, who am less than the least of all saints, is this grace given, that I should preach among the Gentiles the unsearchable riches of Christ *(Ephesians 3:7, 8, King James Version).*

Scripture: Ephesians 3:1-10

As a world-renowned preacher stepped up to the pulpit, the crowd gave him its full attention, waiting for profound words of wisdom. Yet he spoke with great simplicity and humility. Afterwards, a reporter said to him, "Dr. Smith, you have a seminary degree and several doctorates. You've traveled the world and met many great leaders. How does it feel to be so honored?"

The preacher smiled and said, "I'm nothing special. Jesus Christ is the source of my abilities."

This man, like Paul, refused to rely on his heritage or academic background for his effectiveness in ministry. He stressed God's grace in his life, recognizing the ministry as a gifting from God. He was more interested in presenting the gospel than building his reputation.

We can be thankful for men and women like this, who serve the church with pure hearts. They simply give credit where *all* the credit is due.

Father, when I'm tempted to bask in applause, remind me that it's You who have extended blessing. Keep working through me, in Jesus' name. Amen.

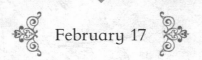

Key Element of Change

All of you, clothe yourselves with humility toward one another, because, "God opposes the proud but gives grace to the humble" *(1 Peter 5:5).*

Scripture: 1 Peter 5:1-5

Her dad had abandoned Liza and her mom before her birth. Further complicating matters, her mom's family rejected them as well. As an adult, Liza was drawn to a lifestyle of partying and drinking. Several failed marriages and ill health left her a broken, addicted, suicidal woman.

But Liza's story has a happy ending. She discovered a church that embraced her with loving hearts. They told her about Jesus and how she could have a fresh start in Him. She gratefully entered the waters of baptism.

Of course, there were many things Liza didn't yet understand in the Word, but she humbly listened, thoughtfully considered, and then tried to practice what she learned. She even began reaching out to others and sharing what Jesus had done for her. Gradually, the sad, devastated woman was transformed by the power of Christ.

The key element in this change was her willingness to receive God's Word along with the counsel of mature believers. Liza's openness and humility helped her find the path of life.

Father, please keep my heart soft and pliable. When things aren't going well, help me listen to the godly counsel of others. In Jesus' name, amen.

_____

_____

_____

_____

_____

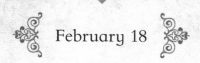

True Relationship with God

You have looked into my heart, Lord, and you know all about me
(Psalm 139:1, Contemporary English Version).

Scripture: Psalm 139:1-6

Children believe that their parents have the uncanny ability to love them and to know every move they make. For instance, Melissa believes, "My parents have eyes in the backs of their heads." Jeff thinks, "No matter what I do, my mom can always tell when I'm lying." And Abbey says, "Mom and Dad love me, no matter what."

The psalmist expressed some of the same thoughts about his relationship with God. David knew he served an all-seeing, all-knowing, and loving God. He believed that his relationship with God was real because God knew his unspoken thoughts, understood his anger, his anxiety, even his depression.

To have a deepening relationship with God, we must believe that He understands us and His love for us is unconditional. A child put it this way, "When you pray, you get a happy feeling inside—like God just walked into your heart and is warming Himself at a cozy fire."

Lord, You know all about me, yet You invite me to come before You, freely revealing the contents of my heart. What a privilege it is to build my life around You, the one who loves me unconditionally. I thank You in the name of Jesus, my Savior and Lord. Amen.

_____

_____

_____

_____

_____

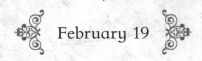

Test of a Disciple

You cannot be my disciple, unless you love me more than you love your father and mother, your wife and children, and your brothers and sisters. You cannot come with me unless you love me more than you love your own life *(Luke 14:26, Contemporary English Version).*

Scripture: Luke 14:25-27

To love Jesus more than life must have seemed unreasonably harsh to many hearers who thought they were Jesus' disciples. And it is not easy for us to hear either. Dr. Phil McGraw, author of *Family First: Your Step-by-Step Plan for Creating a Phenomenal Family,* said, "I love my family more than anything in this world, and I want us all to be safe, healthy, happy, and prosperous in everything we do, both within our family and as we go out into the world."

It is only natural that most of us want to be good parents, and we love those closest to our hearts. Jesus knew that to ask His disciples to put their love for Him above even their closest human relationships meant they were willing to give up everything to serve Him.

Only God can claim this kind of love. Yet, thankfully, when we give Him our all, He gives us every good thing in return: "No mind has conceived what God has prepared for those who love him" (1 Corinthians 2:9).

Gracious God, I want to build my life around You, to love You more than life itself. Thanks for Your Spirit to help me grow. In Christ's name, amen.

_____

_____

_____

_____

_____

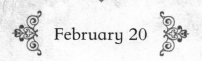

February 20

What Is a Disciple?

So then, you cannot be my disciple unless you give away everything you own *(Luke 14:33, Contemporary English Version).*

Scripture: Luke 14:28-33

Shireen, an Iranian teenager, often listened to the Persian language broadcasts of the Radio Voice of Christ. She wrote the following letter to the station, telling of her wish to follow Jesus:

"One night I saw in a dream that Jesus was telling me, 'My child, I accept you.' I shared these dreams with one of my teachers and one of my friends. They told me if I believed in Jesus I would become an infidel. But when I realized the truth, deep in my heart, I became glad and believed."

She ended her letter with several questions and a request for a Bible and other Christian literature. "Am I a complete Christian now?" She asked. "Is it really true that I am an infidel? And when should I talk to my parents about this?"

Shireen willingly gave up everything to follow Jesus. There must be other stories like hers, because in the past 40 years the Iranian Christian Church has grown from about 5,000 to over 200,000 believers. Her commitment is the kind that Jesus asks from all His followers.

Father, more than anything, I want to be Jesus' disciple. I know that He is always with me, asking me for room in my heart. In His name, amen.

_____

_____

_____

_____

_____

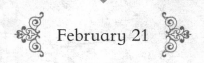

Too Much Money

You still lack one thing. Sell everything you have and give to the poor, and you will have treasure in heaven. Then come, follow me *(Luke 18:22).*

Scripture: Luke 18:18-25

Marzi Muhammadi, an Afghan doctor, hoped to be elected to the parliament in that country's first free election in 30 years. She was battling for a seat from her province, and to finance her campaign she sold everything she owned except her wedding ring. Yet she lost the election. Still, she willingly gave up everything for her goal.

Marzi's commitment was the kind of response Jesus had hoped for from the man in today's Scripture. But he believed his life was blameless because he followed God's Old Testament law.

Jesus knew that the true test of discipleship for this man would be to give away everything he owned and then follow Him. It was a test of character that the rich man failed. He couldn't bring himself to follow Jesus from place to place or give up his wealth to help others.

Jesus continues to say, "Follow me." If we accept His love and follow His example, we are His disciples. But we will not be perfect in our attempts. Only step by step, relying wholly on His grace, do we stay close to Him.

Lord, I hand over the control of my life to You, and I will follow Your Spirit's leading the best I can. Thank You for the free gift of salvation that made this journey with You possible. In Jesus' name, amen.

_____

_____

_____

_____

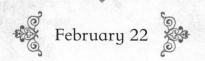

High Cost of Believing

Peter said, "Remember, we left everything to be your followers!" *(Luke 18:28, Contemporary English Version).*

Scripture: Luke 18:28-30

Christians in Vietnam know what it means to give up everything for their faith. Often local authorities try to persuade believers to give up their belief in Jesus. Their tactics include refusing to give monthly support money to poor Christian families. Thus some Christians give in to the pressure and abandon their beliefs; others stand firm.

Peter and the other disciples watched as Jesus spoke to the rich man. The man seemed to have his heart set on the promise of eternal life, but he wasn't willing to make the sacrifice Jesus required of His followers. Disappointed, he walked away.

Later, Peter reminded Jesus that he and the other fishermen had left their homes and families to be with Him. Peter must have realized that what they had given up for Christ would, in a sense, be repaid with eternal life.

To stay or walk away from Jesus is still the choice we face. Each of us must decide whether the benefits of committing our lives to God are worth the hardships we may have to endure. Thankfully, we need never go it alone. We have the fellowship of other believers to encourage us—along with God's own Spirit within us.

Dear God, I come to You in obedience to Your Word, trusting in Your gracious promise to be present with me always. In Christ's name, amen.

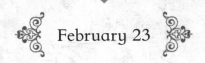

A Better Way to Fish

The men pulled their boats up on the shore. Then they left everything and went with Jesus *(Luke 5:11, Contemporary English Version)*.

Scripture: Luke 5:1-11

What a difference between the response of the three fishermen who had been washing their nets, and the rich man who asked Jesus the way to eternal life! While the rich man apparently couldn't imagine giving away his wealth, Peter, James, and John didn't hesitate. They left their boats, their nets, and all their other equipment by the lake to follow Jesus.

Can you imagine the disciples saying, "Wait a minute, Jesus! After we sell our fish for a good price, *then* we'll come with You." No, the men had listened to Jesus' teaching, they had witnessed a miracle, and Jesus promised they would do much more than catch fish in the days ahead. They were convinced that Jesus was God's messenger, and they were willing to drop everything to follow Him.

When Jesus turns to us and says "Come with me," there's no room for a wishy-washy response. He seeks a yes or no. And once we say "Yes!" He gives us everything we need to live a life that brings glory to His kingdom.

O God, how I long to be counted among those faithful to Your Son in this life! Keep me close through study of the Word, prayer, and fellowship with my brothers and sisters in the church. Thank You, in Jesus' name. Amen.

_____

_____

_____

_____

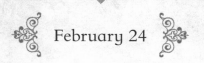

February 24

Results of Obedience

The Lord said to Ananias, "Go! I have chosen him to tell foreigners, kings, and the people of Israel about me" *(Acts 9:15, Contemporary English Version).*

Scripture: Acts 9:1-6, 11-16

While traveling in the Middle East, we decided to take a side trip to Damascus, Syria, probably the oldest continually occupied city in the world. We found the ruins of the ancient Roman city, and after shopping in a crowded bazaar, we walked the bustling Straight Street mentioned in Acts 9:11. Later, we walked down a stairway to an ancient Roman road and entered a small underground chapel. Tradition says we were standing in the home of Ananias.

We don't know much about Ananias or how he became a Christian. But we do know that he swallowed his fear and immediately obeyed God. He left his home and found Saul. As a result of his obedience Saul of Tarsus became Paul the apostle, and the Christian faith spread throughout the Roman world.

Isn't that how God usually works? It may not be clear to us why He wants us to do something. Nevertheless, our task is to trust Him and to do what He has called us to do. He alone is responsible for the results.

Precious Father, forgive me when I ignore You and go my own way. Give me the wisdom to recognize Your will and to do it with a joyful heart. Help me to trust You completely, each step of the way. In Jesus' name, amen.

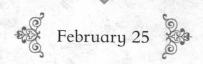

February 25

This Is Shouting News!

Let everything that has breath praise the Lord. Praise the Lord *(Psalm 150:6).*

Scripture: Psalm 150

The book of Psalms comes to us in five sections, each division concluding on a note of praise. In fact, this final psalm not only punctuates the fifth section with praise, but also the entire collection of 150 psalms. Yes, the last psalm has the last word, the word of praise. Yet there is one requirement: We have to be breathing. And if we are breathing, we ought to be praising.

This is very practical. If we get up in the morning, read the newspaper, and can't find our name in the obituary column, we ought to start the day on a crescendo of praise! The book of Psalms begins by inviting us to the law as a way of life and ends by inviting us to praise as the use of our very breath.

Have you considered that there is no better use of your breath than to articulate praises to the God of your blessings? In other words, the many ways God blesses us each day is "shouting news"!

Dear God, I raise my praise for the many and varied ways You bring good things to my life, each and every day. You are gracious and generous, and I am grateful. I praise You now and always; as long as I have breath, I will praise You. In the name of Jesus I pray. Amen.

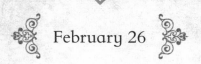

February 26

First, Get Ready

Then David said, "No one may carry the ark of God but the Levites, for the LORD has chosen them to carry the ark of God and to minister before Him forever *(1 Chronicles 15:2, New King James Version).*

Scripture: 1 Chronicles 15:1-3, 11-15

A minister was having difficulty preparing a particular sermon. Finally, he gave up. "Maybe the Holy Spirit will give me something to say," he said to himself. Standing before the congregation on Sunday morning, God did indeed tell him what to say: "Tell the people you are unprepared."

The first time David tried to move the ark to Jerusalem, he made a mess of things. *That will not happen this time,* David vows to himself and promises the people. Every possible preparation will be made, every detail attended to. David will go by the book this time.

Whatever we do for God warrants good preparation. It shouldn't be left to chance or planned haphazardly. After all, God deserves our best. We should do our homework thoroughly, thread our needles carefully, put the stones precisely in place. When we serve God, we are on a high level and in a large place; there, what we do calls for the best we have and the most we are. And before everything else, getting ready is the key to serving God.

Lord, I want to prepare for what You call me to do. Help me ready my mind and my heart through the gifts You give me. In Jesus' name, amen.

_____

_____

_____

_____

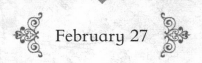

February 27

A Hallelujah Heart

David told the leaders of the Levites to appoint their brothers as singers to sing joyful songs, accompanied by musical instruments: lyres, harps and cymbals *(1 Chronicles 15:16).*

Scripture: 1 Chronicles 15:16-24

David's preparation for getting the ark to Jerusalem included a context for joyful praise. The ark, representing God's covenant with His people, would be lifted to highest glory with shouts of victory and songs of adoration. In each soul would be an amen attitude; in each person gathered, a hallelujah heart.

This dimension of uninhibited joy comes through in the 3-year-old who went to church for the first time. After she and her parents had taken their seats, the lights in the sanctuary were dimmed, and the choir came down the center aisle carrying lighted candles. All was quiet until the 3-year-old started singing in a loud voice, "Happy birthday to you. Happy birthday to you!" Her joy wouldn't stay inside. What was in her heart flowed out everywhere.

Someone asked Joseph Haydn, the composer, why his music was so cheerful. He replied, "I cannot make it otherwise. When I think upon God, my heart is so full of joy, the notes dance and leap from my pen!"

__Dear Heavenly Father,__ there's a joy deep in my heart about who You are to me. May I put it on my face in smiles and laughter. May I put in on my lips in tributes and praises. All praise to You, in Christ's name. Amen.

_____

_____

_____

_____

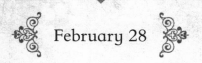
God Strengthens Us

God gave the Levites the strength they needed to carry the chest, and so they sacrificed seven bulls and seven rams *(1 Chronicles 15:26, Contemporary English Version).*

Scripture: 1 Chronicles 15:25-29

A helpful admonition made its way some time ago into books, onto posters, and taped to refrigerator doors. It spoke of God's help in our lives, promising strength and courage: "There is nothing you and God cannot accomplish together today." It's true, isn't it, that such a combination always makes a majority?

David's first attempt to get the ark to Jerusalem failed. The second one did not. The people prepared, and help came from God. It was God who gave them strength to carry the ark to Jerusalem and get it there safely. It was God who guided each step and empowered every move.

When we look at a mountain we need to climb and fear we can't get to the top, God promises to be with us all the way. When we see a road we need to walk, one that stretches long before us and we wonder if we will ever get to its end, God promises to guide our steps and guard our feet. When we put our hands to a formidable and difficult task, we know we are not alone.

Dear God, thank You for being with me in all things and in all places. As I begin each undertaking, I feel Your hand on mine. I am invited by Your presence, I am encouraged by Your promise, I am strengthened by Your power. In the precious name of Jesus I pray. Amen.

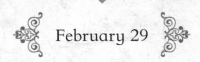

February 29

Blessings All Around

When David had finished offering the burnt offering and peace offerings, he blessed the people in the name of the LORD *(1 Chronicles 16:2, New American Standard Bible).*

Scripture: 1 Chronicles 16:1-6

The day the ark arrived in Jerusalem was a great day in the life of God's people. On that day past failure was forgotten and present accomplishment celebrated. All the preparation had paid off, the objective had been reached. What a day of great blessing!

A man attended a Bible study where the teacher talked of the land promised to Abraham. Thinking about that, the man said, "I already live in the promised land." He didn't have to go anywhere to claim God's promises or gain God's favor. In his daily life he already inhabited the perfect place to enjoy God's goodness. For him, there were blessings all around.

Later on in the Bible study, the discussion focused on the stress people experience these days. This same man commented, "I'm too blessed to be stressed." In a similar vein, an old Russian proverb says, "All days are beautiful . . . when you can wake up." God gives us life, and life gives us so much, if we'll only see it.

Dear Lord, how extravagant You are in Your blessings! With You, the calf is always the fatted calf, the robe the best robe, the pearl a gem of great price. Your peace, too, exceeds my understanding. Every blessing You give me, I give You back in praise. In Jesus' name I pray. Amen.

_____

_____

_____

_____

March

Let everything that hath breath praise the LORD.

—Psalm 150:6

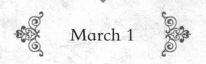

March 1

Credit Is Due

The LORD is great and greatly to be praised; He is also to be feared above all gods (1 Chronicles 16:25, *New King James Version*).

Scripture: 1 Chronicles 16:7-36

With the ark safely in Jerusalem, David weaves a song of praise from three previously penned psalms. He leaves no doubt as to where credit is due. If anyone points a finger of acclaim at him, he deflects it and points straight up to the God of all blessings. He will make everyone aware of source and resource. All will know that God has been on the move on behalf of His people.

If we think, we will thank. Here's what I mean: When we consider how good God is to us, we will surely let Him know how we feel about that. We will use at least some of the 86,400 seconds of each day to say, "Thank You." In fact, I believe we will use more and more of them until we are using all of them (in Heaven). In happy moments, we can praise God. In difficult moments, we can seek God. In every moment, we can thank God. For us, giving God credit is the constant characteristic of our lives.

> *Father,* whatever foundation I stand upon, I know You have put it there. Every road I take You have laid down. All the things I count my own find their origin in Your goodness. Everything I know, everything I have, began in the heart of Your love for me. Thank You, in Jesus' name. Amen.

_____

_____

_____

_____

March 2

A Forever Love

David also appointed Heman, Jeduthun, and the others chosen by name to give thanks to the Lord, "for his faithful love endures forever" (1 Chronicles 16:41, *New Living Translation*).

Scripture: 1 Chronicles 16:37-43

Some 60 years ago, well-known theologian Karl Barth was lecturing at a seminary when a student asked him to sum up his theology in just a few words. The lecturer stepped from behind the podium and began singing, "Jesus loves me, this I know . . ." In a similar vein, holocaust survivor Corrie ten Boom inspired her hearers when she said, "No problem is too big for God's power; no person is too small for God's love."

We love to hear of God's love. After the ark had been successfully delivered to Jerusalem, David made organizational arrangements to insure God's faithful love would be broadcast to the people. He told his staff to draw a circle of God's love so large around the people they could not step outside of it.

Many centuries after David, the great preacher Dwight L. Moody understood the importance of people knowing God's love. He proclaimed: "If we could only make people really believe that God loves them, what a rush we would see for the kingdom of God."

Father, thank You for loving me, no matter what. Thank You for loving me in all circumstances and in every context. Thank You for loving me, even when I don't love You back. In the name of Your Son, Jesus. Amen.

_____

_____

_____

_____

_____

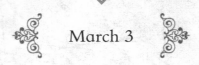
Does God Have You?

He also chose David His servant, and took him from the sheepfolds (Psalm 78:70, *New American Standard Bible*).

Scripture: Psalm 78:67-72

Kristen, my daughter-in-law, had been telling bedtime stories to her two children. She was using some of the passages from her Bible study group and read the segment where Ahimelech gives fugitive David a sword. At the word "sword," Kristen's two-year-old son, Harry, popped straight up in bed and exclaimed, "I know, the big guy! The big guy had the sword!"

"Do you mean David?" Kristen asked. "No, no," said Harry, spreading his arms as wide as he could, "the big, *huge* guy had the sword. Go-li-ath." Harry sounded out the syllables carefully, "Go-li-ath had the sword. David, David was the *little* guy—but he had God!"

Harry, of course, was remembering a previous bedtime story about David and Goliath. As Harry had learned, more important than human strength or size was the extent of one's trust in God. Yes, David had God; or rather, God had David. When God has us, He will take us even through the challenges that are obviously too big for us.

Dear Lord, help me live with a constant sense of Your sovereignty. How thankful I am—how awed I am—that You chose me and took me from my self-centered life into the service of Your kingdom. In Jesus' name, amen.

Pancake Offerings

Go and tell David my servant, "Thus says the LORD, 'You shall not build a house for Me to dwell in'" (1 Chronicles 17:4, *New American Standard Bible*).

Scripture: 1 Chronicles 17:1-6

One Saturday morning as I drove up the road leading to our house, I recognized two bikes lying in the driveway of a new neighbor I hadn't yet met. I stopped just in time to see my 11-year-old twins emerging from the neighbor's house, carrying cans of soda. I asked what they were doing, and Russell answered, "Well, you always told us to welcome new neighbors, so we made something for them."

"What did you make?" I asked.

"Pancakes!"

"And how did you get pancakes here on your bikes?"

"Easy," answered Andrew, demonstrating. "We put them in our pockets!" I tried to picture the new neighbor's reaction to these unwanted gifts, but it must have been gracious, since the twins ended up with sodas.

Sometimes, in my zeal to "do something" for God, I am like my twins. I offer Him my crumpled pancakes, which He hasn't asked for, when He has so much more to give me. If I were a bit more like David, I might check in with God to see if my plans are in line with His plans.

Great Giver, I'm not only blessed beyond imagination but given the power to accomplish what You've planned for me to do. Through Christ, amen.

_____

_____

_____

_____

March 5

House Plans

I tell you that the LORD will build a house for you (1 Chronicles 17:10, *New American Standard Bible*).

Scripture: 1 Chronicles 17:7-10

For years, my mother designed plans for the perfect house while our family of six lived in a tiny, two-bedroom apartment. However, what my parents were finally able to afford radically differed from her dream-house plans. We moved into a rambling, 60-year-old Victorian in disrepair, its paint long faded, covered with vines.

How that house shaped our family for years to come! We learned to adapt to strange creakings, faulty electricity, no central heating, and temperamental plumbing. But our big old house also allowed us to spread out, to develop in ways we would never have experienced in the tidy, modern home my mom had envisioned. In fact, it gave us more than a place to live; it gave us a place to *grow*.

David's vision differed from God's. The king envisioned cedar and stone, but God planned another kind of house, one that would stretch all the way to Christ. Often, we, like David, focus so intently on our own designs that we can hardly imagine God's bigger master plan. Yet He faithfully leads us into His better ways, step by step.

Lord of my life, I am so glad that You are the Master Architect of my future! Let me be like David, quick to change my focus when my plans fall short of Your inestimable glory. In the name of the Father, the Son, and the Holy Spirit, I pray. Amen.

Imperishable Inheritance

I will set up one of your descendants after you, who shall be of your sons . . . . He shall build for Me a house, and I will establish his throne forever (1 Chronicles 17:11, 12, *New American Standard Bible*).

Scripture: 1 Chronicles 17:11-15

My brother farms some of the same land that our great-grandfather worked in the 19th century. In fact, not long ago, my mother and brother received a plaque for having a family farm that has been operating continuously for a hundred years. A plaque is a small hint of past generations' efforts behind their plows, of men and women working hard under a baking sun. It recalls countless freezing mornings, devastating droughts, and the occasional fearsome tornadoes. The plaque proclaims appreciation for our inheritance, not so much of land, but of our ancestors' hope, strength, and persistence.

As God had promised, David's son Solomon did sit on Israel's throne. But God's promise meant much more. It pointed forward to the birth of Jesus—in His humanity, a descendent of David—whose kingdom is eternal. What a heritage we have in Christ! And our inheritance, as it says in 1 Peter 1:4 *(NASB)* can never disappear or be corrupted in any way. It "will not fade away," but is "reserved in heaven" for us.

Lord, I am so grateful that through Jesus I have a part in Your promises and that my inheritance in Christ is imperishable. In His name I pray. Amen.

_____

_____

_____

_____

_____

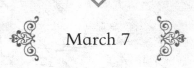

Not Too Far for God

David the king went in and sat before the LORD and said, "Who am I, O LORD God, and what is my house that Thou hast brought me this far?" (1 Chronicles 17:16, *New American Standard Bible*).

Scripture: 1 Chronicles 17:16-19

Most who sing the well-loved hymn *Amazing Grace* probably don't know it was based on 1 Chronicles 17:16 and 17. Nor are many who sing it aware that the author, John Newton, was for many years a slave-ship captain. After his conversion and baptism, though, Newton left the sea, joined the crusade against slavery, and later, in 1764, became an ordained Anglican minister.

Yet, Newton never forgot his sordid past. According to one account, he once exclaimed during a sermon: "My memory is nearly gone, but I remember two things: 'That I am a great sinner, and that Christ is a great Savior!'" Likewise, David, king of all Israel, sat before the Lord in awe at what God had done in his life.

We come from very different experiences, but we too can sit before God. In fact, He calls us constantly to be still and simply acknowledge His lordship in our lives. In our stillness, recalling His greatness, we will be constantly amazed at the grace that has brought us so far into sweet fellowship with Him.

Father, Your grace is truly amazing. You forgave me by Your Son's blood, releasing me to serve You in joy. Praise You, in Christ's name! Amen.

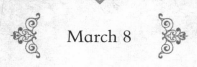

Awesome and Waiting

O LORD, there is none like Thee, neither is there any God besides Thee (1 Chronicles 17:20, *New American Standard Bible*).

Scripture: 1 Chronicles 17:20-22

Annie, rebelling against her family's faith, defiantly maintained that God couldn't possibly care about her—and she didn't believe in Him anyway. In her junior year of college, Annie became pregnant. Following friends' advice, she went to an abortion clinic. However, while she was waiting, Annie asked herself, "If I don't believe in God, then why does this seem so wrong? . . . God, if you are there, help me!"

Annie later said, "It was as if God were waiting for one small sign of seeking from me, because immediately I heard a voice full of love saying, 'Now I can help you.'"

Annie quickly left the clinic. Even though it was difficult, she parented her little girl, finished college on time, and eventually met a wonderful man who loved God—and cared lovingly for Annie and her daughter.

If you are in a difficult place these days, if you have felt that God just doesn't care about you, know that He is waiting for you. Even one little sign of an open heart is enough for Him. Truly there is no God like the Lord. His love waits to enter with healing and peace, no matter how desperate the situation.

Awesome Lord, I love You because You first loved me. I am so grateful that You provided a way to come to You through Jesus. In His name, amen.

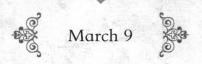

He Hears

Thou, O my God, hast revealed to Thy servant that Thou wilt build for him a house; therefore Thy servant hath found courage to pray before Thee (1 Chronicles 17:25, *New American Standard Bible*).

Scripture: 1 Chronicles 17:23-27

Craig, a new Christian, was knocked from his boat into the waters off the southern California coast. He struggled for five hours to reach a buoy in the 58-degree water, praying and reciting the 23rd Psalm as he swam. Each time he was about to give up, something floated close enough for him to grab—first a blue balloon, and then a piece of driftwood. Craig finally reached the buoy, only to be repulsed by aggressive sea lions.

As he began to sink, he heard a boat engine and was soon rescued—by his brother. Unknown to Craig, his unmanned boat had covered the 25 miles to Catalina Island, crashing on the rocky shore. There a friend recognized it and called Craig's brother, who started a search.

King David's reliance on God's faithfulness gave him courage to come to God, trusting that God would hear his prayer. God extends the same faithfulness to each person who calls upon Him, whether great king or new Christian. He hears and responds with the gift of eternal life.

*Thank You, **Lord,** for not only revealing Your faithfulness in small ways, but for rescuing me by sending Jesus to pull me out of sin's deep waters. In Him, I have the courage to come before You. And in Him I pray. Amen.*

_____

_____

_____

_____

Keeping Promises

The Lord swore an oath to David, a sure oath that he will not revoke: One of your own descendants I will place on your throne (Psalm 132:11).

Scripture: Psalm 132:1-12

Tears shimmered in Janet's eyes as she fled her father's side. Both hands loaded with clothes, Ben watched her leave, sadness causing his mouth to droop. He then turned from his daughter to his wife. "Martha, you know I wouldn't go if the boss hadn't insisted. I'll try to get back in time for Janet's recital Friday night, but I don't know if I'll be able to get away in time."

As the evening's event approached, Janet alternated between anxiety and anticipation. She had worked so hard for this; it was important for her father to be there. Finally, Mom insisted they had to leave without him.

Ben slid into the saved seat beside his wife, just as Janet's group stepped before the lights. He saw his child's beaming smile as she found both parents' faces in the audience. As the music began and the group of girls stepped across the stage, Ben exchanged looks with his wife, leaned closer to her ear, and whispered, "After all, a promise is a promise."

Father, as You always keep Your promises, help me to keep the promises I make to others. In the precious name of Jesus I pray. Amen.

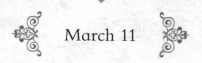

March 11

Plans Gone Amiss

I had it in my heart to build a house as a place of rest for the ark of the covenant of the LORD, for the footstool of our God, and I made plans to build it (1 Chronicles 28:2).

Scripture: 1 Chronicles 28:1-5

Morgana's son, Terry, stomped past her into the hall. "Since you won't let me go to the mall, now I'll have to call Jim and beg off." Just a minor inconvenience for Terry, right? But what if it were something more important, like a move to another city or the purchase of a new car? How often do we make plans, set things in motion, and then run into a brick wall?

"But I prayed about it," we say. Yes, but did we wait to listen for God's guidance, or did we just go ahead, working out the details, committing ourselves to something before really sensing a clear "Go" from above?

When the ark of the covenant arrived back in Jerusalem, King David was so happy he danced with joy before it. He surely spent lots of time planning the temple, collecting materials, designing a resting place for this ark, one worthy of the Lord's presence. Yet, though Scripture doesn't tell us, I suspect David didn't wait to hear all that God had to say about the building—and the builder—of His temple.

Heavenly Father, teach me to seek Your wisdom in everything I undertake. Give me patience to wait for a clear word from You. In the name of Your Son, my Savior, I pray. Amen.

_____

_____

_____

_____

_____

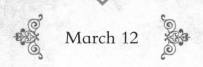

March 12

Learning a Hard Lesson

I will establish his kingdom forever if he is unswerving in carrying out my commands and laws, as is being done at this time (1 Chronicles 28:7).

Scripture: 1 Chronicles 28:6–8

"You're grounded!" said Don, shaking the traffic ticket in his son's face. "There'll be no driving privileges for two weeks, Son." The young man, Joshua, struggled to keep tears of disappointment in check.

Fighting to control his angry response, the father took a deep breath and reached to place an arm around his son's shoulders. "Josh, you know the rules. With privileges come responsibilities. What if someone had been crossing the street when you ran that red light? It could have been much worse."

"I didn't mean to do it, Dad. We were late for the show, and the streets were empty; not another car around. I didn't see the police car until he came up behind me, lights flashing."

"Getting caught isn't the problem, Son. Learning to obey the laws of the land is important. And learning to do that can help us learn to obey God too." Don Morgan tightened his grip. "After all, any authority on earth can only operate with His permission. That's something to honor, right?"

Lord, thank You for giving us civil authorities under Your authority. Please keep our leaders attuned to their responsibilities too! In Jesus' name, amen.

_____

_____

_____

_____

_____

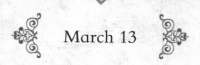

March 13

The Same Hand Provides

Consider now, for the LORD has chosen you to build a temple as a sanctuary. Be strong and do the work (1 Chronicles 28:10).

Scripture: 1 Chronicles 28:9, 10

"But I don't feel qualified to chair the Vacation Bible School program. Find someone who's had experience."

"Mrs. Johnson, as your minister, I've been praying about this for some time, and God keeps bringing your name to mind. I recall you volunteered at the library last summer and helped with their Summer Reading Program. Could this be so much different? And you're good with kids; they really like you. I've noticed how they swarm around you during fellowship time. Just say you'll look over the materials—and get back with me in a couple days—OK?"

Open catalogs and manuals spread around her, Amy felt as if she were drowning. Close to tears, she laid her head down softly. Resting her chin on folded hands, she began to pray, "God, this is such a big job . . ."

Then a familiar Bible verse came to mind: "I can do everything through him who gives me strength" (Philippians 4:13). Maybe, she thought, it wasn't such an impossible task after all.

Father God, I know You empower those whom You call for Your purposes. Help me to remember to look to You for strength and wisdom when I feel overwhelmed. For I know Your hand that points the way is the same hand that provides the way. In Christ's holy name I pray. Amen.

Help When You Need It

"All this," David said, **"I have in writing from the hand of the LORD upon me, and he gave me understanding in all the details of the plan"** (1 Chronicles 28:19).

Scripture: 1 Chronicles 28:11-19

Darrell stepped back and glared at his old tractor. *Why wouldn't that crazy thing run?* He'd tinkered with every part he could get his hands on. And still, the tired engine would just crank over, give a few gasps, and die.

Disgusted with his failed efforts, Darrell packed up his tools and walked away. Later that day, his friend Sam stopped by. Darrell told him about his tractor trials. So they walked, coffee cups in hand, toward the stubborn machine. "I just don't know what else to do. And I sure don't know where I'll find the money for a new tractor."

Sam nodded his head, deep in thought. "Did you set the spark plugs to spec?" Darrell replied in the affirmative. "You know, these old engines get worn after a while," Sam said. "How about adjusting to allow for some wear?" Darrell stopped in his tracks. "You know, Sam, that just might do the trick. I think God brought you over today just to give me that information."

Holy Spirit, You are the promise of God to be teacher of all things. Even before I attempt my own efforts, help me to remember to turn first to You. Teach me to seek Your wisdom whenever I have a problem, for the work of the Kingdom is Yours—and best done in Your way! In the name of God the Father, Son, and Holy Spirit, amen.

_____

_____

_____

_____

_____

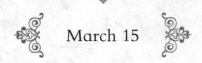

March 15

He Provides the Help

The divisions of the priests and Levites are ready for all the work on the temple of God, and every willing man skilled in any craft will help you in all the work (1 Chronicles 28:21).

Scripture: 1 Chronicles 28:20, 21

"If I could just figure out how to finish off those wings." Gloria reached for another cookie and sipped her hot chocolate. This week's Bible study had produced a lively discussion, and the ladies continued their conversation in the kitchen. "What seems to be your problem?" asked Jane as she settled into the chair beside Gloria.

"Well, I'm working on Margaret's angel costume for the Christmas pageant, but I can't come up with some decent wings."

"I know who can help you," Sally said across the table. "Go to Walden's and talk to the lady in fabrics. She's a whiz. There isn't anything she can't do."

"That's true," said Jane. "She figured out how to attach a veil to my daughter's bridal headpiece last summer. I don't know how many times I've asked for her help. The whole wedding came together like a dream." Gloria smiled her thanks to her friends, as she reached for another cookie. And she silently gave thanks to the Lord for meeting her need.

> *Father, in ancient days King David told his son how You would meet his every need in carrying out Your will. Thank You for this same concern for each need in my own life. How awesome You are! Through Christ, amen.*

_____

_____

_____

_____

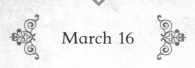

March 16

Preparing Our Dwelling Place

The Lord has chosen Zion, he had desired it for his dwelling (Psalm 132:13).

Scripture: Psalm 132:13-18

Our lease would expire soon, and we had to find a new place that suited our plans. For months we'd searched for property to buy, consulting realtors, scanning ads, and chasing down leads. All to no avail. We were running out of time. Then, while waiting on a dryer load, I scanned the laundromat's bulletin board. A handwritten note caught my attention . . . And the first time I stepped onto that piece of land, I knew I was home.

We were blessed in being able to choose our place of retirement. This will be our dwelling place for the rest of our lives, God willing.

God has a dwelling place too! First Corinthians 3:16 tells us that we are God's temple, that His Spirit dwells in us. God chose us and called us to be the embodied evidence of His reality in the world. Therefore, each day as I look about this beautiful place God prepared for us, I ask His help in keeping His own dwelling place worthy of His abiding presence.

Father, I thank You for sending the Holy Spirit to indwell me, to be my comforter and guide. Remind me, too, that I am Your representative in my world, Your ambassador among my neighbors. Help me show forth Your love in all I do and say. I pray this prayer in the name of Jesus, my merciful Savior and Lord. Amen.

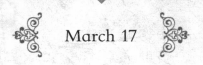

March 17

God's Name

I know that the LORD is great, and that our Lord is greater than all gods. The LORD does whatever pleases him, in the heavens and on the earth, in the seas and all their depths (Psalm 135:5, 6).

Scripture: Psalm 135:1-5

A lady in our study group asked, "Why not call Jesus by the name of Allah or Buddha? They're just other names for God, right?"

"If I called my husband another name," came my reply, "would he be upset?"

"Of course. You're his wife. You should know his name," she said. I nodded. "God has told us His names in the Bible. He never identified himself as Allah or Buddha. Why should we call Him something He has not called himself?"

From the very beginning, Christianity has had to challenge what is known as "syncretism"—the belief that somehow all claims to truth have equal value and must be equally accepted. Yet the Scriptures tell us that one God is greater than all other gods. And we know who this one is: the God and Father of our Lord Jesus Christ.

> ***Almighty God,*** *may I honor You and Your name with heartfelt adoration, realizing You are the God above all gods, the only one worthy of my praise. In the name of Your Son, my Savior, I pray. Amen.*

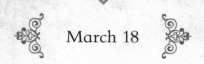

What's in Your Heart?

My father David had it in his heart to build a temple for the Name of the LORD, the God of Israel (2 Chronicles 6:7).

Scripture: 2 Chronicles 6:1-11

Long ago I asked the Lord to help me make a list of the qualities He wanted for my four children's future spouses. Periodically I prayed this list back to God—reminding Him, in a sense, of the list He gave me. Eighteen years separate the first from the last child. As the children grew up, they found the persons described on the list. Today, three are married with children; one to go.

The list didn't call for good looks or big bank accounts, but for good help-mates. It asked for the establishment of godly homes where children are loved and nurtured. It sought a home environment where every family member would hear and heed God's voice.

I truly believe the Lord put these thoughts into my heart, just as He put it into David's heart to build a beautiful temple for Him. I may not live to see that last child marry, but I know I can trust God to work in his life. David didn't live to see the finished temple, but he fervently aspired to lay the groundwork for what was to come. And that attitude was critical. As mystic James Allen said: "You will become as small as your controlling desire, as great as your dominant aspiration."

Father God, may I listen for Your direction as I pray, go with Your flow, and make Your heart glad in all my ways. In Jesus' name, amen.

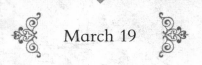

March 19

I Promise

O LORD, the God of Israel, there is no god like Thee in heaven or on earth, keeping covenant and showing lovingkindness to Thy servants who walk before Thee with all their heart (2 Chronicles 6:14, *New American Standard Bible*).

Scripture: 2 Chronicles 6:12-17

"I'm really in a pinch. I promise I'll pay you back on payday," my coworker says. Payday comes. I receive excuses . . . but no repayment.

"Mom, please let me have a puppy. I promise I'll take care of it." But once the puppy grows up, I become its constant caretaker.

"If you'll take the chairmanship, I promise I'll be there to back you up, one hundred percent." The support dwindles to nearly zero by the end of my term of office.

I am guilty of the same kinds of promise-breaking, though. No matter how sincere I may be when I proclaim a promise, I sometimes lose heart before I can fulfill my best intentions.

God is different. He is absolutely, eternally trustworthy. Yet when He promises, He sometimes attaches a condition. And that's where the problem comes in. I'm fickle. I don't have the power to complete my part unless I rely on Him for the strength of heart to carry on to the end. You see, what God *calls* me to, He gives me the *strength* to do.

Faithful One, help me to follow through on what I have promised as I reach out and receive Your strength to finish well. In Jesus' name, amen.

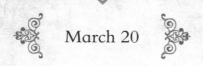

Hearing, Heart to Heart

Hear Thou from heaven Thy dwelling-place, and forgive, and render to each according to all his ways, whose heart Thou knowest for Thou alone dost know the hearts of the sons of men, that they may fear Thee, to walk in Thy ways as long as they live in the land which Thou hast given to our fathers (2 Chronicles 6:30, 31, *New American Standard Bible*).

Scripture: 2 Chronicles 6:18-31

I watch a robin hop over the spring grass in my back yard. It pauses, cocks his head, and listens. With a quick peck, he leans back and pulls a worm out of the ground.

I can't imagine having ears so sharp they can hear a worm crawling underground! God's ears are even better than that, though. He can hear my prayers all the way from earth to Heaven, even if those prayers are unspoken (for He knows my heart, and prayer is more about my open, longing heart than about the words I compose).

He longs to hear from me, heart to heart. Therefore, today I will make time to quiet my heart before Him that He may say:

> My child, come and enter in,
> unburden your soul of cares and sin.
> I long to hear from you today.
> Ask Me; I'll find a way.

Lord, forgive me when I cling to my problems, assuming You're uninterested. Reconnect me today to Your constant presence. Through Christ, amen.

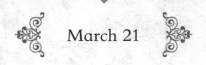

March 21

Homecoming

He got up and came to his father. But while he was still a long way off, his father saw him, and felt compassion for him, and ran and embraced him, and kissed him. And the son said to him, "Father, I have sinned against heaven and in your sight; I am no longer worthy to be called your son" (Luke 15:20, 21 *New American Standard Bible*).

Scripture: 2 Chronicles 6:36-39

At times I have gone into the far land of unforgiveness, greed, or anger. The only solution: name the land, ask God for forgiveness, and come home. Then my prayers sound like this . . .

"Father, You see me from afar. You run toward me, throw Your arms around me, and call for celebration. My heart rejoices in Your strong embrace. You declare I am no longer a slave, but a reinstated child.

"Your mercy flows like honey; Your smile, like sunshine. You wipe away my tears and dress me in fine linen, slipping the ring of rulership on my finger.

"Who am I that You should do this for me? Surely, Your mercy extends to even my generation. I bow before You, who stays closer than a brother, and then I look into Your eyes. My inmost being melts in gratitude before You, my Savior, my Lord, my God.

"And I hear You say, 'Welcome home, child.'"

Father, thank You for Your constant vigilance for my return—and for giving Your Son to provide a way home for me. In His name I pray. Amen.

_____

_____

_____

_____

His Resting Place

Arise, O LORD God, to Thy resting place (2 Chronicles 6:41, *New American Standard Bible*).

Scripture: 2 Chronicles 6:40-42

Imagine being an Israelite surrounded by all the lavish architectural workmanship on the day when Solomon dedicated the temple. Over here, intricately worked solid brass pillars more than 40' high. There, a beautifully fashioned gold overlay box with angels adorning the top. On the far wall, two golden lamp stands created by the finest craftsmen.

On that day, Solomon invited the Lord to come dwell in the Holy of Holies, the divine "resting place." And God graciously answered Solomon's prayer; He filled the temple with His presence in the form of a glory cloud.

In contrast, when Jesus came to earth in a body, He didn't live in a gilded temple. He had no place to lay His head in the very world He'd created. Even after death, He lay in a borrowed tomb.

Now the Lord has risen from the dead—and is still looking for a place to reside. Today Jesus asks, "May I come make my home inside your heart? May I settle in and abide there?"

Dear heavenly Father, make my heart Your resting place. May Your roots sink down deep into me. Let nothing tear me away from You, and help me avoid any distraction that arranges my priorities apart from the kingdom work You've given me. In the name of Jesus, amen.

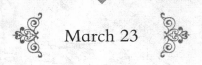

March 23

His Power

I am sending forth the promise of my Father upon you; but you are to stay in the city until you are clothed with power from on high (Luke 24:49, *New American Standard Bible*).

Scripture: Luke 24:44-49

In 1955, I read in *Life* magazine about the five missionaries martyred while they ministered to the Waodani Indians in Ecuador's eastern rainforest. I was a young Christian, and I wondered how people could have the faith to go into such a hostile place, spurning the threat of death, to preach the gospel.

Years later, I understood: They didn't rely on their own strength. They had the power of the Holy Spirit, just as the first disciples did. After Jesus walked on this earth with His followers for three years, He told them they'd receive the promised Holy Spirit to guide them after His resurrection and ascension to Heaven. Obedient, they waited until the Day of Pentecost for the Holy Spirit to come into them in fullness. Then they were ready to be His witnesses, even to death.

You and I need the Holy Spirit operating in our lives today, just as the first disciples did. Thankfully, once we are baptized, the Spirit comes to dwell within us, empowering us to serve in the deepest jungles—or in our neighbor's living room.

Father, thanks for sending Your Holy Spirit that I may be an effective witness in any circumstance You may bring my way. In Jesus' name, amen.

_____

_____

_____

_____

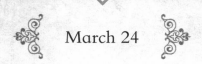

Freedom Through Obedience

I run in the path of your commands, for you have set my heart free (Psalm 119:32).

Scripture: Psalm 119:25-32

My kids, probably like yours, always wanted to do things their way. I remember watching my 2-year-old son as he brushed his teeth one day. This was back in the days when I'd need to help him, so our routine was that he would start the process and I would finish it, or vice versa. On this particular day, I said "How about if I start, and you finish?" He carefully thought about it and then replied firmly, "No, *you* start and I'll finish!"

As children, we think we know it all. However, if you're like me, as a "maturing" adult, I have become painfully aware of how limited my knowledge is. I've also experienced how wonderfully God directs our paths and learned that there is no need to run from Him. In fact, these days, instead of running from His leading, I yearn for it; I seek it.

It's in that safe place that I find the most perfect peace and joy. Strangely, obedience sets my heart free; liberty flows amidst a yielding to His commands.

> **Lord,** *thank You for Your patience with me as I struggle to find my way in this world. And thank You for embracing me when I do eventually come running into Your wide-open arms. I pray in Jesus' holy name. Amen.*

_____

_____

_____

_____

_____

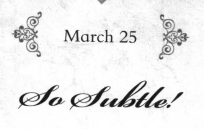

So Subtle!

In his twelfth year he began to purge Judah and Jerusalem of high places, Asherah poles, carved idols and cast images (2 Chronicles 34:3).

Scripture: 2 Chronicles 34:1-7

Ever played the dictionary game? It's a competition in which participants create fake definitions for a word and then read them aloud—including the correct one. They then compete to determine which definition is true amid the false. To score points and win, a good player will create a unique and convincing, close-to-true definition to distract the other players from what is genuinely correct.

King Josiah didn't play the dictionary game, of course, but he was responsible for proclaiming what was true among many false distractions. Twelve years into his rule, he saw his people worshiping powerless idols. His response? He destroyed the idols, eliminating the distractions, and turned the people's eyes to the one true God.

In our day, idolatry is ever so subtle and subversive. Most of us won't turn from the Lord completely; we'll steer clear of the obvious falsities around us. But we may well be distracted by a few choice half-truths—just enough to live a thoroughly lukewarm Christian life. Perhaps that is enough to make the god of this world quite happy.

__Lord,__ I live in a world filled with distractions and subtle heresies. Give me a discerning heart, filled with Your wisdom! In Jesus' name, amen.

_____

_____

_____

_____

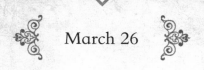

March 26

Mom Too

The men did the work faithfully (2 Chronicles 34:12).

Scripture: 2 Chronicles 34:8-18

I remember it well. The special Bible had a beautiful rendition of Jesus with children on its cover, as well as many colorful pictures inside. A small gold cross hung from the zipper that enclosed it.

Using her meager factory wages, our Primary Department Sunday school teacher had sacrificially purchased five of these Bibles to present to her students. This woman dedicated herself to telling kids of God's love for them. Not only did she faithfully take her own children to church regularly, she determined to help others learn of Him.

She faithfully served in our little country church in whatever way she could. Even with her limited 8th-grade education, she could still invite children to Sunday school. She could still drive them to church. She could still buy a few Bibles with a picture of Jesus-and-the-children on the cover. She could still serve God.

Just like the men in today's Scripture reading, this humble woman quietly and faithfully served God in any way she could. She also built a solid legacy in the process, as that faithful woman was my mother.

Father, how thankful I am for the long train of dedicated men and women who have served you faithfully from the very beginnings of the church! May I someday be added to that marvelous list. Through Christ, amen.

_____

_____

_____

_____

_____

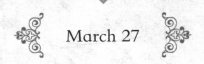

March 27

Personal Faith

Great is the LORD's anger that is poured out on us because our fathers have not kept the word of the LORD (2 Chronicles 34:21).

Scripture: 2 Chronicles 34:19-21

Severe hearing loss is hereditary on my father's side of the family. He had 12 siblings, and many of them shared this "family curse."

My brother also inherited it. He was sent to a school for the deaf as a 6-year-old, where he learned how to read lips.

I have cousins whose children inherited this disability, and I also have second cousins whose children have inherited it. My son hasn't had children yet, but I do worry about them.

Thus far, deafness has missed me personally, and I am thankful for that. But of greater concern to me than my physical heredity is my spiritual heritage. Unlike Josiah, I've truly benefited from my family's good spiritual influence over the years. But unless I personally accept Jesus' sacrificial death on the cross and receive His forgiveness and salvation, I will miss out on that blessing altogether. Whether or not I benefit from my spiritual heritage depends upon my personal choice.

> **God,** thank You for providing eternal life through Jesus. I am grateful for the opportunity to accept Him as my Savior. I rejoice in knowing that Christ has paid the full penalty for my sins. In His precious name, amen.

Jesus, PhD?

Because your heart was responsive and you humbled yourself before God . . . I have heard you, declares the LORD (2 Chronicles 34:27).

Scripture: 2 Chronicles 34:22-28

At work this week, I overheard some coworkers energetically discussing a problem in the hall outside of my office. One person said, "Your opinion doesn't count until you have a doctorate after your name." I couldn't believe what I was hearing! What an arrogant comment (coming from someone with a doctorate, actually).

Not a great way to win friends and influence people. But worse, it's an ineffective way to represent Jesus, isn't it? I think of how our Savior interacted so intimately with the lowliest of people in His day: the woman at the well; the woman who poured expensive perfume on His feet; Zacchaeus, the tax collector, with whom no one else would associate.

In further humble service, Christ washed His own disciples' feet, instead of the other way around. Time after time, Jesus lived out a perfect example of how to humble ourselves before God—with no PhD required.

Almighty and everlasting God, may my heart be humble, realizing that everything I have is from You. Every breath I breathe is because of You. Every day I live is because You've willed it to be so. I praise You and humbly thank You for Your love for me, in spite of my undeserving ways. In the holy name of Jesus, my Lord and Savior, I pray. Amen.

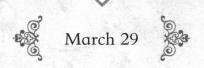

Heart and Soul

The king stood by his pillar and renewed the covenant in the presence of the LORD—to follow the LORD and keep his commands, regulations and decrees with all his heart (2 Chronicles 34:31).

Scripture: 2 Chronicles 34:29-33

I was 15 years old, attending a Christian summer camp for the very first time. Coming from a small rural church with few teens, I thought I'd entered Heaven—along with 150 other young people.

I had such great fun that week! I sang, I swam, I ate, I made lifelong friends. More importantly, I was challenged to deepen my faith in the most practical ways. The special speaker for the week asked, "Whose side will you choose to be on? Will it be God's side, or . . . the *other* side? You can't walk the fence. You must choose."

That was exactly what I had been doing—walking the fence. I was the perfect Christian young lady on Sundays when I attended church, and the typical self-centered teenager when in school. Not surprisingly, few of my schoolmates knew I was a Christian.

In our Scripture reading today, King Josiah renewed His commitment to follow the Lord with all of his heart and soul. That week at camp, I did the same. And I haven't looked back since.

Lord, keep before me this day the precious decrees of Your goodness and love that come to me in the Scriptures. Thank You, in Jesus' name. Amen.

_____

_____

_____

_____

_____

Safe and Sound

Turn my eyes away from worthless things (Psalm 119:37).

Scripture: Psalm 119:33-40

Most autistic people have a hard time looking into another person's eyes. They find it quite difficult and threatening. My daughter has Asperger's syndrome, a high functioning form of autism. She keeps her gaze down when she's with others, rarely looking someone in the eye. That usually only happens when she starts feeling emotionally "safe" with someone.

Today's Scripture reading reminds us to turn our eyes to God's Word for our guidance in daily life. There God reveals what is right and wrong, and what will bring us genuine joy. Turning our eyes from the temporary thrills of this world to the eternal purposes of God is a sure way to stay spiritually "safe," as it will keep our priorities in good order.

It's comforting to know that we can "gaze" into God's heart, isn't it? We do it through prayer, through studying His Word, through listening to that still, small voice as the Holy Spirit guides us through each day. We can feel safe, too, in His returning gaze, knowing that He is completely trustworthy.

My loving heavenly Father, I lift my eyes up to the hills. Where does my help come from? It comes from You, the creator of Heaven and earth. Please remind me that I am safe, forever, in Your care. I pray this prayer in the name of Jesus, my merciful Savior and Lord. Amen.

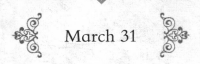

Waiting to Hear from Us

O Lord, I call to you; come quickly to me. Hear my voice when I call to you (Psalm 141:1).

Scripture: Psalm 141:1-4

A. W. Tozer once suggested that the Christian is a rather odd person: "He feels supreme love for One whom he has never seen; talks familiarly every day to Someone he cannot see; expects to go to Heaven on the virtue of Another; empties himself in order to be full; admits he is wrong so he can be declared right; goes down in order to get up; is strongest when he is weakest; richest when he is poorest and happiest when he feels the worst."

We understand David's prayer in similar, paradoxical fashion. We ask the One who is already here to "come" to us. We ask the One who never slumbers, the One who already knows our every need, to "hear" us as we call to Him. Yet David understands that *God wants to hear from us*. He delights in our expressions of dependence upon Him.

The power is in the appeal. God wants to hear from you, is patiently *waiting* to hear from you. He delights in those who take the time to seek His favor, who call upon Him, knowing He hears and answers.

O Lord, I thank You for your comforting presence and that I can turn to You whenever I need. Keep me attentive to Your gentle responses as You guide me each step along Your paths of peace. In Jesus' name, amen.

_____

_____

_____

_____

_____

April

*O Lord, hear my voice. Let your ears be attentive
to my cry for mercy.*

—Psalm 130:2

Evil Empire

The LORD delivered Jehoiakim king of Judah into his hand, along with some of the articles from the temple of God (Daniel 1:2).

Scripture: Daniel 1:1, 2

The New York Yankees are one of the most successful sports franchises ever. That means sports fans either love 'em or hate 'em. Detractors have dubbed them "The Evil Empire"; nothing good ever comes from the Yankees.

Amazingly, we sometimes see God using evil empires for His good purposes. For instance, a stubborn, pagan Pharaoh arose to his position so that God could demonstrate His power. In another case, the prophet Habakkuk discovered that vicious Babylonians would actually be God's instrument to deal with evil in the land of Israel. In the Gospels, Jesus told Pilate that his power to pronounce a death sentence could only come from above.

So we shouldn't be surprised that, in Daniel's day, God used Nebuchadnezzar to discipline his wayward people. To the human eye, Israel fell to a greater kingdom. But Scripture affirms that the Lord himself remained in control. This account gives us a wonderful personal application: Never be quick to assume that evil is winning the day.

Father, I marvel at how You use the unwilling, the uncaring, even the ones adamantly opposed to You. What a sovereign God! Through Christ, amen.

_____

_____

_____

_____

April 2

Worthy by His Grace

Bring . . . young men without any physical defect, handsome, showing aptitude for every kind of learning, well informed, quick to understand, and qualified to serve in the king's palace (Daniel 1:3, 4).

Scripture: Daniel 1:3-7

Mighty Moses thought he couldn't speak in public. The great King David's brothers once ridiculed him as a child and tried to send him home. And valiant warrior Gideon initially saw himself as the weakest of all the Israelites.

In our Scripture passage today, Daniel, Hananiah, Mishael, and Azariah were selected for training in order to enter the Babylonian king's service. Only those who met the highest physical and intellectual standards were chosen. So imagine the boost to one's self-esteem should he "get the call."

We often doubt ourselves, our abilities, or our worthiness to serve God. Yet God sees all that is hidden from our view. He looks past outward appearances and into our hearts. Yet He does not save us based on our potential or any human quality within us. He calls us by pure grace and prepares us for His service through the working of His Spirit within us. Bottom line: We are "worthy" only as He makes us so.

Lord, You have selected and gifted each of us for Your service. No ability, no talent, no matter how meager it may seem, is insignificant. Help me to use all that You have given me for Your glory alone. In Jesus' name, amen.

_____

_____

_____

_____

_____

Resolved!

Daniel resolved not to defile himself with the royal food and wine, and he asked the chief official for permission not to defile himself this way (Daniel 1:8).

Scripture: Daniel 1:8-10

It has been estimated that most New Year's resolutions are broken within a few short days. Some apparently don't even last the night! But not so with Daniel. He resolved not to defile himself with any food God had declared unclean, and he stuck to it. For him, even the demands of a king took second place to the laws of God.

God's people have always realized that sin defiles them in the sight of God and weakens their fellowship with Him. There really are no justifications that might excuse us from obedience to our loving Lord. And that is good—for our own good—because of sin's destructive power.

In the book of Genesis, Joseph faced temptation, day after day, from Potiphar's wife. But he resolved not to sin against God.

Let us consider today: What special circumstances tend to make it difficult for us to obey God? Do certain acquaintances bring temptations with them? Do certain environments put us at risk? May we rightly proceed with caution amidst circumstances that will try our souls. Thus may our resolve never be defiled.

Lord, I can be weak, easily tempted, so quick to make poor choices. May the resolve of Daniel inspire me to stand firm this day. In Jesus' name, amen.

April 4

Daniel: A+

Please test your servants for ten days: Give us nothing but vegetables to eat and water to drink (Daniel 1:12).

Scripture: Daniel 1:11-14

While some may enjoy watching a film like *Arachnophobia,* one friend of mine can't even stand to watch the previews. For someone who actually suffers from that particular phobia, there's no entertainment value in watching marauding spiders intent on inflicting mayhem. But the people I feel for most are those stricken with testophobia. Nothing fancy in this word; it's exactly what it sounds like—a fear of taking tests.

Though he didn't face a classroom setting, Daniel welcomed his special test, a test of faith in God. What an opportunity to demonstrate the superiority of God's wisdom in all things—even nutrition! So Daniel proposed a 10-day test between those eating the rich, royal foods and the four young Hebrew men (Daniel included) who would eat only what God had declared appropriate.

Daniel understood that God's laws aren't meant to restrict us, but to enhance us. Royal food would defile; God's way would bless. In other words, pass the test of obedience . . . and reap your blessing!

Dear Lord, when the way seems cloudy, when it seems another way holds greater promise, remind me of the wisdom of Your ways, of the blessings inherent in Your plans for me. For this day, keep me walking in obedience as You assure me of Your constant presence. In Jesus' name, Amen.

April 5

It Is Enough

To these four young men God gave knowledge and understanding of all kinds of literature and learning. And Daniel could understand visions and dreams of all kinds (Daniel 1:17).

Scripture: Daniel 1:15-17

John Murray lay in bed ill, and his son was reading the Bible to him. Upon hearing the words of Psalm 8:8, "All that swim the paths of the seas," Murray asked the boy to repeat the phrase. Hearing it the second time, Murray said, "It is enough if the Word of God says there are paths in the sea; they must be there, and I am going to find them." Within a few years he had discovered and was charting ocean currents. This 19th-century Canadian is now considered the father of modern oceanography.

Notice Murray's faith: If the Word of God says it is so . . . It was enough, too, for our four young men, that God said it was so. Daniel and his friends trusted the wisdom of God's dietary laws and were blessed accordingly.

To those with faith, God's Word is more than a guide for getting to Heaven. It is also the wisdom of God for successful living in this present world. And, most wonderfully, such wisdom remains readily available, as the apostle James tells us: " If any of you lacks wisdom, he should ask God, who gives generously to all" (James 1:5).

*Help me, **Father**, to stand upon Your Word as firmly as those who have preceded me in the faith with such laudable lives. In Christ's name, amen.*

_____

_____

_____

_____

_____

April 6

None Equal

The king talked with them, and he found none equal to Daniel, Hananiah, Mishael and Azariah; so they entered the king's service (Daniel 1:19).

Scripture: Daniel 1:18-21

We measure intelligence with a test that gives us a numeric rating we call our "intelligence quotient," or IQ. Marilyn vos Savant achieved the highest IQ ever recorded, 228. I enjoy reading her newspaper column, in which she answers various questions posed by readers. I've yet to see her struggling to answer, and I marvel at her wit and wisdom.

In this way, I can relate to an ancient king who enjoyed talking with four young Hebrew men. To this mighty ruler, the young men surpassed all the other supposed wise men of his kingdom. The king's discerning investigation was the only "IQ test" that mattered, and his word was this: there were none wiser than these four youths.

Few of us can say there are "none equal" to us in any particular field. And, of course, we may never stand before a king. But God's wisdom, encased within His Word, will bring His blessing to those who live accordingly. Build your house on the solid foundation of His Word, and others may well marvel at the depth of your wisdom and understanding.

Lord, guide me in Your wisdom lest I go astray. As I heed Your indwelling Spirit, may Your glory be my only claim to fame. Through Christ, amen.

_____

_____

_____

_____

_____

April 7

The Lord Our Helper

My help comes from the LORD, who made the heavens and the earth! (Psalm 121:2, *New Living Translation*).

Scripture: Psalm 121:1-4

As Hurricane Katrina blew across Louisiana, Annie's husband, Mack, was air-lifted to safety from his room in a New Orleans hospital. Not knowing where Mack had been taken, Annie was forced to live for weeks by herself in the downtown convention center. After the waters receded, Annie searched for two weeks and finally found Mack in a Lafayette hospital, 160 miles west of New Orleans. Annie lost her home, all that she owned, and almost lost her husband.

Lafayette overflowed with evacuees, as shelters and churches housed thousands. Many took strangers into their homes, including my niece, Pixan. She met Annie at an ice cream parlor near the hospital and could almost hear God whisper, "She's the one I want you to help." Pixan prayed with Annie, brought her home, and cared for her needs. After Frank's release from the hospital, God miraculously led them to the last available rental house in Lafayette. When you are lost, hurting or alone, God knows right where you are. He'll send help.

Lord, when I despair of finding any help amidst my daily difficulties, refocus my vision on Your infinite power and love! Through Christ, amen.

_____

_____

_____

_____

_____

April 8

Sudden Trouble

As soon as they heard the sound of the horn, flute, zither, lyre, harp and all kinds of music, all the peoples, nations and men of every language fell down and worshiped the image of gold that King Nebuchadnezzar had set up (Daniel 3:7).

Scripture: Daniel 3:1-7

A great raging wall of water crashed into the Gulf Coast with a fury unknown in U.S. history, destroying everything in its path. Living in Louisiana, I watched with horror as our stunned government officials bowed in fear before the devastation of Hurricane Katrina. While many shuddered at the magnitude of the damage, God was raising up a mighty force, the church, to respond with compassion and practical help. Thus, in a sense, God was the "first responder."

God shows His love and care amidst the worst catastrophes. Surely God's people felt it a sudden, tragic turn of events when King Nebuchadnezzar set up his golden image for idolatrous worship. In horror they heard the sound of the horns and knew that death could be imminent. Yet God used King Nebuchadnezzar's fearsome decrees as part of His plan to bless Daniel and the captive nation. Whether nature harasses us—or even our own secular leaders—we can remain confident amidst every raging wind: God's will prevails.

__Lord,__ instead of bowing down under the weight of my problems, let me rise up, strong and courageous, in Your strength. In Jesus' name, amen.

_____

_____

_____

_____

_____

In Flood or Fire

If you do not worship [the idol], you will be thrown immediately into a blazing furnace. Then what god will be able to rescue you from my hand? (Daniel 3:15).

Scripture: Daniel 3:8-15

My brother, Billy, and sister-in-law, Delores, are from St. Bernard Parish, Louisiana. For them, Katrina's floods came even more unexpectedly than for others. You see, they thought they were safe living in an area that *never* floods. But their front door burst open one morning, and within two minutes they stood waist deep in water.

They broke down the back door and climbed up the outside garage stairs onto the roof, barely making it out before the entire house flooded. A neighbor with a boat rescued them and brought them to a local community center, where they stayed for three days without food or water. All the while, the family was praying for them, not knowing where they were or if they were even alive. (Billy has diabetes and could have been in really big trouble.)

Six days later we found them all in Baton Rouge. They were extremely dirty and starving, but "OK." Billy had no medication for the entire time. He could have died in a diabetic coma, but our God was able to deliver him. What a miracle! No matter what troubles you—freezing flood waters or a blazing furnace—God can rescue you.

God, I won't be forced to worship an idol today, but I am often tempted by lesser gods. Help me cling to You a bit tighter! Through Christ, amen.

_____

_____

_____

_____

April 10

Best Defense: None

If we are thrown into the blazing furnace, the God we serve is able to save us from it, and he will rescue us from your hand, O king (Daniel 3:17).

Scripture: Daniel 3:16-23

Marty works for a large corporation where He manages dozens of salesmen. He is honest, hardworking, and well-regarded by his superiors. But two years ago, his work situation changed drastically. Marty's new supervisor was "offended" by his Christianity and did everything she could to make him look incompetent, even embarrassing him publicly at a large manager's meeting.

Marty's response? He prayed for her, determining to trust in God's favor. By the end of the year, he was worn out, but at the last sales manager's meeting, the CEO announced Marty's group as the top sales group in the entire company. They honored him with a large bonus and a nice vacation. And . . . the CEO transferred Ben's supervisor to another area of the company—she has not been heard of since.

Notice in our Scripture today that the three Hebrew men didn't defend themselves. They allowed God to do the talking for them. It seems that when we stand up for God, even in total silence, He will fight for us.

*   **Almighty Lord,** *You see my trials and You are fully able to defend me when I can not defend myself. Thank You, my rock, my shield, my strength, and my redeemer. In Christ's holy name I pray. Amen.*

_____

_____

_____

_____

He's There!

He said, "Look! I see four men walking around in the fire, unbound and unharmed, and the fourth looks like a son of the gods" (Daniel 3:25).

Scripture: Daniel 3:24-27

I hope you aren't tired of hearing about Hurricane Katrina. For those of us who lived in Louisiana during those howling winds, fearsome memories still linger. At the moment, I'm thinking of the six pine trees that smashed through Ron and Caron's roof. Every room in the house was ruined as trees and water burst through.

The couple went into shock, totally overwhelmed, but God held them in His hands. Ron and Caron moved in with a family friend and, one by one, work crews from churches around the country began to show up for them. People they didn't know cut trees, cleared the yard, and removed the damaged sections of the house. Months later, after many tears and many prayers, the house stands rebuilt.

The trials have been great, the stress difficult, but God walked with them in the midst of their "fiery furnace." They are coming up out of the fire without even the smell of smoke on their clothes. What was impossible for human strength, God accomplished with divine power. In fact, He was right there with them the whole time.

God, You've promised to walk with me through flood or fire. Even if I perish, I'm determined to walk with You through it all. In Jesus' name, amen.

_____

_____

_____

_____

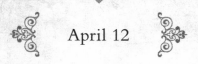

April 12

Amazing Reversals

I decree that the people of any nation or language who say anything against the God of Shadrach, Meshach and Abednego be cut into pieces and their houses be turned into piles of rubble, for no other god can save in this way (Daniel 3:29).

Scripture: Daniel 3:28-30

Decades ago, Sara received a letter warning, "Do not return to East Germany, or you will be arrested. And don't smuggle any more Bibles into this country." She prayerfully obeyed God, however, and on her next trip she entered another communist country, Poland. I went with her—on my first mission trip.

Sara knew God was able to deliver her from her enemies. Once, while crossing into Germany (before the wall came down) an SS officer interrogated her. As he drew back his fist to strike her, she prayed for God's protection. The officer's arm froze in mid-air, and Sara shared the gospel with him. The upshot was that Sara soon had a friend to protect her whenever she came through his checkpoint at the border.

God Almighty has been working such amazing reversals among His people for centuries. A blaspheming king becomes defender of Israel's God; a Gestapo torturer turns compassionate helper. Who but the Lord could save the day in this way?

Lord, keep me trusting You, even in dangerous situations. Help me recall the miraculous ways You deliver Your children. In Christ's name, amen.

_____

_____

_____

_____

April 13

Storm Protection

The LORD will keep you from all harm—he will watch over your life (Psalm 121:7).

Scripture: Psalm 121:5-8

The house moaned—I could see the walls moving in and out with the force of Katrina. The winds screamed as they passed between the houses. Three mighty oak trees groaned an unearthly cry as they were torn from their roots, falling on the left side of the house. They toppled over, one after another, like heavy giants, shaking the world with their impact.

Next the winds whipped around the house, and a tree came crashing down in the backyard. But instead of falling in the same direction as the others, it had fallen at a 90-degree angle across the back. An eternity seemed to pass while the terror went on and on. Then several large branches tore off the trees in the front yard, falling in front of the door.

When the winds finally ended, my house stood safe amidst a mass of uprooted and broken trees. I don't know why some suffer such tragedy and why some are untouched, but I know God is faithful to all who call on Him. He watches over their lives, preserving them here in the reality we know on earth—or taking them to be with Him in the ultimate reality that awaits all who love Him.

> **God,** *You deliver from trials, not by always changing the circumstances but in transforming my heart. Thanks for Your peace! Through Christ, amen.*

_____

_____

_____

_____

_____

April 14

No Excuse, Please!

Though the wicked bind me with ropes, I will not forget your law (Psalm 119:61).

Scripture: Psalm 119:57-64

"He hit me first!" offers 8-year-old Steven, who had just been fighting with his brother. Typical childhood explanation for less than exemplary behavior, right?

But don't we adults often apply this "because he did a bad thing to me" logic to justify our sins? We may well feel justified in forgetting what's truly right when someone seriously wrongs us. We drop a tidbit of juicy gossip about her, we make it hard for him, we overestimate the damages, or we exaggerate (or underreport) on our tax forms. Yet, two wrongs do not make a right.

The psalmist understood this. Daniel understood it too: Obedience to God offers no loopholes or compromises. Hard times, insults, injuries—none justify evil on our part. If, like the psalmist, we promise to obey God, seek God with all our hearts, consider all our ways, and are quick to obey God's commands, then—if we have integrity—we will not forget God's law, even though the wicked bind us with ropes.

Father, You know my desire to love and obey You—and my tendency to forget Your law, especially when others have hurt me. Help me to respond as Your Son always did, in obedience and love. Through Him, amen.

Character, or Just Position?

Daniel so distinguished himself among the administrators and the satraps by his exceptional qualities that the king planned to set him over the whole kingdom (Daniel 6:3).

Scripture: Daniel 6:1-4

Most of us know the story of Daniel in the lions' den, which unfolds here in chapter 6. We know of Daniel and his obedience, and we recall how God rescued him from hungry lions' jaws.

We may be less familiar with King Darius, who plays a key role in this story. In these next few days, let us consider and contrast Daniel and King Darius. I believe we'll gain some insights into the differences between the kingdom of God and human kingdoms, between a man who knows, loves, and obeys God, and a man who knows power, loves himself, and obeys his own desires.

Today's passage reveals a difference in the origins of their power. Darius had power because of his position, because he ruled the kingdom and could direct the affairs of his subjects as he pleased. He assumed he was accountable only to himself. Daniel, on the other hand, had power because of his exceptional qualities, because he was trustworthy, incorruptible, conscientious, and skillful. Kingdom people are known not so much by their *position,* but by their *character.*

> **Lord,** *develop in me the qualities shining so brightly in Daniel's life. May I too come to be known as a person of character. In the name of Jesus, amen.*

_____

_____

_____

_____

April 16

Really Number One?

Anyone who prays to any god or man during the next thirty days, except to you, O king, shall be thrown into the lions' den (Daniel 6:7).

Scripture: Daniel 6:5-9

O King / Queen _____ (fill in your own name), live forever! The world has agreed that you deserve the best and most luxurious house, car, vacations, toys, tools, games, and pleasure. You deserve to be adored and admired by everyone for your accomplishments, your good looks, your good deeds, your power, and your possessions. You are, in effect, King Darius.

This vain monarch found it perfectly natural that everyone should bow to him, and so he happily wrote a decree that he alone must be worshiped for a solid 30 days (for starters). In contrast, Daniel humbly worshiped God alone, coming before Him with praises and petitions.

Hundreds of advertisements each day—and many well-intentioned people—try to convince me that I deserve the best, that I should live luxuriously, and that, really, the world ought to worship me. It makes me wonder: How tempted am I to secretly agree, like King Darius, that I'm Number One in the universe?

O God, help me to center my life around You, for You alone are worthy of devotion and praise. Help me to resist the world's temptations to vanity and pride. I come humbly to You daily to seek Your presence, Your will, Your power, Your grace, and Your mercy. In Christ's name, amen.

_____

_____

_____

_____

_____

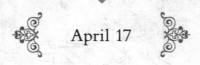

April 17

Impractical Behavior

[Daniel] went home to his upstairs room where the windows opened toward Jerusalem . . . [and] got down on his knees and prayed . . . just as he had done before (Daniel 6:10).

Scripture: Daniel 6:10-14

While clearly an excellent administrator, Daniel isn't primarily a "practical" man. He does not compromise his walk with God or his testimony in order to be politically correct or to protect his personal interests. He does not selfishly conceal his relationship with God for 30 days until the decree expires.

There was nothing magical about praying with open windows towards Jerusalem three times a day. Yet, to hide his prayers in this circumstance would be to give in to his enemies' attack on his integrity as servant of the living God.

The world says, "Be practical. Compromise your walk with God in order to get along and fit in. Talk about sports, the weather, politics, and even sex, but don't talk about Jesus, sin, or salvation. Gossip about people's outrageous lifestyles, but don't pass moral judgment on them. Worship the world's idols, but not the Lord God."

It won't be easy, but I hope today to follow Daniel's impractical example. Will you join me?

Living God, I want to grow in my walk with You, and I want my life to testify to Your glory and goodness. May the manner of my life today humbly testify to the world that You are Lord of All. In Jesus' name, amen.

_____

_____

_____

_____

Its Too Late

The king returned to his palace and spent the night without eating and without any entertainment being brought to him. And he could not sleep (Daniel 6:18).

Scripture: Daniel 6:15-18

You slam on the brakes, but you know it's too late. In a few seconds you'll hit the car in front of you, and you can do nothing to prevent it. Or you speak angry words that you immediately regret. Those words hurt the one you love, but you can't take them back.

There comes a time when we can't undo what we've done—and when we can't *stop* doing what we've always been doing. That's when we may realize our helplessness and cry out to God for help, as did King Darius. Probably only sickness, wars, or rumors of wars ever prevented the king from enjoying his nightly sensual indulgences. But this night was different. The king, who seemed accustomed to sending people to the lions' den, suffered helplessly in a trap he himself had set.

If we must be caught, let it be like Daniel, entwined in righteousness, wrapped up in obedience to God—not like the king, who languished in the jaws of foolish vanity.

> *Lord God of Heaven and earth, You know my weaknesses and vanities and, Lord, You know my desire to serve You in righteousness and obedience. Purify my heart. Help me to walk with You along the pathways of life, free from the chains of my sins. I pray this prayer in the name of Jesus, my merciful Savior and Lord. Amen.*

_____

_____

_____

_____

April 19

Winning a Heart

The king was overjoyed and gave orders to lift Daniel out of the den (Daniel 6:23).

Scripture: Daniel 6:19-23

Eager children run into the living room on Christmas morning to see what presents await them. Distraught women went early on the third day to the tomb where Jesus was laid. And the anguished King Darius got up at the first light of dawn, hurrying to see whether Daniel was still alive.

Clearly, the king cared deeply for Daniel, not merely as a valued administrator, but apparently as a close friend. Daniel and the king obviously had very different religious beliefs and value systems. Yet Daniel's excellence, loyalty to the king, and consistent service to God bridged the gap between them. He so touched the king's heart that Darius thrilled to find Daniel alive.

The king observed genuine faith in action. Even in this most trying situation, Daniel treated King Darius not with coldness, bitterness, or disdain, but with warmth, grace, and respect. What an example for us today! A godly life benefits not only believers but also our relationships with, and testimony among, those with seeking hearts.

Dear God, help me to love the world as You love it. Help me to be its salt and light for Your glory. And thank You for the example of Daniel's life, of a believer who won the heart of a king through excellence, loyal friendship, and continual service to You. I pray in Jesus' name. Amen.

God Is More Than We Know

I issue a decree that in every part of my kingdom people must fear and reverence the God of Daniel. For . . . his kingdom will not be destroyed, his dominion will never end (Daniel 6:26).

Scripture: Daniel 6:24-28

Have you ever been introduced with words that seemed to leave out a lot of information? Maybe you were introduced as a gifted musician or a smart student, yet you wanted to say: "But I'm *more* than that!"

We generally first grasp new ideas by relating them to familiar concepts, although these limited concepts do not enable us to fully comprehend the new ideas. Here's what I mean: Daniel knew God deeply from a lifetime of walking with Him. In contrast, it appears that powerful King Darius was just beginning to know God, and in his proclamation he began with what he readily grasped: God's *power*. Yet, while God is powerful, He is also much more.

As Daniel knew, God is also faithful, righteous, compassionate, forgiving, just, gracious . . . the list could go on forever. For God will always be greater than our limited understanding of Him.

Let us walk constantly with Him, then, as Daniel did, so our lives and testimonies will grow fuller as we come to know God more deeply. That adventure has no end.

__Almighty,__ You are great and awesome, infinitely beyond my understanding. Nevertheless, I love and worship all that You have revealed of Yourself. Thank You for showing me Your goodness this day. In Jesus' name, amen.

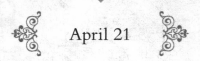

April 21

Wait in the Cherry Tree

I wait for the LORD, my soul waits, and in his word I put my hope (Psalm 130:5).

Scripture: Psalm 130

In the beloved literary classic *Anne of Green Gables,* we meet the charming waif, Anne, as she waits alone at a train station. Another child might have been frightened, but not Anne. When Matthew finally arrives, she cheerily informs him that she didn't mind his tardiness a bit. She had made up her mind to climb into a wild cherry tree and spend the night entranced by moonlight and white blossoms, confident that someone would come for her in the morning.

The life of faith often feels like a long wait at a train station. We think God must have forgotten us, and we begin to fret. We wonder why He's late. But God is never late; He holds the master schedule, and He knows exactly when to move. Meanwhile, we wait, and if there is nothing else to be done about it, we may as well wait with all our might, like Anne. Confidence in the one for whom we wait gives us the freedom to wait with joy. Thus we clamber into the boughs of a wild cherry tree and perch there, deeply content among fragrant, moonlit blossoms.

Lord, today give me the patient attitude of trust. So much of what I'll experience today depends on what I choose to experience. In Christ, amen.

April 22

Look at Me!

I turned to the LORD God and pleaded with him in prayer and petition, in fasting, and in sackcloth and ashes (Daniel 9:3).

Scripture: Daniel 9:1-3

"Mommy!" A small boy has been trying unsuccessfully for several minutes to get his mother's attention. Finally, he drags a chair next to her and climbs up on it, raising him to his mother's eye level. Placing both hands flat against her cheeks, he pulls her face in his direction and demands, *"Look* at me!"

God isn't hard of hearing, nor does He become distracted, as an earthly parent might. However, the principle of persistent prayer abounds in Scripture. God strengthens our faith by making us flex our prayer muscles.

Seemingly unanswered prayer can make believers feel like that small boy. But when the answer seems overly long in coming, it's time to dig in with all the determination of the undaunted child. To fast, mourn, and pray as Daniel did is like dragging a very big chair next to our Father. Then, with the daring of a child who knows that he's loved, we place our hands on His strong face and demand, "Look at me!" Well pleased at such trusting audacity, a smiling Father-God turns to regard His child.

> *Father, I know You always hear me. You are El Roi, the God Who Sees Me. You love me with an indestructible love, and no one can snatch me from Your hand. Knowing this truth, let me be determined in petition and sacrificial in intercession for others. In the precious name of Jesus I pray. Amen.*

Reinvent Yourself?

We have sinned and done wrong. We have been wicked and have rebelled; we have turned away from your commands and laws (Daniel 9:5).

Scripture: Daniel 9:4-10

"It's never too late to reinvent yourself," the speaker assured his audience. A weary and disillusioned young woman straightened in her chair. Something about the phrase "reinvent yourself" snagged her imagination. Could she really make herself into someone new?

No, not from the inside out. Our inability to do so stands at the heart of our need for God's amazing grace. Through our baptism and by the power of the indwelling Holy Spirit, though, we can indeed enjoy soul-deep reinvention. But to benefit from God's beautiful offer of a fresh start, we must first be willing to look frankly into our lives and see the truth: "I have sinned."

Daniel admitted that painful truth on behalf of an entire people, and it was the first step to a brand new day for them. For God reveals our faults not to punish, but to correct that which keeps us from experiencing all the fullness of His good plans for us. Alone, we are helpless to reinvent ourselves. In Christ, we are new creations.

My God, I thank You for loving me too much to settle for mediocrity. Help me to abandon my life into Your strong and creative hands. Mold it like soft clay in the hands of the master craftsman. Wonderful Lord, reinvent my life; make me more like You. In the name of Jesus I pray. Amen.

Training His Child

The LORD did not hesitate to bring the disaster upon us, for the LORD our God is righteous in everything he does; yet we have not obeyed him (Daniel 9:14).

Scripture: Daniel 9:11-14

Children dread this statement: "This is going to hurt me more than it hurts you!" They doubt the claim, but a good parent knows that discipline supplies healthy boundaries—and sometimes painful corrections. Without limits, a child will stay self-centered and remain incapable of growth.

God is the ultimate good parent, isn't He? He wants the very best for his children and won't hesitate to apply whatever encouragement is required to reap the essential changes. Some of his children are particularly obstinate and require firmer training. But the wise realize the futility of refusing their Father's correction, for it would go against their own best interests.

God's training program is a permanent facet of life. For He longs to give His children good things, as they learn to follow their own deepest longing to its ultimate Source. And consider this: Providing our adoption into His family (via the cross) really did hurt God more than it hurt us. Would such a loving Father then leave us to raise ourselves?

My loving Father, I trust You to know what is necessary for my training. Help me bend to Your loving discipline. In Jesus' name, amen.

_____

_____

_____

_____

_____

April 25

We Have Heard

Give ear, O God, and hear; open your eyes and see the desolation of the city that bears your Name. We do not make requests of you because we are righteous, but because of your great mercy (Daniel 9:18).

Scripture: Daniel 9:15-19

The dusty traveler stands before the imposing doors of a great man's house. "I beg an audience with your master," he tells the servant who answers his knock. "Who are you to beg favors of my lord?" the servant asks. "Why should my master see you?"

"It's true," the traveler says. "I'm not an important man. But I am a man in great distress, and I believe your master may help me, if only he will hear me. I have heard of his reputation. They say he is merciful as well as wise."

"Why should he hear you? What have you to give him?"

The traveler bows his head, clutching his hat in his hands. "Truly, sir, I have nothing to offer except . . ."

"Except?"

"Except my gratitude and eternal devotion."

The servant smiles. He pulls the great doors open and stands aside to admit the dusty traveler.

"That is the price of admission, good sir. What you have heard is true; enter, and ask what you will."

Great and merciful God, I come before You with nothing to offer but gratitude and love. I ask for Your favor not because I deserve it but because of who You are, my powerful and gracious Savior. Through Christ, amen.

_____

_____

_____

April 26

What a Confidence Builder!

As soon as you began to pray, an answer was given (Daniel 9:23).

Scripture: Daniel 9:20-23

Matt's heart pounded so hard he thought it would burst out of his chest. There she was—the girl he loved—sitting alone at a library table. He had to ask her to the youth-group party before somebody else did. *Just do it!* he coached himself. The worst she can say is, "Why would I want to be seen with a guy like you?"

Matt swallowed hard and strolled over, trying to look casual and confident. "Hey, Tina. So, uh . . . how's it going?" *I can't think of anything to say! Why is she just sitting there? I think I'm going to be sick.* "So . . . got a date for the party yet?"

"Nope. You?"

"Nope." Now, now! *Ask!*

Most of us can recall similar adolescent scenes of reticence to step forward, fearing to ask, avoiding assertion. And in most every area of life, as grown-ups, we've learned to move forward, confidently, with any legitimate request. But can we do so in approaching our God?

Angel Gabriel told Daniel that, even as his lips began to ask, the answer was already given. When it comes to prayer, what better confidence-builder can we have than that?

Lord, I believe You are waiting with answers even before I ask. Help me trust Your love enough to ask boldly for every need. In Jesus' name, amen.

_____

_____

_____

_____

Moment by Moment

Seventy "sevens" are decreed . . . to finish transgression, to put an end to sin, to atone for wickedness, to bring in everlasting righteousness, to seal up vision and prophecy and to anoint the most holy (Daniel 9:24).

Scripture: Daniel 9:24-27

Why does human nature so predictably resist a deadline? Students wait until the last minute to write their term papers, often pulling an "all-nighter." Tax payers send in their returns at midnight on the final day—or file for an extension. We keep saying to ourselves, "There's still a little more time . . ."

The phrase "seventy 'sevens' are decreed" suggests there is only so much time, and then the time runs out. A sense of urgency pervades this passage. "Time is limited," it shouts. "Act now!" God does have a timetable, and He's not inclined to accommodate stragglers.

Each of us has a limited span of time to use while we're visiting planet Earth. We may spend it as we please, but when it's gone, it's gone. The end of our opportunity to serve in God's great rescue effort will arrive, and none of us knows when. We are wise, then, to ponder carefully the best use of our precious time. Not just for the week ahead, but for the next few moments.

Sovereign Lord, how comforting to know that Your plans for the universe cannot be thwarted. You have determined times and seasons for all things, and You've given me a part to play. Thank You, in Jesus' name. Amen.

Accept This Blessing

Blessed are those who dwell in your house; they are ever praising you (Psalms 84:4).

Scripture: Psalms 84:1-4

I can't remember ever being hugged by my father. He was an unhappy man, quick to anger, slow to praise. It's no surprise, then, that I grew up believing I had to earn my heavenly Father's love and affection. I just couldn't wrap my mind around the idea of unconditional love.

One weekend, when my husband and kids were out of town, I called an older couple in the church to see if I could spend the night at their house. What they did for me that weekend changed my life forever. From serving my favorite food to moving the recliner so I could sit in front of the fireplace, Vic and Carol treated me like their favorite child.

I'd never been so "loved on" in all my life. I went home and cried like a baby, finally realizing that God loves me that much, and so much more. Since then, I've grown in God's love—so blessed to be one of His favored kids. The same love and favor of God is there for all of us who call upon Him. We need not earn it, but only accept it.

Father, help me grasp how wide and long and high and deep Your love is for me. Reveal Your love that goes beyond knowledge—that I might be utterly filled with Your sweet presence. In Christ's name, amen.

April 29

Choosing Your Thoughts

This is what the LORD Almighty says: "Give careful thought to your ways" (Haggai 1:7).

Scripture: Haggai 1:1-11

"You are what you think." True statement? A Christian counselor once explained to me that thoughts heavily influence feelings and actions. When I think on happy things, I am likely to become more happy. When I replay painful events in my mind, I struggle with grief, anger, and even bitterness. These feelings then help determine how I behave.

There's a story about Ronald Reagan, as a kid, going into town with his aunt to order a new pair of shoes. But Reagan couldn't decide whether he wanted round or square toes. To his surprise, when he returned to the store a few days later, the shoemaker handed him one shoe with a square toe and the other with a round toe. "This will teach you not to let people make your decisions for you," the shoemaker cautioned. Reagan said that he learned right then that "if you don't make your own decisions, someone else will." Rather than sitting passively by, take charge of your life by choosing your thoughts carefully. Every action needs a thought to get it started.

Father Almighty, as I realize the power of my thoughts, I pray You would reveal any false beliefs that might negatively affect my actions. Teach me to line up my thoughts with Your Word, that I might walk in the freedom of Truth. In the name of Your Son, my Savior, I pray. Amen.

April 30

God Never Lets Go

Haggai, the LORD's messenger, gave this message of the LORD to the people: "I am with you," declares the LORD (Haggai 1:13).

Scripture: Haggai 1:12-15

Have you ever taught a child how to ride a bicycle? Most likely, you ran alongside, holding the bike upright as the child learned to balance, pedal, and steer. Eventually, you slipped behind the bike where the child could no longer see you. "I'm still here," you promised, as the child repeatedly turned to check. Finally, when the child acquired enough confidence and skill, you let go of the bike to show the child that he could, indeed, keep going on his own, even far out of your sight.

Not so with our heavenly Father! He will never let go. Deuteronomy 31:8 promises that "the Lord himself goes before you and will be with you; He will never leave you nor forsake you."

Why wouldn't God want us to be able to keep going on our own? Because He desires to achieve His will and purpose in our lives by working through us. As He holds us with His righteous right hand, His Spirit more fully influences our lives, enabling us to continue with confidence and skill while relying on His power.

Dear Father, thank You for Your promise to stay by my side—to love, guide, and support me. I give myself to the leading of Your Holy Spirit that I might accomplish all that You have planned for my life. Teach me to listen to Your voice and trust Your direction. Through Christ I pray. Amen.

My Prayer Notes

May

*I will praise you, O Lord, with all my heart . . .
and will praise your name for your love and your
faithfulness.* —Psalm 138:1, 2

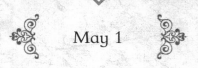

God Glasses

Many . . . who had seen the former temple, wept aloud when they saw the foundation of this temple being laid, while many others shouted for joy (Ezra 3:12).

Scripture: Ezra 3:8-13

A remnant of Jewish people had returned to Jerusalem to rebuild the destroyed temple. With the foundation laid, the people stopped to give praise to the Lord. Some shouted for joy; some wept.

What made the difference in the people's reactions? I believe it had something to do with their perspectives. No doubt some looked back to what once was and mourned the loss, while others looked forward to what was to be and rejoiced with excitement. What they already held in their hearts determined what they saw.

Too often, we judge solely by what we see on the surface. Thankfully, our heavenly Father looks much deeper. We may see failure, while God appreciates effort and improvement. We might see hopelessness while God sees the first small steps toward a bright future. It's been said that we only see what we are *prepared* to see. We would all do well, then, to reflect often on the character of God. As we do, we will learn to see all things through His eyes.

Father, search my heart and examine my thoughts. Remind me to focus on others' hearts more than outward appearances. Through Christ, amen.

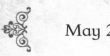

Faith—My Working Energy

Then the peoples around them set out to discourage the people of Judah and make them afraid to go on building (Ezra 4:4).

Scripture: Ezra 4:1-4

If anyone ever owned the right to be discouraged, it had to be Helen Keller. In her book *Let Us Have Faith,* Helen said, "I know that faith made my life possible and that of many others like me. . . . Reason hardly warranted Anne Sullivan's attempt to transform a little half-human, half-animal, deaf-blind child into a complete human being. Neither science nor philosophy had set such a goal, but faith, the eye of love did. . . . In my doubly shadowed world, faith gives me a reason for trying to draw harmony out of a marred instrument. Faith is not a cushion for me to fall back upon; it is my working energy."

Anne Sullivan stepped into Helen's life and cared enough to stay and make a difference. No doubt Anne, herself, suffered great discouragement in the process. But she didn't give up.

In your life these days, who needs a friend to step in and make a difference? Might you be just that person? Refuse to give up as you allow your faith in God to become your working energy.

Dear Father in Heaven, may I keep on doing Your will, even in the midst of discouraging circumstances. Help me remember that my strength comes from You as I strive to make a difference in someone's life today. In the name of the Father, the Son, and the Holy Spirit, I pray. Amen.

_____

_____

_____

_____

_____

All in a Day's Work

Then Zerubbabel son of Shealtiel and Jeshua son of Jozadak set to work to rebuild the house of God in Jerusalem. And the prophets of God were with them, helping them (Ezra 5:2).

Scripture: Ezra 5:1-5

Having explained the meaning of *humility* to my fourth-grade class, I asked whether the students knew anyone who was humble. When one child named her pastor, another raised his hand and blurted, *"My* pastor humiliates himself every Sunday!"* Out of the mouths of babes . . .

In our Scripture passage for today, God had spoken to the Jewish people, instructing them to rebuild the temple. The people immediately went to work, including the prophets of God.

What a great example of humility in leadership! Colossians 3:23, 24 says, "Whatever you do, work at it with all your heart, as working for the Lord, not for men, since you know that you will receive an inheritance from the Lord as a reward. It is the Lord Christ you are serving." Whether spreading peanut butter on bread for the kids, cleaning restrooms for a booming corporation, or speaking at an international religious conference, we can serve Jesus, if that is our goal.

> *Dear Father, once again, I surrender my life to You. Take my hands, my mouth, and my feet. Use my whole being to accomplish Your purposes in my world today. In the name of Jesus, my Savior, I pray. Amen.*

May 4

Mission Impossible

If it pleases the king, let a search be made in the royal archives of Babylon to see if King Cyrus did in fact issue a decree to rebuild this house of God in Jerusalem. Then let the king send us his decision in this matter (Ezra 5:17).

Scripture: Ezra 5:6-17

Enemies of God's people, determined to stop the rebuilding of the temple, wrote a letter to the king, asking him to confirm that the work was authorized. Unable to deter the work with their own lies and threats, these enemies attempted to stir up strife at the very highest level. But their efforts backfired when King Cyrus supported the work and further authorized that all expenses be paid from the royal treasury.

I recall praying about a situation that seemed incredibly hopeless. "I don't even know what to ask for," I told the Lord. And immediately these words of Scripture came to mind: "[He] is able to do immeasurably more than all we ask or imagine, according to his power that is at work within us" (Ephesians 3:20).

When we know we are doing God's will, we know we have His power within us. We may not know exactly what to ask, but we can certainly imagine the Lord having the power and the plan to set everything right, in spite of any determined opposition. Isn't that enough?

> ***Dear Father,*** *I am sure to face opposition today in a society bent on leaving all moral absolutes behind. Work through me, in Christ's name. Amen.*

Homesick

By the rivers of Babylon we sat and wept when we remembered Zion (Psalm 137:1).

Scripture: Psalm 137:1-7

I suffered my first bout of homesickness at the age of 5. During a visit, my aunt and uncle persuaded my parents to send me with them to play with my favorite cousin for a few days. My relatives lived in another town, and it was my first extended time away from Mom and Dad. During the day I was fine, happily playing with dolls and coloring books. At night, however, my spirits sagged.

Things were different here! My aunt sewed button eyes on my teddy bear, even though I liked him just as he was. When bedtime came, we said our prayers, and Aunt Fran tucked us in. Then my thoughts again turned toward Mom and Dad. What were they doing right now? Did they miss me?

In the darkness, I buried my head in the pillow and quietly cried. My wise aunt and uncle recognized the symptoms, and the next day my parents picked me up. Homesickness can debilitate, but it displays the strength of ties to home and family. Surely the Israelites had every reason to weep in their foreign land of captivity.

Father, thank You that someday I'll change addresses, and all the comfort of this house will pale compared to living in Your presence. In Christ, amen.

_____

_____

_____

_____

_____

May 6

Good Grief

"**The wall of Jerusalem is broken down, and its gates have been burned with fire." When I heard these things, I sat down and wept** (Nehemiah 1:3, 4).

Scripture: Nehemiah 1:1-4

"Dad's gone." I heard my sister-in-law's voice over the phone, but struggled to accept her words. "Oh no," I responded, disbelieving.

For months we'd expected this news. Doctors said the congestive heart failure was terminal. A counselor helped Daddy plan his funeral and set his finances in order. He was almost 93 years old, after all, but it still seemed too soon to lose him. And my brother and I worried about our mother. Dad had always been the strong one, and she went along with his decisions. How would she manage?

In the grief that followed, Mom struggled with loneliness, often feeling hopeless. The protective "walls" of her marriage were gone, and the "gates" of decision-making provided by her husband were destroyed. She felt deeply sad and helpless. Attending a class for widows comforted her, however, and helped her learn how to survive the hard work of grieving. To our surprise, she regained her gentle cheerfulness and even began to make her own choices. A few years later she moved into a retirement center . . . and thrived.

Father, Your Son was "a man of sorrows and acquainted with grief." Thanks for staying close when we lose our loved ones. In Him, amen.

_____

_____

_____

_____

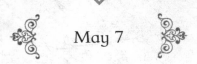

May 7

Pray the Scriptures

Remember, I pray, the word that You commanded Your servant Moses (Nehemiah 1:8, *New King James Version*).

Scripture: Nehemiah 1:5-11

Wednesday night prayer meetings were anything but boring at San Jose Christian College, when I attended in the late 1960s. Woodrow Phillips, our beloved president, brought the sessions to life. Woody, as we knew him, always opened a chapter of the Bible, read a section, and explained it. Then he'd apply it to our lives and invite us to "pray it" with him.

The way he linked the Bible to dating, studying for finals, and curfews made it uniquely personal for us. He'd alternate reading, then praying through the Word, for the entire meeting, drawing from his deep well of relationship with God. He encouraged us to bring God's Word before Him in prayer, just as Nehemiah did, "reminding" the Lord of what He'd already said about our concerns.

God certainly doesn't need reminders! But we do, especially when a situation looks bleak from all outward appearances. "Lord, You said . . ." is a great way to build our faith when we pray, helping us embrace His will in His presence.

__Wonderful Counselor, Powerful Healer, Loving Father,__ remember now Your promises to me and to others who need Your touch. Though You really need no reminder, please remind me of Your close presence throughout this day. In Your Holy name I pray. Amen.

May 8

Amazed, Astonished, Astounded

The king said to me, "What do you request?" (Nehemiah 2:4, *New King James Version*).

Scripture: Nehemiah 2:1-10

I really needed a job. Even though I stayed busy with substitute teaching, I needed the stability of full-time work. Besides, I wanted my own classroom, my own kids to nurture. Then one afternoon the phone rang, and the principal of the Christian school my grown kids had attended invited me to interview for a position.

Invited . . . *me!* I was amazed. After the interview, I talked to a teacher on the hiring committee, seeking feedback on how I'd come across. She said mine was the strongest interview she'd seen.

Recalling my nervousness, I was astonished. When I got the job and went for the initial meeting with the principal, she confided that she'd been wanting to hire me for three years, ever since I'd earned my degree in education. She'd known me as a parent at the school and believed I'd make a fine teacher.

I was astounded. And Nehemiah must have felt the same way when he allowed the king to see his sorrow after concealing it for four months. How could he have known the king would extend such wonderful favor?

Jehovah-jireh, You truly are the one who provides in overwhelming ways. I thank You so much for the wonderful way You brought me to my school. I don't deserve Your favor—but thank You for it anyway! In Christ, amen.

_____

_____

_____

_____

First Step, Diagnosis

And I went out by night . . . and viewed the walls of Jerusalem which were broken down and its gates which were burned with fire (Nehemiah 2:13, *New King James Version*).

Scripture: Nehemiah 2:11-16

My youngest son has an impressive orthopedic history. Before he reached high school, he broke bones in a foot, a thigh, an arm (a couple of times) and his other elbow—twice. In all those trips to the emergency room and follow-up visits to the Orthopedic and Facture Clinic, I learned the importance of X-rays.

Always the first step in treating my son involved taking an X-ray. Then the doctor would slide the large film into the clips and turn on the light box behind it. "Here is the fracture," he'd say, pointing with a pen to the jagged edges of some misshapen bone. It wasn't difficult to accept his diagnosis, seeing it pictured in stark black and white, and I had no trouble agreeing to the treatment plan.

Nehemiah recognized the importance of diagnosis as a first step and took a donkey ride by moonlight to survey the damage to Jerusalem's wall. It's a good strategy for tackling any problem. Take time to gain a good understanding of what's amiss before proceeding to fix it.

Lord, help me pause when troubles surface. Help me move into quietness that I might ask Your expert advice—and then spend plenty of time listening for Your still, small voice of guidance. May I always trust Your plan for overcoming any obstacles in my journey with You. In Jesus' name, amen.

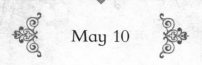

May 10

Recruit a Team

I said to them . . . "Come and let us build the wall of Jerusalem" . . . So they said, "Let us rise up and build" (Nehemiah 2:17, 18, *New King James Version*).

Scripture: Nehemiah 2:17-20

As a new teacher, I'm learning all the time. This year I took an idea from a magazine and created a long list of jobs for my fifth-grade students. They eagerly volunteered to clean the white board, lead the pledges, and hand out papers. I was a little surprised at their willingness to help, but recognized a good thing when I saw it.

When their parents came for Back to School open-house night, the trend continued as moms and dads volunteered to drive on field trips, make copies, and grade papers. So many signed up that I had to create a calendar scheduling them for alternating weeks!

Needless to say, it's been a wonderful year. I bring less work home and leave school earlier. Chatting with moms when they come in has built strong relationships, and the classroom runs smoothly because all the students share the workload.

Nehemiah's dynamic leadership followed the same principle: recruiting an army of volunteers for the task at hand. Rarely can we do it all alone.

*   **Lord,** *thank You for calling Your people to work together in the kingdom. We'd miss so much if we tried to manage everything without help. May we always work hand-in-hand for Your glory. Through Christ, amen.*

_____

_____

_____

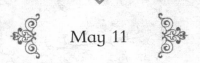

May 11

A Crying Prayer

In the day when I cried out, you answered me, and made me bold with strength in my soul (Psalm 138:3, *New King James Version*).

Scripture: Psalm 138:1-5

During a short-term missions trip to Brazil, I spent three weeks living in the home of a family who welcomed us with overwhelming graciousness. Our hostess, Nair, eagerly helped me learn a little Portuguese and taught me how to cook the savory black-bean mixture she served over rice.

My most memorable lesson, however, occurred not in the kitchen but in a garage. She took me to a prayer meeting of women from the church, held in the white stucco carport of one of the church women. As usual, with ladies everywhere, the gathering began with enthusiastic chatter. Then they started to pray.

Although I understood only a few words of the language, there was no mistaking the fervor of their intercessions. Nair squinted her eyes shut and cried out in a loud voice, tears streaming down her face. I watched in wonder. It wasn't the volume of her voice, nor the lowliness of the setting, but the intensity of her spirit that ignited mine. My hostess cried out to God, just as the psalmist did.

O God, when Your Son prayed in the garden, He prayed so intently that drops of blood fell from His brow. Make me bold, Lord, and give me courage to open my heart in all sincerity to Your love. In Christ I pray. Amen.

Trust This Rock

I call as my heart grows faint; lead me to the rock that is higher than I (Psalm 61:2).

Scripture: Psalm 61:1-5

The children squeal with delight as I push the merry-go-round. "Faster—faster!" they cry, hanging on with all their might. Their innocent trust is so precious.

As for me, sometimes I feel life is a merry-go-round that goes too fast. Problems come one upon another, and my heart grows faint. I can't see the next step, and my soul cries, "Stop the world; I want to get off!"

Then I can drag my feet in a desperate attempt to control my own destiny. I can announce to Heaven that my problems are too big for God, that I must handle them myself. Or I can abandon myself to God, trusting that He will never fail or forsake me.

Yes, I can hold tightly to Him, my strong tower, my refuge, my rock. I can rest under the shelter of His wings and cry with Job, "Though He slay me, yet will I trust Him" (13:15, *NKJV*).

God is in control, either way. But when I choose trust, I end up having more peace, more hope, more joy—and I soon learn again just how much I'm loved.

Lord of my life, today I want You to have control of my every word and deed. And keep reminding me that You are capable of handling each problem that comes my way. In the name of Jesus, my Lord and Savior, amen.

_____

_____

_____

_____

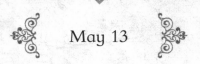

May 13

Its the Little Things

What they are building—if even a fox climbed up on it, he would break down their wall of stones! (Nehemiah 4:3).

Scripture: Nehemiah 4:1-6

If I were a senior devil instructing less-experienced imps as in C. S. Lewis's *Screwtape Letters,* I know just what I'd say. "Remember, the little foxes spoil the whole vineyard! Don't attack your assigned believer with major catastrophes; he will just run to our Enemy. Send in the little foxes, the everyday irritations. Bring misunderstandings into his relationships, get him into debt, fill his life with a thousand minor distractions. Those are the things he'll consider too small to bring to You Know Who.

"And keep him busy, busy, busy! Don't allow him any time for fellowship, prayer, or reading that horrible black book. He'll soon become tired, confused, and begin to believe the Enemy doesn't care for them. In next to no time . . . he'll be yours."

My point: Don't assume that anything in your life is beneath God's attention. It's the little discouragements that do so much damage, if we let them. That is how Sanballat and his friends hoped to wear down the builders of Jerusalem's walls. But Nehemiah and his people refused to give in. We, likewise, can stand firm in God.

> *Father,* help me never forget how much I matter to You. Today I commit my life into Your hands, even amidst naysayers and discouragers. Thank You for Your loving care in all situations. In Jesus' name, amen.

May 14

Not So Formidable

When Sanballat, Tobiah, the Arabs, the Ammonites and the men of Ashdod heard that the repairs to Jerusalem's walls had gone ahead . . . they were very angry (Nehemiah 4:7).

Scripture: Nehemiah 4:7-11

Sanballat, Tobiah, the Arabs, the Ammonites, and the men of Ashdod—formidable enemies against a handful of God's elect. Yet God's people have often faced insurmountable odds. David stood before nine-foot-tall Goliath with five stones and a sling. Moses stood against Pharaoh with only a wooden staff. Elijah confronted a wicked queen and 450 prophets of Baal with a simple stone altar and a stack of wet wood. And Jehoshaphat defeated the armies of Ammon and Moab simply by standing still and waiting on God.

Our Lord's victories do not depend on our strength, but they do make use of our faith. Even today, He can still walk through fire with us, shut the mouths of lions, and knock down walls—or build them up again. Our Lord can divide the Red Sea as easily today as He did so many years ago. He is the same yesterday, today, and forever. Remembering this truth makes it easier to calm my spirit, to allow His perfect love to cast out my fears as I face my own daily giants.

Precious Lord, I thank You that victory in Jesus does not depend on my strength but on Yours. Guide my thoughts and actions today. Help me remember to wait on You, for You are my strength. In Jesus' name, amen.

_____

_____

_____

_____

_____

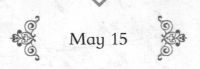

May 15

Do Something!

Don't be afraid of them. Remember the Lord, who is great and awesome, and fight for your brothers, your sons and your daughters, your wives and your homes (Nehemiah 4:14).

Scripture: Nehemiah 4:12-15

Some time ago a teacher in Colorado was fired for keeping a Bible on his desk. It was not a teaching aid. He simply kept it there to read while he ate his lunch.

And in a case that was later overturned, the Ninth Circuit Court of Appeals ruled the Pledge of Allegiance unconstitutional because of the words, "under God." Hearing of the case, Jay Leno quipped, "With hurricanes, flooding, fires, earthquakes tearing up the world from one end to the other, are we sure this is a good time to take God out of the pledge of allegiance?"

British orator Edmund Burke said, "All that's necessary for the triumph of evil is that good men do nothing." Nehemiah must have known that doing nothing in the face of his enemies would lead to their assured triumph. Instead, he called the people to bring swords, spears, and bows to the wall. They'd need to form a strong defense.

Even today, Christians under attack will often have to rouse themselves. Doing nothing as a once great culture crumbles will bring no honor to themselves or to the God who ultimately governs all peoples.

Lord, help me to be Your hands, Your voice, Your heart within a struggling society that's dying to find Your salvation. In Jesus' name I pray. Amen.

May 16

How Are You Today

From that day on, half of my men did the work, while the other half were equipped with spears, shields, bows and armor (Nehemiah 4:16).

Scripture: Nehemiah 4:16-23

"How are you?" my friend asked politely as I entered the church building. Smiling, I gave the standard reply, "Fine!" Actually, I was screaming inside. I'd just moved, boxes filled the house, and my daughter was seriously ill. I felt overwhelmed and hopeless, on the verge of despair. Had I been honest with my friend, she stood ready to offer prayer, compassion, and practical help. But I allowed pride to keep me from the warm support of Christian fellowship.

No doubt here's where we can learn from Nehemiah, who designated half of his people for support while the others worked. Yet we can't support one another if we don't know what's needed—and what help is available.

One day a small child was trying to lift a heavy stone as his father watched. The rock wouldn't budge, and the boy began to weep. "Are you using all your strength?" his father asked.

"Yes, I am!" the frustrated boy cried.

"No, you're not," the father said evenly. "You haven't asked me to help you."

Lord, deliver me from any pride that keeps me from the support I need from my Christian brothers and sisters. Thank You, in Jesus' name. Amen.

_____

_____

_____

_____

_____

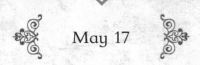

Grapes and Diamonds

I prayed, "Now strengthen my hands" (Nehemiah 6:9).

Scripture: Nehemiah 6:1-14

A grape must be crushed before it can be made into wine. Silver must withstand the hottest part of the fire to become pure. Diamonds form only through prolonged exposure to high pressure and temperature. And believers grow spiritually mature and complete through trials and testing.

Men and women of God aren't formed overnight. Joseph suffered in Pharaoh's dungeon. David faced Goliath and even death at the hand of his king. Daniel was taken captive and carried hundreds of miles from home before he became counsel to a pagan king. Even Jesus learned obedience from the things He suffered (see Hebrews 5:8). Every trial brings a choice. We can shake our fist at God and ask, "Why me?" Or we can humbly pray, "Now, strengthen my hands."

Lilias Trotter writes in her *Parables of the Cross:* "Take the hardest thing in your life—the place of difficulty, outward or inward—and expect God to triumph gloriously in that very spot. Just there He can bring your soul into blossom."

__Heavenly Father,__ I trustingly place myself in Your hands. Help me wait patiently for the unfolding of Your purposes in my life. I present my body a living sacrifice that You might make it holy and acceptable. In the name of Your Son, my Savior, I pray. Amen.

_____

_____

_____

_____

Impossible? His Specialty

When all our enemies heard this . . . [they] were afraid and lost their self-confidence, because they realized that this work had been done with the help of our God (Nehemiah 6:16).

Scripture: Nehemiah 6:15-19

The orphans had dinner and were tucked into bed. They had no idea the orphanage had no money or food for breakfast the next day. But God had called George Mueller to care for these children. Though he did not know how, he was confident the Lord would provide.

Committing the care of the orphans to God, Mr. Mueller went to bed. The next morning he went for a walk, praying for God to supply the needs. During his walk he met a friend who asked him to accept some money for the orphanage. Mr. Mueller thanked his friend, but didn't tell him about the pressing need. Instead, he praised God for the answer to prayer and went back to the orphanage for breakfast.

God finishes what He starts. He can tear down walls and build them up again. He opens doors no one can shut and closes doors that can't be opened. As Nehemiah's enemies learned, no one can change God's plans or force His hand. God specializes in the impossible.

Dear heavenly Father, thank You for Your faithfulness. My heart trusts in You, and You have never failed me—nor will You. Please help me to walk by faith in joyful anticipation of the blessings that await me. In my precious Savior's name I pray. Amen.

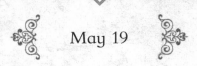

Is a Quick Fix Worth It?

Wait for the LORD; be strong, and let your heart take courage; yes, wait for the LORD (Psalm 27:14, *New American Standard Bible*).

Scripture: Psalm 27:11-14

While visiting my niece, I was accused of "trying to control everything." I accepted the fact that what I had done upset my niece. But I could not accept her characterization of the motive. I felt the motive was love.

I was hurt and went to my room to read my Bible and pray. Soon it became clear to me that I must not defend myself but wait upon God to heal this breech.

Nevertheless, I still tried to fix the problem! And you can imagine what happened; the hurtful words we said to each other caused even more pain on both sides.

Eventually, we "agreed to disagree" and parted with hugs. God in His own time healed both of our hearts, but my attempt at a quick fix had contributed little. I learned much, though: Waiting on God isn't always easy, but the benefits far outweigh the consequences of impatient and misguided controlling behaviors.

Lord, let me realize the fulfillment of Your promise—that if I wait on You, my heart can take courage and I can have strength to obey You. Thank You for showing me mercy and forgiveness when I rush ahead of Your will. In Christ's precious name I pray. Amen.

_____

_____

_____

_____

_____

It Didn't Happen

All native-born Israelites are to live in booths so your descendants will know that I had the Israelites live in booths when I brought them out of Egypt. I am the LORD your God (Leviticus 23:42, 43).

Scripture: Leviticus 23:33-43

One day while I was walking my 5-year-old grandson, Kevin, home from the park, I noticed a big dog watching us from across the street. Knowing Kevin's fear of dogs, I immediately shielded him from seeing the dog. Kevin joyfully went on his merry way, unaware of the potential danger.

I wonder how many times God has sheltered me that way. When I pray in thankfulness to Him, I'm reminded these days to include gratitude, not only for the blessings I've received, but for the unknown tragedies from which God has surely shielded me.

God's people in the days of Moses enjoyed the great blessing of God's direct protection, as He even instructed them in building their shelters. This reminds me of the Scripture in Psalm 61:3, where David says to God, "You have been my refuge, a strong tower against the foe." It also helps me form a picture of Jesus, who shelters us from every form of spiritual opposition.

Dear God, help me to remember that You have provided shelter for me, just as You sheltered the Israelites in the wilderness. Teach me a daily, heartfelt gratitude for Your loving care. Through Jesus Christ my Lord, amen.

May 21

Frazzled or Joyful?

The LORD your God will bless you in all your harvest and in all the work of your hands, and your joy will be complete (Deuteronomy 16:15).

Scripture: Deuteronomy 16:13-17

While attending a writer's conference, I ran into a friend I hadn't seen in years. As we were eating lunch, I noticed how nervous and exhausted she appeared. She shared with me that she wished she could be more joyful about serving God . . . but she was simply worn out.

I sensed that she'd overextended herself in church activities. "When do you have time to write?" I asked.

"That is exactly my problem," she said. "I really thought God wanted to use my writing to encourage others, but I can't find time to do it! I feel I am disobeying God."

A few months later I ran into her again. This time, she shared that she'd read Eugenia Price's book, *A Woman's Choice,* and it had spoken deeply to her heart. She even quoted these lines: "Millions of women are simply expecting too much of themselves. God does not expect us to be superwomen. He only expects us to be His women and to take the daily provision He yearns to give us."

I couldn't have said it better!

Heavenly Father, just as You helped my friend, let me stay tuned to the Holy Spirit's leading so I too can have my joy complete in You. I pray the work of my hands today will glorify You. In Jesus' name, amen.

_____

_____

_____

_____

Bow to Him

Ezra blessed the LORD**, the great God. And all the people answered, Amen, Amen, with lifting up their hands: and they bowed their heads, and worshipped the L**ORD **with their faces to the ground** (Nehemiah 8:6, *King James Version*).

Scripture: *Nehemiah 8:1-6*

They worshiped with their faces to the ground? What do you make of that?

Meditating on what genuine renewal means, my thoughts drifted back to my treasured Sunday school teacher in Deland, Florida, years ago. Her every word and action demonstrated a heart consumed with Jesus. With humble countenance and demeanor, she ministered His love to everyone. Mrs. Thompson had true humility because she sat at the feet of Jesus daily.

Andrew Murray in his book *Humility* says, "We may find that we have been delighting in beautiful thoughts and feelings, in solemn acts of consecration and faith, while the only sure mark of the presence of God—the disappearance of self—was all the time wanting. Come and let us flee to Jesus, and hide ourselves in Him." Perhaps this principle might motivate a people to worship with faces—or knees—pressed to the ground. But when did you last bow, literally, to God at a worship service?

> **Lord,** *often I think more highly of myself than I should. Help me pray today in a posture that shows my willingness to hear Your voice and submit to Your will. In Christ's name I pray. Amen.*

_____

_____

_____

_____

May 23

Still Hearing the Word?

They read from the Book of the Law of God, making it clear and giving the meaning so that the people could understand what was being read (Nehemiah 8:8).

Scripture: Nehemiah 8:7-12

My husband and I had moved to a new city and were searching for a church home. We didn't realize that we hadn't been "fed" very well from the Bible—until we heard clear and powerful proclamation from the Book, just as in Nehemiah's day. We were like sponges; we couldn't get enough of the Scripture in this new church.

Is it harder to find such good preaching today? I've certainly noticed many preachers embellish the Word by decorating it with their own favorite spin.

Ezra and Nehemiah awakened a hunger in the people to know more about God—directly from the Word of God. And, thankfully, the Word that so powerfully convicted the people of Nehemiah's day is the same Scripture that convicts and blesses us today; plus, we have the New Testament too. What a shame it would be to ignore this treasure or listen to explanations of it that fall short of its glorious message: the word of sin and repentance, of forgiveness and eternal salvation.

*I praise You, **God the Father, God the Son, and God the Holy Spirit,** for the many preachers who continue faithfully to feed their flocks with the precious Word that leads us to Christ our Lord. Help me faithfully lift up our pastors and teachers in prayer. In Christ's name, amen.*

Let Us Keep the Feast

[Ezra] read the book of the law of God daily, from the first day to the last day and they celebrated the feast seven days, and on the eighth day there was a solemn assembly according to the ordinance (Nehemiah 8:18, *New American Standard Bible*).

Scripture: Nehemiah 8:13-18

One of my favorite authors is the 19th-century preacher Charles Spurgeon. He has such a way of giving us word pictures to help us understand Scripture. In one of his books, *Twelve Sermons on Holiness,* he enlightens us regarding the word *feast:* "Let us keep the feast, nourishing souls with Christ's sacrifice, making our hearts glad by reflecting upon the blessing which this has brought us. It should always be feast time with God's servants. Let's feast by feeding upon Christ; he was slain to be fed upon. Only Jesus is the true feast. Our keeping of the feast is not a matter for times and seasons, for festivals and holidays, it is always our position, our daily lifelong fellowship with Jesus."

As we see Ezra and the people feasting for seven days on the law of God, and as we see how Spurgeon offers such a beautiful view of what holy feasting is, we can learn also to feast on God's Word daily.

My awesome Father, thank You for Jesus the Lamb who was sacrificed for my sins. And thank You for speaking to me through the Bible, which I treasure so highly. As I feast on the written Word and the living Word, grow me into the kingdom servant You call me to be. Through Christ, amen.

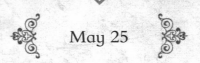

Help or Harm?

Keep back thy servant also from presumptuous sins; let them not have dominion over me: then shall I be upright, and I shall be innocent from the great transgression (Psalm 19:13, *King James Version*).

Scripture: Psalm 19:7-14

Most mothers like to think they have "the gift of helps" in relation to their children. We love to help our children—but do we love it too much? Once our married children leave the nest, they may see our helping gift in a whole new light.

One holiday while visiting our daughter, I started to do what I always do: match my grandson's socks. Since our daughter has a large family, I always thought that doing something practical like that was quite helpful. But this time, as I picked up a sock to take upstairs, my daughter said, "Don't do that."

I was shocked. It came out that I was offending her by getting into the children's dresser drawers.

A presumptuous sin? I began to see it that way. Yes, after much embarrassment and agonizing, I finally saw it from my daughter's viewpoint—and apologized. Of course, I hope I'll keep back from presumption with God too. That may be harder to see, harder to define. I'll ask Him to help me here!

> **Lord,** let me not offend You or others with my words and actions. Thank You for being my friend always, even when I goof! Through Christ, amen.

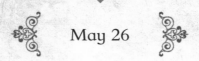

Needing Wisdom Today?

The child grew and became strong; he was filled with wisdom, and the grace of God was upon him (Luke 2:40).

Scripture: Proverbs 8:22-31

Our small group members began sharing their prayer requests. One by one, they made their needs known.

"Our daughter's new neighbors are spreading lies about her. She needs wisdom regarding how to deal with the situation."

"We found drugs in our son's room. Pray that we'll know how to talk to him about it."

"Our daughter-in-law was taken to the hospital after a drug overdose. Pray for wisdom for our son."

All these friends had knowledge of God and His promises. They knew the Scriptures. But now they needed more; they needed to know how to *apply* the Word to the situations they faced.

We all need such wisdom. Solomon asked the Lord for it, believing it was more important to him than vast riches. And even Jesus, in His human nature, grew in wisdom.

What crisis are you experiencing today? It may be a family illness, a broken relationship, a spiritual dryness. Ask the Lord for wisdom, and He will give it to you.

Dear Lord, I am so thankful for Your promise to guide me into Your wise ways. Keep my heart attentive to Your leading. In Jesus' name, amen.

_____

_____

_____

_____

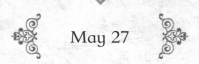

God Speaks, Even to Me

In the past God spoke to our forefathers through the prophets at many times and in various ways (Hebrews 1:1).

Scripture: Hebrews 1:1-5

I caught my breath as I drove through the beautiful northern Michigan hills, passing lush pine trees on both sides. I could almost hear God's whisper, "I created this beauty for you."

Years earlier, tears had come to my eyes as our son-in-law held up our first grandchild. I'd thought back to our daughter's illness during the first three years of her life, and I could almost hear God whisper, "I healed Janet so she could be the mother of this precious baby."

And in 1984, doubts filled my heart as I stood by the side of my comatose mother. "Why, Lord?" I implored. "She's such a good woman." And I could almost hear God's whisper, "She's been faithful to me all these years. It's time for her to come home."

God speaks to us in many ways: in the beauty of nature, in the wonder of childbirth, even in the valley of death. Thankfully, no matter the trial we face, we can always take a moment to listen for His voice. For God has been speaking to His beloved human beings down through the centuries, calling them to himself. He is just that good, just that personal, and just that interested in you and me.

Lord, *as the psalmist says, let me be still today and know that You are God. I pray to listen more closely, through Christ, my Savior. Amen.*

_____

_____

_____

_____

Just Add Light

The light shines in the darkness, but the darkness has not understood it (John 1:5).

Scripture: John 1:1-5

What a dark time in the life of my friend Charles! First, his mother died. Shortly afterwards, he lost his younger sister to pneumonia. Then one day he came home to find his grandmother lifeless on the kitchen floor. Adding to his problems was an inability to keep a job because of his addiction to alcohol.

But then Charles met the Lord. "When my grandma died," he told me, "I knew that if I didn't change the way I was heading, I would very quickly be next."

The months following his baptism weren't easy for Charles, but he determined to leave his old ways behind. When I saw him a year later, he was sober, neatly dressed, and fully employed.

When the darkness of our tough times seems to overwhelm us, we can remember that Christ came not only to give *life*, but to give *light*. After all, He is the light of the world (see John 8:12). And the best way to fight any darkness is simply to add more light.

Dear Father, I am so thankful that You have brought the light of Christ into my life. And I am thankful, too, that no matter how hard the prince of darkness tries, he can never gain a complete victory. Through Christ and His cross, the war against sin and death has been won. I give all glory to You, in the name of the Father, and the Son, and the Holy Spirit. Amen.

_____

_____

_____

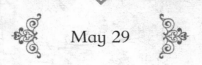

May 29

He Reigns!

About the Son he says, "Your throne, O God, will last for ever and ever, and righteousness will be the scepter of your kingdom" (Hebrews 1:8).

Scripture: Hebrews 1:6-9

I once read a story in a Sunday school paper that ended with these words: "She prayed, and everything turned out all right." While I definitely know that prayer changes things, I'm more inclined to go along with the saying that "prayer changes people, and people change things."

More powerful than both these statements, however, is the promise in God's Word that no matter how rough the situation we're going through, His Son is still on the throne, and His rule makes everything right.

His rule took Joseph out of prison and made him prime minister of Egypt.

His rule delivered Daniel from the lions' den.

His rule brought three Hebrew men out of a fiery furnace, without even a trace of smoke remaining on them.

His rule brought down the walls of Jericho after the Israelites had marched around the city seven times.

Are you in a prison today of illness or depression? walking through the fire? facing a wall? God is still on the throne. In due time, He will make everything right.

Father, thank You that every situation may be redeemed for Your glory—even if only as a way of purifying me through fiery trials. Keep me strong and faithful, then, amidst all circumstances! In Your Son's name, amen.

_____

_____

_____

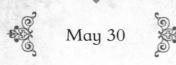

Some Things Never Change

You remain the same, and your years will never end (Hebrews 1:12).

Scripture: Hebrews 1:10-12

I walked into the empty chapel on the campgrounds. Things didn't look the same as they did when I was a teen and my family spent 10 days there every summer. Gleaming restrooms replaced the wooden structures across the road. A beautiful nursery made it convenient for mothers to enjoy the services. No more ceiling fans; air conditioners had taken their place. "Everything's different," I thought wistfully.

No, not everything. For across the front of the chapel stretched the grey stone altar rail, stained with the tears of many seekers over the years. I thought of all the prayers offered at that altar: for salvation, for renewal, for guidance in ministry and mission. There were so many prayers of intercession for loved ones or prayers for strength and encouragement. And one more thing hadn't changed: The God I met summer after summer at those camp meeting services is the same God I serve today.

Perhaps things have radically changed in your life. You've lost a family member; you've had to make a move; your children are gone. Take heart. God is still there for you, and He never changes.

Father, the older I get, the harder it is to accept changes in my world. Yet how reassuring is Your unchanging faithfulness! In Jesus' name, amen.

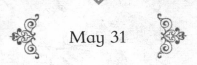

May 31

Jesus Is Here with Us

The Word became flesh and made his dwelling among us. We have seen his glory (John 1:14).

Scripture: John 1:14-18

The baby girl wasn't expected to live through the night. But when a friend walked into the hospital room the next morning, the infant was cooing and smiling. The friend looked at the exhausted, but thankful, parents and said, "Jesus must have been here."

A young woman who had suffered from depression for 18 months awoke one morning and told her husband, "I'm going to make it." Joy filled the room. Jesus must have been there.

A teenage girl arose from prayer and shared with those gathered around her, "The aching loneliness I had inside is gone." Jesus must have been there.

It's true that none of us has seen the face of God, nor His Son, in the flesh. But who can deny that we have seen His glory over and over again—in His touch on our bodies, our minds, and our hearts? How God must love us—to become one of us and to let us see like that!

I am going to look around me today and make a note of all the places where I might see glimpses of His glory. I know it will encourage and strengthen my heart.

Dear Father, thank You for loving me so deeply. Thank You for sending Your Son to live on this earth that He might understand all the things I'm going through. I love You, in Jesus' name. Amen.

_____

_____

_____

_____

June

He is the image of the invisible God, the first-born over all creation.

—Colossians 1:15

Angelic Encouragement

Are not all angels ministering spirits sent to serve those who will inherit salvation? (Hebrews 1:14).

Scripture: Hebrews 1:13, 14

I sat in Detroit Metro airport, exhausted. Shortly after my mother's death, my elderly stepfather had come to spend five months with us, and I had just taken him home. On the plane I was seated next to a gentlemen who turned out to be a Christian singer. I shared with him my reason for the trip, and he promised to pray for me.

When I changed planes in Chicago, my new seatmate was reading a book written by an inspirational author I knew. We, too, had an uplifting conversation. Then, as I embarked on the third leg of my flight—from St. Louis to Phoenix—my new seatmate and I discovered we had a mutual friend in the church she attended.

Back home, my husband greeted me and said, "You must be tired."

"No," I replied. "God sent three 'angels' to minister to me. I feel renewed!" And I wondered: Who might need my own angelic encouragements in the week ahead?

Dear Father, sometimes I get so caught up in my own problems, I fail to look for those who may need my help. Lead me to someone today who needs encouragement, just as You have ministered to me. I pray this prayer in the name of Jesus, my merciful Savior and Lord. Amen.

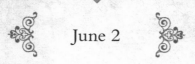

June 2

Something God Forgets

I will forgive their iniquity, and their sin I will remember no more (Jeremiah 31:34, *New King James Version*).

Scripture: Jeremiah 31:31-34

How is your memory? Ever forget anything? I have forgotten so many things that . . . I could never remember them all! At least I've never forgotten my wife's birthday or our anniversary.

However, I did forget her name once. Yes, shortly after our wedding, I was leading worship and wanted to say something about my new wife. Since I was nervous anyway, my mind seemed to go blank at just the wrong moment. How did I recover? I spoke of "my beautiful bride" (avoiding saying her name at all). She thought I was being romantic; I didn't tell her otherwise!

Has it occurred to you that nothing "occurs" to God? God knows everything, yet our passage says that He chooses not to remember our sin. Unlike us, God can choose what to remember and what to forget. And when God forgets, it really is gone, forgotten right out of existence.

Dear Father, how thankful I am that You have chosen to deal with my sin problem through Your own personal sacrifice in Jesus, Your Son. I lift my heart in praise for the saving work He did for me at Calvary. Thanks to You for loving sinners and forgetting their sins. In my Savior's name, amen.

_____

_____

_____

_____

_____

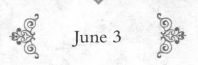

God Is So Generous

Abraham took a tenth of all he had captured in battle and gave it to Melchizedek (Hebrews 7:2, *New Living Translation*).

Scripture: Hebrews 7:1-3

I've heard it said that if you want to clear a church building, just announce you'll be taking up an offering. And, apparently, there is no subject worse than tithing in certain churches. But I hope I haven't lost you, faithful reader, because of this topic. Like it or not, our Scripture discusses giving a tenth.

Our passage today has Abraham giving a tenth of all he had gained to Melchizedek. And just who is Melchizedek? Just the priest who is "like the Son of God" (see verse 3). Abraham knew it was God who provided the victories and spoils in all his battles. So as an act of worship, Abraham gave back a tenth of all he had graciously been given. Similarly, it is God who has blessed us with everything we have, even the air we breathe.

I know it can be difficult to follow and trust God completely. But we can begin by returning at least some portion of that with which He has blessed us. That portion will no doubt grow much larger over the years. For God is faithful, always overwhelming His children with a generosity that goes far beyond what they expect.

Dear Father, help me to view everything in my life as on loan from Your gracious hand. As I lift up a thankful heart for all Your goodness, help me, as well, to give back with genuine gratitude. In Jesus' name, amen.

Conquering Who?

Blessed be God Most High, who has defeated your enemies for you (Genesis 14:20, *New Living Translation*).

Scripture: Genesis 14:17-20

"Don't count your years. Make your years count." That's what my refrigerator magnet says. An older couple (older than we are) had left us that magnet as a gift when we bought their house. My wife and I noticed it there on the frig almost immediately. And I've taken the advice to heart, trying to make my years count rather than counting the years as they seem to fly by, ever faster and faster.

It helps to learn to slow down each day, to pay attention—not just to the days but to moments within those days. Thus God calls to us in the Psalms: "Be still, and know that I am God" (Psalm 46:10).

It is this God who helps us through every day, every moment, every situation. He never fails us in our times of need.

But what particular "enemy" will you face today? Will it be a genuine thwarter of God's will or just an unnecessary obstacle of our own making? I like to remember the pithy words of writer Elbert Hubbard along these lines: "An enemy is anyone who tells the truth about you." In such a case, may God help us to conquer ourselves.

Heavenly Father, help me to remember that all of my resources are sacred gifts, as they come from Your hand. Use me to make a difference today, by the power of Your indwelling Spirit. Through Christ, I pray. Amen.

_____

_____

_____ _____

_____

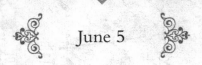

June 5

Who Is Really Blessed?

Without question, the person who has the power to give a blessing is greater than the one who is blessed (Hebrews 7:7, *New Living Translation*).

Scripture: Hebrews 7:4-17

On my mission trips to Romania, I always took tissues, shampoo, soap, pain relievers, and an assortment of common things we easily find at our local discount stores in America. These items were to be delivered to the "gypsies" (the Roma) of Romania.

Upon entering the homes of many of the Roma, I was humbled to recall how richly blessed I have been over the years, beyond measure, from God's hand. While I was a blessing to them, they ended up being such a blessing to me.

What an awesome challenge—to *bless* someone else! When we have the resources to bless others, we should do so. I opened my heart to the Roma of Romania, and they opened their homes to me. I gave them supplies, but they gave me friendship. Really, who received the greater blessing? As Victor Hugo once said: "As the purse is emptied, the heart is filled."

Almighty and gracious God, You have blessed me beyond all measure. Now help me to be a blessing to someone today. May I open my eyes to the needs around me— and also open my heart and billfold to the people You bring across my path. In the name of the Father, the Son, and the Holy Spirit, I pray. Amen.

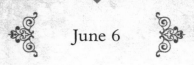

Satisfaction Guaranteed

(For the law made nothing perfect), and a better hope is introduced, by which we draw near to God (Hebrews 7:19).

Scripture: Hebrews 7:18-24

The song says it best: "My hope is built on nothing less than Jesus' blood and righteousness." Quick question: Which would you prefer? The law or the grace of Jesus? We are made perfect through Christ Jesus, while the law can only show us our shortcomings. (I prefer the grace of Jesus.)

Christ Jesus is our better hope. When He comes into our lives, He gives us purpose. Through the work of the Holy Spirit, we draw near to God. When we accept Christ's sacrificial death on the cross for the remission of our sin, we gain that better hope for all eternity. Entering the waters of baptism in His name, we will be with Jesus forever.

Not only do we gain eternity, we gain Jesus as our "priest." He is our intercessor before God the Father, ever guaranteeing that our covenant with God stays in place. I like that word: *guarantee*. I can build my hope of eternity on Him, satisfaction guaranteed.

O great merciful Father, thank You for Jesus, my Savior. He is indeed my hope and my guarantee of eternity. I praise His name. Help others to see Jesus living in me so that You will be glorified in my life—and become the hope in others' lives. I pray this prayer in the name of Jesus, my Savior and Lord. Amen.

Save to the Uttermost

Therefore He is also able to save to the uttermost those who come to God through Him, since He always lives to make intercession for them (Hebrews 7:25, *New King James Version*).

Scripture: Hebrews 7:25, 26

Of all household duties, doing the laundry is arguably one of the least favorite chores. First you sort the dirty clothes, then place them in the washing machine. Following the wash, you throw the clothes in the dryer (unless you hang them out to dry). Finally, you must fold them or hang them up in their proper places. And this chore never seems to end.

But what would you do if that shirt you placed in the washing machine came out still dirty? You would probably wash it again, since you want your shirts completely clean, not just partially clean.

Now, I don't want to equate laundry with our souls, because the analogy will soon break down. But when Jesus comes into our hearts, He does cleanse us completely. That is what it means "to save to the uttermost" in our passage today. *Completely* saved, not just partially. This is no halfway job, since He washes away our sin. And who could imagine the Lord of All doing a less than perfect work for us?

***Merciful Lord,** thank You for saving my soul and cleansing me from sin. Help me to live the Christian life so that others can see You, the living Christ, living in me. In Your name, I pray. Amen.*

_____

_____

_____

_____

_____

June 8

Just Once

Unlike the other high priests, he does not need to offer sacrifices day after day, first for his own sins, and then for the sins of the people. He sacrificed for their sins once for all when he offered himself (Hebrews 7:27).

Scripture: Hebrews 7:27, 28

April 15 comes just once a year. We all know the date as "Tax Day" in the United States, the deadline for paying our income taxes (unless we file for an extension). Either I pay my taxes by that deadline, or I must pay "late penalties" for missing the date. I'm just glad this day comes around only once a year.

While I still pay my taxes every year, Jesus paid my "sin debt" once and for all when He died on a Roman cross. He doesn't have to die "all over again" every time I sin; that debt is paid in full. And while Jesus intercedes on my behalf with His precious blood, He doesn't have to sacrifice Himself anymore.

That truth, "He sacrificed for their [my] sins once for all when he offered himself," leads me to praise God on this Lord's Day. As we worship today, we can offer thanks to a loving God who would sacrifice himself on our behalf. We deserve death; He gives us life. Once and for all!

> *Dear heavenly Father, thank You so much for loving me and saving my soul. Thank You for Jesus! Help me to radiate Christ in my life today, that others may come to know Him. In the name of the Father, the Son, and the Holy Spirit, I pray. Amen.*

_____

_____

_____

_____

_____

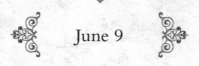

June 9

Lost in the Crowd

God is spirit, and his worshipers must worship in spirit and in truth (John 4:24).

Scripture: John 4:21-26

"There was a much better spirit in our old church," the man complained. "Now I just feel like a number."

"Yeah, I know what you mean," the other man agreed. "The number zero."

What had happened? These two church members apparently felt they had gotten lost in the crowd. While they supported the construction of their new church building, they weren't enjoying the change.

Jesus explained to the Samaritan woman that the *place* of worship was not as important as the *spirit* of worship: "A time is coming when you will worship the Father neither on this mountain nor in Jerusalem" (John 4:21).

Our two modern-day worshipers were facing the question that lay heavy on the Samaritan woman's heart. *Where is the best place to go for closeness to God?* Thankfully, God has chosen to dwell in us; He goes with us to our various places of worship. If only we will keep our spirits open to Him there!

*Thank You, **Lord,** for Your love and Your Spirit of truth. Help me learn to look within before I look out into the crowd and feel lost. In Jesus' precious name, amen.*

_____

_____

_____

_____

_____

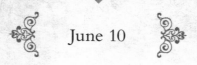

Truly Everlasting

When Christ came as high priest of the good things that are already here, he went through the greater and more perfect tabernacle that is not man-made (Hebrews 9:11).

Scripture: Hebrews 9:11-15

The batteries I'd placed in my portable radio lasted so long that I wondered whether the brand name could be taken literally. But the batteries couldn't really last forever; they were merely man-made. (Besides, so often, just when I needed them most—zap, they'd go dead.)

All man-made products will eventually stop working, even when they're "built to last." (Actually, I sometimes wonder what, exactly, that claim can mean. Is the product built to last for . . . a week? a month? a year? or indefinitely? The phrase simply hangs in the air, uncommitted to any specific length of time.)

What a contrast with Christ, our high priest! With His precious blood as an offering for our sins, He entered a tabernacle that was not man-made: Heaven itself. Now He sits at the right hand of the Father, evermore making intercession for us. Thus He is our advocate, always available to plead our case before the throne. No man-made tabernacle and no more man-made sacrifices. Only the everlasting accomplishment of Jesus will do for our salvation.

Heavenly Father, *thank You for sending Your Son, Jesus, to offer an eternal sacrifice for the sins of the world. In His name I pray. Amen.*

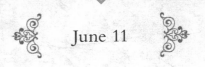

June 11

Why Blood?

He said, "This is the blood of the covenant, which God has commanded you to keep." In the same way, he sprinkled with the blood both the tabernacle and everything used in its ceremonies (Hebrews 9:20, 21).

Scripture: Hebrews 9:16-24

Moses told the people in his day about the covenant that God expected them to keep with Him. Then the covenant was "ratified," so to speak, by blood. Why? The answer comes by analogy. Think of a will. It can only go into effect once someone has actually died. Similarly, God's promises of our inheritance can only go into effect if the perfect sacrifice for sin has been accomplished for us.

Before the coming of Christ, in Moses' day, the law required that everything be cleansed with the blood of animals. Today, we look back to the blood of Jesus, the perfect Lamb of God, for the cleansing of salvation. As the Scripture reminds us, without the shedding of blood there is no forgiveness (see Hebrews 9:22).

Sadly, many people today consider it crude or unenlightened to speak of Christ's mission in the world being a sacrificial offering. They prefer to consider Jesus a great teacher, a moral influence, or simply a good man. But in light of the clear teachings of Scripture, we do not have that option, do we?

O God, I seek Your cleansing and forgiveness, and I lift up a thankful heart that Jesus has shed His blood for just this longing. In His name, amen.

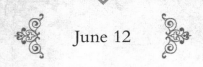

Can't Earn This

Just as man is destined to die once, and after that to face judgment, so Christ was sacrificed once to take away the sins of many people (Hebrews 9:27, 28).

Scripture: Hebrews 9:25-28

In ancient Israel, the high priest entered the Most Holy Place every year with blood that was not his own. Although the sacrifices came only once a year, they still had to be offered over and over again. They were temporary "coverings" for the sins of the nation.

In contrast, Christ died *once* to take away the sins of the world. Furthermore, He rose from the dead and will appear a second time. His mission will be different at that time, but it will still be the result of the one sacrifice, eternally offered before the Father.

What great salvation Christ has accomplished for us! And the most wonderful thing of all is that we do not need to try to earn it. Instead, let us be so grateful for this gift to us that we serve our Lord with joyful and thankful hearts. This is always the motive for our good works—not that we could become worthy of Christ's sacrifice, but that we might proclaim it's surpassing goodness by our own manner of life. And even this we can only do by His spirit working within us.

Heavenly Father, I know that I can pray no prayer more fitting than to simply thank You for Your Son, Jesus, whom You sent into this world as the ultimate sacrifice for sin. In His name I pray. Amen.

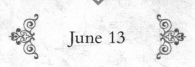

June 13

Pointing to the Ultimate

The law is only a shadow of the good things that are coming—not the realities themselves (Hebrews 10:1).

Scripture: *Hebrews 10:1-10*

When I first saw the old man's cluttered little office, I thought the plaque hanging above his desk referred to his profession. Actually, no one seemed to know the old man's line of work. He'd just always been there in the neighborhood to lend a listening ear and to occasionally give advice. "*Good* advice," everyone agreed.

Everyone also agreed it was a "good thing" the old man had remained in the neighborhood all those years. In explaining the plaque above his desk, he said, "I just saw it one day, and I liked it." What did the plaque say? I moved closer to read the small print: "Good things come in small packages."

True! And it's also true that sometimes good things are foreshadowed before they actually appear in reality. That's the idea in our Scripture today. The Old Testament sacrificial system served the good purpose of pointing to Christ. It could never match the greatness of the perfect, eternal sacrifice of the cross. However, it could hint.

Sometimes when I leave the office of that kind old man I lift up a prayer to my heavenly Father. The man seems to point me there . . .

Lord God in Heaven, *may I use every opportunity to point to my Savior in all I do or say this day. Thank You, in Jesus' name. Amen.*

_____

_____

_____

_____

_____

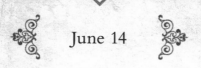

June 14

An Exciting Drama

Day after day every priest stands and performs his religious duties; again and again he offers the same sacrifices, which can never take away sins (Hebrews 10:11).

Scripture: Hebrews 10:11-14

Did the priest mentioned in our Scripture ever get bored with his everyday duties? If so, we can no doubt identify with seemingly never-ending duties, especially the ones we have to do day after day. However, it's been said that doing the hard part first will make our work seem easier.

Jesus, the perfect priest, came to do what everyday duties couldn't accomplish: take away our sins. And He certainly did the hard part first—He went to the cross, giving up all His heavenly privileges, to die like a common criminal. Then came the resurrection, the ascension, and His eternal reign in glory. Thankfully, He then sent His Spirit to dwell in our hearts until His coming again.

Nothing boring here! That's because this is the greatest drama ever enacted in the history of the universe. The key for you and me is to ask ourselves daily: Am I a vital part of this drama? Does my own life show that all Christ did for me makes a practical difference?

Lord, thank You for forgiving my sins. May I now serve You with a joyful and thankful heart, realizing it's a privilege rather than a duty. And when I become bored with my daily routines, give me a fresh awareness of Your indwelling presence. In Jesus' name, amen.

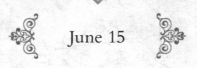

June 15

Once and for All?

Their sins and lawless acts I will remember no more (Hebrews 10:17).

Scripture: Hebrews 10:15-18

The young mother had spoken stern words. "Now, you listen to me, Tyler. I'm telling you once and for all—behave yourself. Stop bothering your sister!"

While dining at a local restaurant, I overheard such words from a mother to her son at least 10 different times. The "once and for all rule" just hadn't held up—no matter how many times it was proclaimed. (I could identify with her. I've used this same rule with my own sons on occasion—with similar result.)

According to the author of Hebrews, in God's unfolding plan of salvation, no sacrifice of animals could *once and for all* remove human sin. Only Christ, the perfect sacrifice, could do that. Being fully human, He could atone for humans. And being fully God, He could atone with eternal result. So you see, He removed the need for animal sacrifices once and for all.

When we're forgiven, our wrongdoings are remembered no more. As someone has said, "God buries our sins in the deepest sea, and puts up a sign: No Fishing!"

Dear Father, when I'm tempted to resurrect all my old failings and sins, draw me nearer to the cross of Your precious Son. There my sins were nailed with Him. There all of Your love and acceptance come to me forever. Thank You, in the name of my Savior, Jesus Christ. Amen.

_____

_____

_____

_____

_____

June 16

Barn Choir

He will fill your barns with grain, and your vats will overflow with good wine (Proverbs 3:10, *New Living Translation*).

Scripture: Proverbs 3:5-12

During a severe winter cold-snap, I was in the milking parlor at 2:00 AM preparing to milk 250 cows lounging in the attached barn. I was frustrated, struggling against the cold weather. But in my heart raged an even bigger wrestling match—with God. I resented my financial pressures. Despite all I was doing, it seemed as if God just wasn't providing enough. "Where is Your provision when I need it?" I questioned. "What more can I do? " I railed.

As the hours passed, the parlor slowly warmed with the heat given off by the cattle. Then I noticed a new sound. I turned to see first one, then several, and eventually dozens of sparrows descending from the barn's rafters to eat grain that had spilled on the parlor floor. Not seeming to notice the cold, dark night, they began to sing.

Songs of thanksgiving? Songs of praise? A sparrow choir had arrived to thank God for His provision. My heart soared.

Dear Father, thank You for every simple reminder of Your care for me and for every one of Your creatures. And please melt the coldness and hardness in my heart that grips me when I forget You are the only sustenance I need. Through Christ my Savior, I pray. Amen.

_____

_____

_____

_____

_____

For Now, the Author Allows

Let us fix our eyes on Jesus, the author and perfecter of our faith, who for the joy set before Him, endured the cross, scorning its shame, and sat down at the right hand of the throne of God (Hebrews 12:2).

Scripture: Hebrews 12:1-3

What kind of author writes stories that include personal tragedy, sickness, accidents, and even death? Apparently, the same storyteller who authors my life story. So, I ask myself whether that is really very good news.

Often, I pray about how I'd like the next sentences and paragraphs of my story to read. My prayers never include confusion or darkness, pain or disappointment. But Jesus, the author of my faith, allows these elements into my earthly days and invites me to follow Him right through to the same joy that He entered. Yes, His story included injustice. Yes, His story included sorrow, pain, and death. But His story didn't end there. Death led to a life at home alongside His Father.

Can you and I accept this kind of storyteller as the author of our lives? He called His story good. Can you and I call our stories good? We can, if we see that this is not yet the best of all possible worlds for us. We are not yet home.

Lord, I know that in Your wisdom You are allowing the forces of evil to have some sway here on earth. Remind me that sin's power is temporary and that nothing enters my life without Your approval. In Jesus' name, amen.

_____

_____

_____

_____

_____

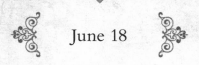

June 18

Downward Mobility

God is educating you; that's why you must never drop out. He's treating you as dear children. The trouble you're in isn't punishment; it's training (Hebrews 12:7, *The Message*).

Scripture: Hebrews 12:4-7

To be pursued by someone who loves me is a great experience. It makes me feel important. Yet it surprises me, because sometimes I don't feel I'm *worth* pursuing. So when I read a story about Jesus loving me so much that He took the hard downward path of humility, suffering, and punishment to the death, my heart perks up.

Because He took the descending path, I am made clean and acceptable. I don't have to prove that I am worthy of love; I am now God's adopted son. Writer Henri Nouwen speaks of it this way: "My whole life I have been surrounded by well-meaning encouragement to go 'higher up—you can do so much good there, for so many people.' But these voices calling me to upward mobility are completely absent from the gospel." As I take time to reflect on various circumstances in my life that are difficult to understand, I may need to view them differently. Was that recent loss of my job, for instance, really a *punishment?* Or was it *training*—and an opportunity to grow in faith? In other words, isn't downward mobility a good thing?

My Pursuing Father, thank You for the intensity of Your desires toward me. I rest in Your presence with me on paths that I don't understand right now—paths of learning and training. Sustain me, through Christ. Amen.

_____

_____

_____

_____

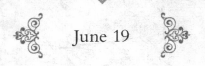

June 19

Untamed God

No discipline seems pleasant at the time, but painful. Later on, however, it produces a harvest of righteousness and peace for those who have been trained by it (Hebrews 12:11).

Scripture: Hebrews 12:8-11

I love the story of the interaction between God and Job in the Old Testament. Job was being severely tested, and I see myself in him as he tries to get God to recognize his righteousness and end his sufferings. Finally, God responds to Job's complaint and begins a beautiful history lesson for him (and me): "Where were you when I laid the earth's foundation? Tell me, if you understand" (Job 38:4). At the other end of this history lesson, Job discovers that the two things he's been trying to produce on his own—peace and righteousness—can only come from God.

I don't think God is angry with me when I complain and try to convince Him to change my circumstances. But He isn't a tame God. In a very real sense, He is wild and uncontrollable and . . . good.

Like Job, when you and I come to the end of our futile attempts to manage and manipulate God, can we find what we've always longed for? His peace? His righteousness? If so, it will be because we have received these blessings as gifts from His generous heart.

Father, help me see that the discipline You bring into my life has a good purpose. You wish to produce a harvest of peace and righteousness in me. So help me give up my efforts at total control. In Jesus' name, amen.

_____

_____

_____

_____

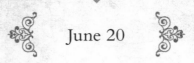

June 20

My Weakness, His Strength

Wherefore lift up the hands which hang down, and the feeble knees (Hebrews 12:12, *King James Version*).

Scripture: Hebrews 12:12, 13

The river was flowing swiftly as I let it carry me toward the safety of a small island. "I'll be OK," I thought—until I discovered the current had carried me downstream past the lower end of the island. At that point, the strength of the current doubled. I was in trouble. I turned to swim back to shore, but when I saw the distance, I panicked.

My energy was sapped, and now, filled with fear, I felt helpless. My friends and family, watching my flailing efforts, were concerned, but unaware of how weak and vulnerable I felt.

Eventually, I made it far enough out of the strong current to be able to stand, shakily, in knee-deep water. Bent over, my hands on my knees, I gasped for the oxygen I craved.

What swift current of circumstances in your life makes you feel threatened, out of control, vulnerable, foolish, or ashamed at the moment? Join me in lifting a weary, discouraged, struggling heart to God. He's a Lord who loves to come through for us. How has He met with you in your weakness?

God of my salvation, I come before You acknowledging my inadequacies, my sins, my failures. In this place of neediness, I lift up my hands that hang down, and on feeble knees I look to You. Through Christ, amen.

_____

_____

_____

_____

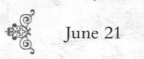

Make Beautiful Harmony

Fulfil ye my joy, that ye be likeminded, having the same love, being of one accord, of one mind (Philippians 2:2, *King James Version*).

Scripture: Philippians 2:1-4

I love it when my son, Zach, returns from guitar lessons. He shares with me things he's learned—like how to listen to the *texture* of music; how to enjoy the way different instruments blend with each other to make a sound bigger and more beautiful than they can produce individually.

In a similar vein, my friend Tim loves to talk about musical harmony. Then he makes his point, explaining how relationships between people include differences in personalities, differences in opinion, differences in perspective. Yet these differences can work in harmony too.

I admit that being "likeminded" with people is hard for me. I often feel threatened by others' viewpoints as I argue for my own. My feelings can get hurt, and many times I've lashed out at those who disagree with me.

Yet have you noticed that the people we most often disagree with are those closest to us? usually family or friends? Join me in asking God for help to move towards these folks with humility and love rather than withdrawing into relational disharmony.

God, *Your love for me penetrates my heart and helps me see how I can harmonize with others whom You also dearly love. Through Christ, amen.*

June 22

Never Alone

Surely I am with you always, to the very end of the age (Matthew 28:20).

Scripture: Philippians 2:5-11

Close friends invited my wife and me to join them in their anniversary celebration. Their relationship has been filled with serious challenges. But instead of evaluating whether their marriage had gotten better, they chose to speak about how they enjoyed being together, even through the most difficult times.

I have heard many say that our attitudes spring from our choices. I agree, but honestly, I really struggle with making consistently right choices. And there is something deeper that my heart longs for than just "getting it right."

As I look at the closeness Jesus enjoyed with the Father, even as He moved into suffering, I realize that's the deep thing my heart longs for. Closeness with God.

What are the biggest challenges in your life these days? Are you worn out trying to make life better, easier, more comfortable? Join me in thanking Jesus, not only for His incarnation, but for His promise of continued closeness. Let Him come alongside you.

> ***Dear God,*** *I don't want to face today's struggles alone. Please forgive me for attitudes that come across as a demand for You to make my life better. I do thank You for pursuing me and walking alongside me, for my heart can only truly rest in Your presence. I pray in Jesus' holy name. Amen.*

_____

_____

_____

_____

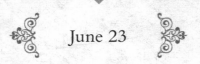

June 23

Can God Provide?

It is better to trust in the Lord than to put confidence in man (Psalm 118:8, *New King James Version*).

Scripture: Psalm 118:5-9

My husband and I responded to the call of God to serve Him in overseas missions. There was no salary, though, and my husband suggested we sell our house to finance the first trip.

Sell the house? I rebelled. We had worked hard on that house, and it was our security. I fought with God and was miserable. Then I thought: If I were killed on the road tomorrow, the burden of the house would be lifted. So . . . why not let it go today?

We never regretted our decision. When our own money ran out, there was always just enough for us—and for others with very great needs. Fifteen years later we retired to a home of our own—all we need and more—absolutely amazed at the way God provides for all things.

Now we live on a pension from my husband's former job in the British Health Service, but our faith clings ultimately to God. A pension merely relies on the stability of the stock market. God is much more reliable than that!

*Thank You, **Father,** for the ability to earn my own living. But my trust goes far beyond my own skills. It is You I can trust to provide for my family and myself, even when all else fails. Through Christ my Lord, amen.*

_____

_____

_____

_____

_____

Jesus, Supreme

He is the head of the body, the church; he is the beginning and the firstborn from among the dead, so that in everything he might have the supremacy (Colossians 1:18).

Scripture: Colossians 1:15-20

When the queen of England decides to visit a city, great preparations ensue, and no expense is spared to make her visit a happy one. Parks and gardens are trimmed to perfection, roads and buildings repaired. The red carpet of welcome comes out, the mayor waits, and we welcome the queen in our best new clothes.

The city is at her disposal as we honor her. City leaders stop looking important and bow down. The security men get headaches when she goes walking around among her people, but she decides, and they follow. Nobody argues with, or walks ahead of, the queen.

But kings, queens, and presidents live under the authority of our Lord Jesus, whether they acknowledge the fact or not. He is supremely in control, and nothing escapes His notice. Ironically, men and nations struggle for power—which has already been given to Him!

Today's reading delights my heart. How good to know that ultimate control rests in Christ's capable hands. Let us never be ashamed to acknowledge Him and give Him all the honor He is due.

Father, I am so glad that Your Son reigns supreme over all. In this quiet moment, I joyfully bow before Him, and in His holy name I pray. Amen.

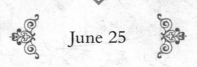

June 25

Opening Our Home

Do not forget to entertain strangers (Hebrews 13:2).

Scripture: Hebrews 13:1-6

Manchester, my city in England, is full of political asylum seekers, foreign students, and people of various nationalities and cultures. In theory, this should enrich and challenge us, but we do tend to withdraw into our own cultural groups, because we feel more comfortable there. Nothing wrong with that, I suppose. But if we never open up our hearts and homes to strangers, we miss something important and blessed.

Overseas students like to visit a home in the country, but if Christians don't invite them, those students may lose an opportunity for hearing the gospel. And so many of these folks are delightful people!

Perhaps we are wary of inviting desperate asylum seekers who may take advantage of us. But I read in the Bible that God actually *favors* the poor and defenseless. And I have no doubt that extending simple human kindness and hospitality is a great way to show our faith in action. Even if I have only one small room, I can offer that to Jesus—and to the stranger He loves.

Father, I would exercise my faith in these things too. Yet I need Your wisdom and protection for my family members, as they are willing to participate. Continue to guide and encourage me as I remember that whatever I offer to You, You will pour back into my life with even greater blessings. I pray this prayer in the name of Jesus, my merciful Savior and Lord. Amen.

_____

_____

_____

_____

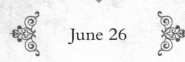

June 26

Be Yourself in Him

Remember your leaders who spoke the word of God to you. Consider the outcome of their way of life and imitate their faith (Hebrews 13:7).

Scripture: Hebrews 13:7-9

I'm thinking of a man who once brought the Word of God to our church in a powerful way. He was much loved and revered, and he certainly lived the life that he preached. In fact, some young men revered him so much that when they preached, they copied our friend's mannerisms, even his tone of voice. Someone said, "They're just his clones!"

Time, however, showed that they were not clones, because they had their own deep faith in God. Eventually their own personalities came through in their living and preaching. The same message, the same God, was proclaimed. But each could be himself in Him.

It is the *faith* of the leader we are encouraged to follow, as we see that faith lived out. We need not imitate the man or woman, but follow their faith in the one who never changes. My faith, like the leader's faith, must rest solely in Jesus.

Dear heavenly Father, I thank You for all the men and women who have helped me grow in my Christian life. I pray for my present church leaders and Sunday school teachers—and for all of us—that we may be good examples to those who follow You. In the name of the Father, the Son, and the Holy Spirit, I pray. Amen.

_____

_____

_____

_____

Outside the Camp

Let us, then, go to him outside the camp, bearing the disgrace he bore. For here we do not have an enduring city, but we are looking for the city that is to come (Hebrews 13:13, 14).

Scripture: Hebrews 13:10-16

I recall the story of a mother who watched her soldier son marching in a parade. She observed to her friend, "Why is everybody out of step but my Jamie?"

As Christians in this world, I suppose we have all experienced times when we feel "out of step" with everyone else. Our interests, values, and perspectives often don't mesh with the "man on the street," do they?

One of my young friends was expected to attend an office party. As a Christian, she felt totally out of place among all the drunken revelry and soon ordered a taxi home. "Now some of my colleagues avoid me, and I feel like such an outsider," she complained. But she was in good company. Jesus was also rejected, just for being true to himself. And He calls us to follow Him and live with Him "outside the camp."

Of course, my friend still loved her colleagues and prayed for them. But she finally had to admit that she was not one of them. She belonged with Jesus.

Dear God, You have won my heart. This world has its attractions and delights, but You are better to me than all of them. Your Son was despised and rejected by this world, and I will follow Him, even if I am the only one. In the holy name of Jesus, my Lord and Savior, I pray. Amen.

_____

_____

_____

_____

Taking Possession

I press on to take hold of that for which Christ Jesus took hold of me (Philippians 3:12).

Scripture: Philippians 3:12-16

On his daughter's 21st birthday, a very rich man gave her a present. It was an envelope containing the deed to a house. She flung her arms around his neck and thanked him, then put the deed in a drawer and just left it there. Her father was very disappointed, because he intended the house to be lived in.

A house is for possession. God, at great cost, gave me the "deed" of my salvation. I didn't have to earn it, but I do have to take hold of it and live in it.

The apostle Paul was obviously enjoying the salvation God had given to him. But he knew there was more, and he intended to take hold of everything God had meant for him.

I know there is more for me to take hold of in my life: more doors and windows to open up, more rooms to be filled with God's presence, more of my garden to clear so that good works may flower and blossom. It's easy to let gifts lie in a drawer; possession takes some effort.

*Thank You, **Father,** for all the blessings of the past. But I want to take hold of everything You have given me in Christ Jesus. I open up all the doors and windows of my heart and life to You and ask You to come and fill this house. May Your love in me flow out to all I meet this day. In the name of Jesus, Lord and Savior of all, I pray. Amen.*

_____

_____

_____

_____

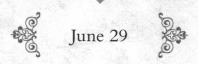

June 29

Avoiding the Shame

As I have often told you before and now say again even with tears, many live as enemies of the cross of Christ (Philippians 3:18).

Scripture: Philippians 3:17-21

The Scottish Covenanters, severely persecuted for their faith, sang hymns in the carts that carried them to the gallows. They sang farewell to earthly sun and moon; they sang of the doors of Heaven opening before them and of seeing Christ in all His glory.

Many in our present day face death for their faith in Christ, and all Christians experience some kind of rejection in this world. As Jesus said, we must take up our cross and follow Him.

When someone carried a cross in those ancient days, everyone knew he was on his way to crucifixion. We, too, will often face the choice of suffering rejection or evading the shame of the cross. Sadly, at those times, we may opt for living comfortably with the world.

It's sobering to realize that the "enemies of the cross of Christ" were believers—but with their minds set on earthly things. So it's no wonder Paul wept. Nevertheless, by grace, I want to be like our Lord, who scorned not the cross but the shame of avoiding it.

> **Dear God,** *keep me from professing Your name while still living as though the cross never existed. Let the cross of Your Son mean everything to me! If I am privileged to suffer for You, let me even rejoice. In Jesus' name, amen.*

_____

_____

_____

_____

_____

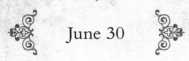

June 30

Delighting in the Lord

He will delight in the fear of the LORD. He will not judge by what he sees with his eyes, or decide by what he hears with his ears (Isaiah 11:3).

Scripture: Isaiah 11:1-3

Best-selling author Stephen King once spoke of a story concept that occurred to him: "I was too overawed with delight to do more than think about it for days." I understand his emotion. As a fiction writer, I recently had an inspiration for an intriguing novel. Excitement grew as I discussed possible plot points and characters with fellow writers. I enjoyed thinking about it and writing down ideas as they surfaced.

I may never achieve novel-writing success, but I can dream of making this book a reality. Perhaps someday I'll hold the complete manuscript in my hands, and then I'll probably do a "Snoopy Dance" over the achievement— even though the book may never make it to the bookstores.

As I've grown in my Christian faith and become more familiar with my Savior, I've learned to rest in Him and His wisdom. As I bask in His love this day, I realize that Jesus is truly worthy of my delight.

God, I delight in Your love and mercy. Help me to keep You foremost in my mind, even in the midst of ordinary tasks. In Jesus' name, amen.

My Prayer Notes

July

God is one and there is no other but him. . . .
love him.

—Mark 12:32, 33

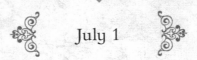

July 1

Need Recharging Today?

Jesus returned to Galilee in the power of the Spirit, and news about him spread through the whole countryside (Luke 4:14).

Scripture: Luke 4:14, 15

Apparently, Jesus relied on the power of the Spirit to energize Him for His mission on earth. I would love to take up that habit! In fact, I sometimes wish I came with an alarm that would beep when I get spiritually, emotionally, or physically drained. I do need constant re-energizing.

God created us with amazing stamina, but we're not little pink bunnies that can bang a drum forever. We need to check our energy levels daily. Have we spent time with the power source of the universe to recharge our spiritual batteries? Do we power up emotionally by taking time to examine a rose or admire a sunset? Or are we hunched over a steering wheel in a never-ending traffic circle of errands?

My prayer is that I'll learn to rely on the recharger of my life, rather than depending on the all-too-weak batteries of my own strength.

Father, thank You for Jesus' example of relying on Your power rather than His human strength. In His divine nature, He was all-powerful, but in His human nature, He showed the way for every human: to depend on heavenly help in all endeavors. In His precious name I pray. Amen.

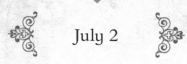

July 2

Power or Timidity?

All the people were amazed and said to each other, "What is this teaching? With authority and power he gives orders to evil spirits and they come out!" (Luke 4:36).

Scripture: Luke 4:31-37

The people of Palestine had never heard such a speaker. Here was an uneducated carpenter from the wrong side of the tracks, and he was a better orator than their usual synagogue teacher. And something else made them scratch their heads. His message had authority, backed by powerful action.

I'm usually a timid witness when someone asks me about the hope within me. I don't want to offend. I don't want a potential friend to turn her back on me. And I certainly don't welcome ridicule—or being labeled as a religious fanatic. So I whisper that I'm a Christian and often act as if I'm ashamed.

Yet the same Lord who ordered demonic forces to flee now lives within me, ready to calm my anxiety and enable me to speak boldly for Him. Through His Holy Spirit, I can stand strong against real or imagined opposition.

We serve an awesome God. He has the authority to act in our lives and has the power to motivate us to action too. That's a message worth shouting from the rooftops.

Lord, help me throw off the shackles of my timidity and serve as a courageous witness for You. Yet may my words always be seasoned with gentleness and my actions wrapped in love. Through Christ, I pray. Amen.

_____

_____

_____

_____

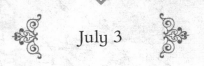

July 3

In His Grip

The people all tried to touch him, because power was coming from him and healing them all (Luke 6:19).

Scripture: Luke 6:17-23

Dr. Fritz Talbot of the Children's Clinic in Düsseldorf, fought against infant mortality in the 1940s. When a child was hopelessly wasting away, the physician would scrawl a prescription on the chart: Old Anna.

Anna was a grandmotherly woman on the ward, often seated in a large rocker with a baby on her lap. She held and stroked the failing patients. In most cases, those children began to thrive. In fact, she had more success with her "rocking chair therapy" than any of the doctors in the clinic.

Jesus knew the power of touch. He could heal with a word, and sometimes did. More often, though, He accompanied his healing with touch.

I used to view God working only through intermediaries—His encouragement through the written Word, His "hug" from a friend, His challenge from a sermon. Now I experience Him as personally reaching into my life. My prayers aren't directed merely to a so-called higher power in the clouds, but to the Lord who stays ever so close. He touches me on the shoulder, reaches out to grasp my hand, and holds me steady in His grip.

Jesus, thank You that You love me personally and up close. Help me to sense Your presence and rely on Your grip. Through Christ, amen.

The Measure of Success

Woe to you when all men speak well of you, for that is how their fathers treated the false prophets (Luke 6:26).

Scripture: Luke 6:24-26

I like approval. I love to receive compliments about my clothes, appreciation for my writings, and gratitude for my delicious dinners. However, I know that I need to seek approval from the right people. For example, some less-than-sincere folks may speak kindly of my "fashion sense" when they really mean that I tend to hide my excess pounds pretty well.

True friends won't steer me wrong. A comment about my weight stings, but a friend will encourage me when I finally pass up the French silk pie.

One youth worker described to me a tough-looking teen: he was wearing black clothes and chains, had tattoos, and sported a Mohawk gelled into six-inch spikes. As the worker talked with him, he discovered a sensitive and deeply spiritual young man. After a while, the worker asked him why he dressed as he did. "So I know who my friends are," he responded.

Ouch. Do I wear my designer blouses to get the approval of people who aren't real friends? Or am I willing to act contrary to custom in order to win approval from God, the one who really counts?

> **Lord,** *too often I've craved the spotlight of others rather than a "well done" from You. Help me to put You first! In Jesus' name, amen.*

_____

_____

_____

_____

_____

July 5

Holocaust Forgiveness

Love your enemies and pray for those who persecute you (Matthew 5:44).

Scripture: Matthew 5:38-45

On February 28, 1944, the Nazis arrested the ten Boom family. Their crime: hiding Jewish refugees and helping them escape German-occupied Holland. Corrie ten Boom and her sister, Betsie, were sent to the Ravensbrück concentration camp in Germany. Betsie died; Corrie was released in December 1944, weak and emaciated.

When she recovered, Corrie began speaking on the theme of forgiveness throughout Europe. After one meeting in Germany in 1947, a man approached her—one of her cruelest Ravensbrück guards. Could Corrie now practice what she preached?

She prayed for the ability to forgive this man, then reached out to clasp his hand. In her book, *Tramp for the Lord,* she wrote, "For a long moment we grasped each other's hands, the former guard and the former prisoner. I had never known God's love so intensely as I did then."

Although our natural inclination is to seek revenge, Jesus commanded us to love our enemies. How radical! It's only possible through the love God supplies to us.

Lord God, *I am helpless in the face of hatred. Yet through Your Son, You forgave the sins of the world, though You had no part in them. Please work Your forgiving ways into my own soul, day by day. Thank You, in the holy name of Jesus, my Lord and Savior. Amen.*

July 6

More Surgery!

"Tell us by what authority you are doing these things," they said. "Who gave you this authority?" (Luke 20:2).

Scripture: Luke 20:1-8

Recently a doctor told me I needed surgery, a second operation in 10 months. Although the news distressed me, I was glad the surgeon who performed the first operation was the one who called. I trusted her, and I preferred her scalpel to anyone else's.

I now have three small incisions from the laparoscopy procedure, in addition to my hip-to-hip scar from hernia repair. My surgeon jokingly offered a "buy-one-get-one-free" deal on any future operations, but I declined. (Hey, I'm running out of parts.)

If a truck driver had told me I needed surgery, he would have been correct, but a truck driver has no training in making accurate diagnoses; he has no authority in that area. And though it's true that a self-proclaimed expert could tell us all kinds of things about our health, I want to know that the person has genuine credentials to back up his claims.

Jesus is no pretender with a mail-order diploma. He's the authority on spiritual life and death. Although I might cringe at the thought of "spiritual surgery," I know and trust the Great Physician to work wonders on my soul.

God, I acknowledge Your sovereignty in this world and in my own life. I yield myself to You as the ultimate authority. Through Christ, amen.

_____

_____

_____

_____

_____

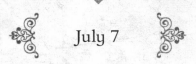

Living in His Favor

The time of the LORD's favor has come (Isaiah 61:2, *New Living Translation*).

Scripture: *Isaiah 61:1-4*

As a young wife I sat in my bedroom reading Romans 8:1, which says there's no condemnation for those who belong to Christ Jesus. I remember a strange feeling, as if the Spirit wanted to communicate something I didn't quite grasp. Frustrated, I set my Bible aside. Later, God revealed to me what I hadn't understood in 20 years as Christian: God completely accepts me. He doesn't look at me with condemning eyes, but with eyes of favor.

Somehow, I'd gotten the wrong message. I believed Jesus forgave sins and gave me an eternal inheritance, but that my job was to "live up" to that gift. Perfection eluded me, though, and I wrapped myself in a cloak of self-loathing. I just couldn't be "good enough."

What a joyous day when I finally realized that Jesus came not only to give me Heaven in the future, but also His peace in the present. When He stood in the synagogue and read the prophecy of Isaiah, Jesus proclaimed His mission to my approval-hungry heart.

Dear Lord, help me more fully grasp Your favor and live as one unconditionally loved. Thank You for setting my heart free and turning the ashes of my life into something beautiful for Your glory. In Jesus' name, amen.

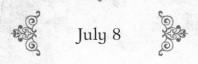

July 8

No Longer a Victim

He cast out many demons (Mark 1:34, *New Living Translation*).

Scripture: Mark 1:29-34

I don't know whether I believe that demons can live in a Christian—all the theology of the spirit world is bigger than I can grasp at the moment. But I do know that for many years I was in bondage to what I can only describe as demonic lies. Were they indeed lies of the devil? In any case, it seemed I was being "told" that I was unworthy to serve Jesus—that I was a failure. I thought God must grow so tired of my constant mistakes.

I also kept recalling past hurts, so that, too often, my thoughts swirled with anger and fear. I felt my heart was in prison.

One day some caring people spent several hours praying with me. They encouraged me to confess my sins of pride, unforgiveness, and perfectionism. As we shared together, they explained some of the misconceptions I'd held about God and myself. Then they showed me the truth: the chains I'd been living in were shattered at the cross. They had no power over me. I no longer needed to be victim to the demons who'd chased me.

Heavenly Father, thank You for setting me free from perfectionism and pride. Keep me close to You throughout this day. And make me ever more wise to the ways of the enemy, so that my thoughts reflect only the truths of Your eternal Word. I pray through my deliverer, Jesus. Amen.

July 9

Time for a Time-out?

Everyone is looking for you (Mark 1:37, *New Living Translation*).

Scripture: Mark 1:35-39

My friend was on the phone, crying, while my teenage son kept giving me "the look"—the one that says, "Get off the phone; I need you, Mom."

Then my daughter poked her head in and whispered, "I really need to talk to you." The doorbell rang as I heard a thud downstairs, followed by a wail, and the shriek of my younger children calling for me. I wanted to scream.

Either I'm a very important person . . . or my life is totally out of control. It feels like the latter.

I once read that John Wesley's mother would throw her apron over her head when she couldn't take it anymore (she gave birth to 19 children in all). That was the signal to her brood that Mom needed to pray and not be interrupted.

Jesus, too, spent His days being pulled in a million directions. But it didn't seem to ruffle Him as it does me. He always seemed to know which cries to answer immediately, and which ones could wait. And I notice that when people pulled at Him, He often slipped away by himself and prayed. Did He understand the great value of a time-out?

Father, help me to recognize the signal when I need a time-out from the demands of my world. Instead of blowing my cool, help me to choose time alone with You. Thank You, in Jesus' name. Amen.

_____

_____

_____

_____

Touched

Moved with compassion, Jesus reached out and touched him (Mark 1:41, *New Living Translation*).

Scripture: Mark 1:40-45

The doctor raised an eyebrow as I cuddled my fevered child. "It's very contagious," he said. But I couldn't help it. My little one needed the comfort of his mother's arms.

I washed my hands, took lots of showers, and changed my clothes often, but I refused to ignore the longing in Sam's eyes. He was hurting. I couldn't make the virus go away, but I could hold him.

When I hurt, I long for the touch of Jesus. Unlike me, Jesus has the power to make all the pain go away, but sometimes He doesn't do that. In those times it can be hard to trust Him.

I've been known to whine, complain, and even throw little fits about the hard stuff in my life. But as I've grown in my relationship with Jesus, I've come to understand that even when He doesn't take away the difficult circumstances, my pain always moves Him. He doesn't stand aloof, afraid of the germs in my life. He gets right down there in the middle of my messes and holds me. For that I am eternally thankful.

Lord God in Heaven, *thank You for caring about every single thing I go through. Your touch is what I need, so please help me to slow down long enough to experience it. In the name of the Father, the Son, and the Holy Spirit, I pray. Amen.*

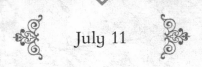

July 11

With Us

Soon the house where he was staying was so packed with visitors that there was no more room, even outside the door (Mark 2:2, *New Living Translation*).

Scripture: Mark 2:1, 2

When the president visited our town, we got tickets to the rally held in an amphitheater nestled in the Red Rocks outside of Denver. As the day grew closer, our anticipation mounted. We arrived early. Standing in line for an hour didn't faze us; we waited patiently for the security check.

The afternoon progressed as the excitement heightened. Secret Service men positioned themselves all around the stage, hiding in the rocks above us, their weaponry both menacing and comforting. Then a low buzz started at the front of the crowd and moved our way. He was coming! The crowd went wild, and we cheered with the best of them, our children's eager faces alight with the thrill.

People flocked to Jesus too. Only He didn't hire Secret Service men with swords or make those who came to see him stand in a security line. He let them crowd around Him. He ate with them, laughed with them, healed their diseases, cast out their demons, and blessed them. He modeled the heart of our Father who wants always to be near to us.

O God, I'm amazed that You don't hold yourself aloof or lock yourself away behind celestial guards. You long to be with me—so much that You choose to dwell in my heart. Thank You, in Jesus' name. Amen.

_____

_____

_____

_____

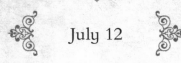

Crowded Out

They couldn't bring him to Jesus because of the crowd (Mark 2:4, *New Living Translation*).

Scripture: Mark 2:3-5

Last summer I went through a crazy, busy season. Company, Cub Scout camp, conferences, and family demands kept me rushing around at full speed. I didn't get much time alone with the Lord, and guilty feelings descended upon me.

Jesus seemed to be standing on the other side of the crowd of my life. I couldn't push through to Him. Finally, I asked Him whether He was displeased. He showed me that loving my husband, my company, and my children was a way of being with Him at this time. Jesus wasn't far away; He was with me in every moment of those days.

I'm awed by the story of Brother Lawrence, who said he felt as close to God when he washed the dishes in a busy kitchen as when he prayed in solitude. I'm not there, though. My time alone with God feels so much sweeter than any other time. But I'm learning that Jesus is always with me, and I shouldn't evaluate our relationship by missed quiet times. He's there whether I'm curled up in my recliner reading my Bible or rushing around loving His people. Nothing can crowd out the presence of the one who lives within me.

Dear Lord, thank You that You are always with me. Help me to focus on Your presence in both solitude and service. In Christ's name, amen.

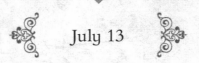

Wonderful Acts of Jesus

Everything he does is wonderful (Mark 7:37, *New Living Translation*).

Scripture: Mark 7:31-37

Though a young woman, Kim used to walk with a cane. She had a perpetual stomachache, dizziness, and frequent memory loss. She was also consumed with the shame of enduring 13 years of sexual abuse, which began when Kim was 3 years old. When she asked for prayer, Kim always appeared wounded and frightened.

A friend prayed for Kim, identifying both her emotional scars and physical disabilities, and God answered. The first thing Kim noticed was that her stomach didn't hurt anymore. Within a few days the dizziness was gone. Kim put her cane on the shelf and never again picked it up.

Before God healed her, Kim's lips were sealed. She didn't tell anyone of the abuse, and speaking in front of people petrified her. Her ears were closed to hearing God's whispers of affirmation. Now, though, she's open to God's loving words and tells people across the country how He set her free, not only from serious medical conditions, but also from the shame that haunted her for so many years. When I think of Kim, I can see that, indeed, God does everything well.

> *Thank You, **God,** for Your wonderful acts of love. You heal broken hearts and bodies, opening souls to the wonder of yourself. I pray in the name of Jesus, the great physician. Amen.*

_____

_____

_____

_____

_____

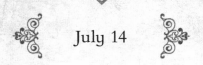

July 14

Love Hurts

The punishment that brought us peace was upon him (Isaiah 53:5).

Scripture: Isaiah 53:4-6

When I was young, my parents frequently disciplined me for doing wrong. I often deserved reprimand, and my parents did so out of love, patiently teaching me right from wrong.

They always said that punishing me hurt *them.* And I remember thinking, "Sure it does!" Now that I am a parent, I understand what they meant. I cannot express the deep love I have for my child; I want him to be happy, never to feel pain or sadness, and always to know my love. When my child has done wrong, we punish him from our deep desire that he live life on the right pathways—for his own good. But, yes, it does hurt us to punish him.

When we sin, it surely grieves God's heart. After all, sin is the ultimate form of self-destructive behavior, and no parent enjoys watching his child hurt himself. It must be horrible for God to see it happening all the time. Thus He actively did what was necessary to heal our self-destructiveness: He took our sin and its punishment upon himself. What a great God is ours!

Father, thank You for Jesus. I can't imagine the pain it caused You to send Your Son to the cross. Have mercy on me, in Christ's name. Amen.

_____

_____

_____

_____

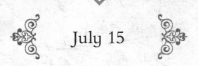

Cleansed by Love

He got up from the meal, took off his outer clothing, and wrapped a towel around his waist. After that, he poured water into a basin and began to wash his disciples' feet, drying them with the towel that was wrapped around him (John 13:4, 5).

Scripture: John 13:1-5

While recovering from surgery, I required assistance for a simple bath. Thankfully, I knew three people I could ask for help with such a private task without owing anything in return—my husband, my mother, or my sister. I could have asked my brothers, too, but that just wasn't an event they'd care to share with me!

Jesus had loved His disciples as family, but the time had come for Him to return to His heavenly Father. So He reached out to the disciples in a simple but deeply personal gesture—He washed their feet. Not merely to help with their hygiene, but to demonstrate the principle of servanthood that should characterize all Kingdom leadership in the centuries that would follow. It was an act of pure love and humble service, offered with no strings attached.

God's love comes to us freely and unconditionally. No matter what we have done or where we may go, His love will be with us. In response, let us reach out to others through the power of that love. All it takes is a simple act of service done in His name.

Father, thank You for living out Your love on earth through Your Son. Please help me to share Him with others today. In His name, amen.

_____

_____

_____

_____

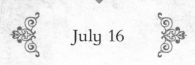

What Great Humility!

"No" said Peter, "you shall never wash my feet." Jesus answered, "Unless I wash you, you have no part with me." "Then Lord" Simon Peter replied, "not just my feet but my hands and my head as well!" (John 13:8, 9).

Scripture: John 13:6-11

"What is Your direction for my life and work?" In prayer, I waited for God's guidance. Several times over the coming months, an answer presented itself, one that seemed perfect, and I eagerly jumped into what I thought was a wonderful opportunity. Yet down the road a bit, I discovered that I had jumped too quickly!

Rather than hearing or heeding a humble solution, I dove into the grander schemes. I would compare all the perks and choose the very best. In doing so, I seemed to miss God's point. How was I to grow in faith, if I never faced any daunting challenges?

Jesus had no grand plan by the world's standards. To the very end, some of His disciples failed to grasp that. The idea was to model humility in the smallest acts of service. And the sobering fact is this: If we refuse such servanthood, we refuse Christ as well.

Heavenly Father, Your Son, Jesus, taught that Your grand plan is not of this world. Yet I so often limit my vision to the here and now, making my decisions based on personal comfort and advantage. I thank You for using my mistakes to teach me that Your plans are perfect. Draw me closer to You this day, I pray, in the name of Christ my Lord. Amen.

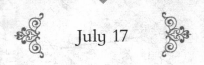

July 17

Its Beautiful

Now that I, your Lord and Teacher, have washed your feet, you also should wash one another's feet. I have set you an example that you should do as I have done for you (John 13:14, 15).

Scripture: John 13:12-17

I grew up in a small town where my parents owned and operated their own business, always treating their customers with care and respect. We heard the Golden Rule often: "Do unto others as you would have others do unto you." And my parents lived it. Everywhere my siblings and I went, people expected proper behavior because of our parents' example and stellar reputations. We learned not only from their words but also from their actions.

Jesus' disciples were, in a sense, a big family. Therefore, anyone observing from afar probably expected certain behavior to come from them. And Jesus knew that a key indicator of their character would be this: How they treated one another.

The same is true today for the followers of Christ. People will often "tune out" a sermon, but it is quite difficult to ignore a group of people who sacrificially serve one another with the purest of motives. In them, the surpassing beauty of Christ shines through.

Father, Your Son left a legacy for me to live—a legacy of love for You and for others. Please help me to carry out that legacy with grace, every day of my life. In Jesus' precious name, amen.

July 18

Where Betrayal Can't Live

I am not referring to all of you; I know those I have chosen. But this is to fulfill the scripture: "He who shares my bread has lifted up his heel against me" (John 13:18).

Scripture: John 13:18-20

I am blessed with many friends whom I hold close to my heart. I share just about everything with them, considering their love and support to be priceless. These precious folk know my heart—sometimes better than I know it.

Jesus' disciples were not only His friends, they were like a family. He knew them, through and through, just as He knows our own hearts. We cannot hide from Him, and this ought to make great impact on how we pray. For example, when we are tempted with selfishness or lust, we often say in our prayers, "Lord, you know I don't want to do that." But, really, wouldn't it be more honest to let the Lord know that, at some level, we really *do* want to do it?

The key is to keep our true hearts always open to Him. In closing off any part of our lives to Him, we hinder the growth of the relationship. And a deep and abiding relationship with us is exactly what the Lord seeks. In such a context, betrayal has no chance.

Heavenly Father, when I falter in my faith, please forgive me and protect me from evil. Heal my life and my heart, and use me to show Your glory to the world. In Jesus' precious name, amen.

_____

_____

_____

_____

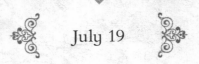

July 19

Safe and Secure

"What is it you want?" he asked. She said, "Grant that one of these two sons of mine may sit at your right and the other at your left in your kingdom" (Matthew 20:21).

Scripture: Matthew 20:20-23

As new parents, my husband and I sat down to prepare a will. We named a guardian for our son and outlined financial matters in the event something should happen to us. Our estate may not amount to much, but we wanted to provide him with as much stability as we could.

There are more important matters than earthly security for our son. By being involved in church, reading the Bible, and praying with him, we pass on the tools for living a strong Christian life. We cannot secure a place in Heaven for our son, but we can do all within our ability to show him the right path.

The mother of James and John, understandably, wanted a secure future for her sons with Jesus. The three only dimly understood the kingdom, however. It was a realm in which servanthood would be the goal, in which giving up one's earthly life would be the means to eternal life. Yes, security would follow but only as a blessed result of pursuing the Lord's will, first and foremost.

O God, I know that my time on this earth is limited. It is not a secure existence—and sometimes not a pretty one. Thank You for preparing a place in Heaven for me to spend eternity with You. As I grow in faith, keep my thoughts on bringing glory to You. In Jesus' precious name, amen.

_____

_____

_____

_____

_____

July 20

Life Worth Living

Whoever wants to become great among you must be your servant, and whoever wants to be first must be your slave (Matthew 20:26, 27).

Scripture: Matthew 20:24-28

Having made many job changes, I began to pray diligently, seeking to find the "me" God intended—and the perfect vocation to go with it. Yet with each promising new move, I found little peace.

When motherhood finally became my "career," I heeded the deep desire to be at home with my child. I thought I'd finally found my life's purpose. However, the yearnings barely diminished.

Only when I stopped my human reasoning could I begin practicing what I like to call "faith reasoning." Have you tried it? The upshot was that I began helping with ministries at church and opened up my life for God's use. Much of what I do now is volunteer work, even though money is tight. But I wouldn't trade my newfound areas of service for anything. They make use of the "real me" (my spiritual gifts) as nothing ever has before.

In all my previous years of employment, I was successful with the help of my heavenly Father. But nothing ever satisfied me until I used my life in joyful, wholehearted servanthood.

Lord, You plan blessings for me far greater than I can imagine. Help me to live my life as Your servant today and always. In Jesus' name, amen.

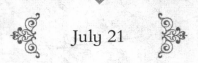

July 21

Watch Out for Flying Plywood

When you pass through the waters, I will be with you; and when you pass through the rivers, they will not sweep over you. When you walk through the fire, you will not be burned; the flames will not set you ablaze (Isaiah 43:2).

Scripture: *Isaiah 43:1-7*

When I saw the plywood fly by the window, I knew it was time to stop looking for flashlight batteries and get downstairs with my husband and crying children. When the sirens stopped and we exited our home, we saw where the tornado had been. One neighbor's roof was in our front yard. On the other side of him, homes were completely demolished, with chairs, underwear, and other items draped in the trees. Amazingly, our home was fine; we just lost a couple of trees.

I thought of that tornado when I read Isaiah 43:1-7. Though these words were written to the Israelites, they also apply to us. Sometimes bad things will happen. Storms will cover us, or we'll swirl in rivers of troubles up to our neck. God never promised to keep the storms and tragedies of life out of our neighborhoods. But He does promise to be with us when they strike.

Lord, when I see the plywood flying and feel the winds blowing in my life, help me remember that You are the Master of all literal and figurative winds. Help me trust in You. Through Christ, amen.

_____

_____

_____

_____

_____

Jesus from A to Z

"But what about you?" he asked. "Who do you say I am?" (Matthew 16:15).

Scripture: Matthew 16:13-16

About a dozen or so teenagers gathered in the unfinished basement of one teen's home. It wasn't the best setting in the world, but the minds of the teens in the Bible club were able to go beyond the setting.

Our activity was to go from A to Z. As each letter was named, teens called out words that described Jesus to them. Sure, the kids used a lot of the expected names: Savior, Lord, Emmanuel, Holy One. But they also used words we may not think about: Rescuer, Compassionate One, Eloquent, and more. Seventeen-year-old Dennis grinned mischievously as he announced "Xtra Special" for the letter X.

It's been 20 years since I cosponsored that Bible club. But sometimes I still see those teens' reverent faces as they thought about all Jesus meant to them. It still encourages me to line a paper with A to Z sometimes and list all the things Jesus is. In fact, that might be a good spiritual exercise for all of us today.

> *Dear heavenly Father, just as Peter had the discernment to know exactly who You are in a world that was confused about You, open my eyes to the many facets of Your eternal being. And as I come to know You better, increase my ability to speak of You to others. Thank You, in the name of Jesus, Your incomparable Son. Amen.*

_____

_____

_____

_____

_____

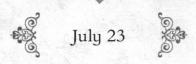

July 23

Blurt the Good Stuff

Jesus replied, "Blessed are you, Simon son of Jonah, for this was not revealed to you by man, but by my Father in heaven" (Matthew 16:17).

Scripture: Matthew 16:17-20

Peter is probably the disciple I relate to most closely. You see, I'm also likely to make mistakes, get myself into trouble, or just plain sin by thoughtlessly spouting the wrong words. Likewise, Peter seemed to put his foot in his mouth regularly. He bragged about never leaving Christ—and then abandoned Him, even lied about Him. On the mountain when Elijah and Moses talked with Christ, Peter was the one who wanted to settle down there with those legends permanently. So Jesus, once again, had to correct this impulsive disciple.

However, in our Scripture passage today, blurting out an answer was a good thing for Peter to do—in fact, Jesus told him that God was working through him at just that moment. Peter might have had some issues with his mouth, but he apparently also kept his mind contemplating Christ and pondering what God was doing. As he kept his thoughts trained on God, God revealed the most marvelous truths to him. Maybe I'd like to be more like Peter, after all.

Dear Father, how thankful I am for Your incarnate Son! Please help me to focus on Him so that if I must blurt out things, they'll be words that reveal His wonderful qualities. In His name, I pray. Amen.

_____

_____

_____

_____

Who's Making the Plans?

Jesus turned and said to Peter, "Get behind me, Satan! You are a stumbling block to me; you do not have in mind the things of God, but the things of men" (Matthew 16:23).

Scripture: Matthew 16:21-23

In his few unkind moments in life, my husband has said that I'm bossy, that I think my way is the only way to do things. In his kinder moments, my easygoing husband sits back and lets me make the plans—knowing that otherwise nothing may ever happen in our family!

I do have administrative gifts. I'm quite analytical, and I'm pretty good at planning things, thinking through the details to figure out the best way to proceed. But I guess the downside is that I get used to being in control. Also, I'm often reluctant to think outside my own plans.

In today's Scripture, Peter didn't like what Jesus was saying about the future. Perhaps it didn't line up with his plans on how things really ought to unfold.

As I've often been reminded—and as Peter was reminded—it's OK to make our plans, or perhaps nothing will ever get done. But even as we make our plans and envision our futures, we still have to keep God in the center of the equation. That way, we'll be ready for Him to reveal more of His perfect will at any moment.

Dear God, help me remember to make no plans without consulting You and to accept Your ways as the best ways. When I don't understand, give me Your peace that surpasses understanding. In Jesus' name, amen.

_____

_____

_____

_____

July 25

On the Mountaintop

Peter said to Jesus, "Lord, it is good for us to be here. If you wish, I will put up three shelters—one for you, one for Moses and one for Elijah" (Matthew 17:4).

Scripture: Matthew 17:1-4

My 17-year-old stepdaughter spent most of her time last summer at a place called God's Mountain. She worked there for a week in the early summer helping with a kids' camp. While she worked with the children, God touched her own heart, leading her to dedicate her life to Christ.

We saw the change in her life as soon as she arrived back home. And for most of the summer, she returned often to the camp to help with the different sessions and simply to relish the atmosphere—being with people who focused on Christ. She didn't want to leave that mountain when the summer ended, because so many amazing things happened there in her spiritual growth.

We've all had our "mountaintop experiences" with the Lord, times when we've just wanted to stay in His presence forever. Like Peter, we want to pitch permanent tents and bask in the glory. But life goes on and demands that we join it. However, we can ask God to keep His glory alive in our hearts.

Heavenly Father, help me find the "glory stops" in my days—moments when I can bask in Your presence without any other agenda. Then energize me by Your Spirit to walk into my world with the matchless message of Your goodness. In the precious name of Your Son, Jesus, I pray. Amen.

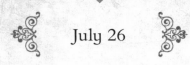

July 26

He's Pleased with You

While he was still speaking, a bright cloud enveloped them, and a voice from the cloud said, "This is my Son, whom I love; with him I am well pleased. Listen to him!" (Matthew 17:9).

Scripture: Matthew 17:5-8

I was as pleased as could be when I saw my 8-year-old son tenderly helping his 3-year-old sister. I was so proud that he was watching out for her without being asked. I love those moments in parenting when I'm just so happy with my children that I could burst.

Apparently God the Father was pretty pleased with God the Son in the Scripture for today. Just as at Jesus' baptism, the Father's voice broke through the sky, proclaiming His pleasure with His Son. The Father didn't wait until Jesus had finished the whole task set before Him on earth. He was proud of His Son and pleased with His daily obedience and commitment.

Have you ever thought about God's pleasure with you? He doesn't wait until we're finished with our work here on earth; He's pleased with us now, as we walk in day-by-day commitment to Him. He's pleased each time we make right choices and go where He leads. And even when we fail, His love never lessens, His care is never withdrawn.

*Thank You, **Lord,** for loving me as tenderly and joyfully as a mom and dad love their kids. Help me to live in the power of this love, especially when I'm tempted to see nothing but my failures. Through Christ, amen.*

_____

_____

_____

_____

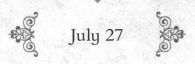

Ready to Burst!

As they were coming down the mountain, Jesus instructed them, "Don't tell anyone what you have seen, until the Son of Man has been raised from the dead" (Matthew 17:9).

Scripture: Matthew 17:9-13

Has anything so exciting ever happened to you that you were just ready to burst with the telling? I have felt that way a few times, especially a few years ago when I learned I was pregnant with my youngest child. I couldn't wait to proclaim the news to my friends and family.

Can you imagine how excited Peter, James, and John were? They'd watched Jesus glow with an internal fire, they'd actually seen Moses and Elijah, and then they heard the literal voice of God. Wouldn't their report just blow away a small group meeting? Jesus held them back though, until finally, after the resurrection, they could spread the good news far and wide.

Poet Robert Frost once said: "Half the world is composed of people who have something to say and can't, and the other half who have nothing to say and keep on saying it." We can be different from either group; we have something eternally worth saying, and we *can* say it, as the Spirit gives us the will and the words.

Lord, I thank You for revealing yourself to human beings through such creative ways. When You work in my life and I'm ready to burst, give me opportunities to tell others—Christians or not—about the marvelous things You've done. In Jesus' name, amen.

_____

_____

_____

_____

July 28

Perfection in the Fire

Let patience have her perfect work, that ye may be perfect and entire, lacking nothing (James 1:4, *King James Version*).

Scripture: James 1:1-4

Our minister told of being in a pottery class, fashioning a colorful bowl. A four-step process was required, in which the bowl would be glazed, then baked, and then baked a third and fourth time. Impatient to see the final product, he only put the bowl in the kiln twice, at the beginning and at the end of the process. The first time he used the bowl, it cracked, and all of his hard work went to waste.

We too are like bowls in a potter's hand, and James tells us that our trials can help mold a stronger faith in us. Our hard times can be like a fire that, though painful, works to strengthen our commitment to the Lord.

It is easy to praise the Lord when circumstances unfold to our liking, and everything happens according to our own "perfect" time schedules. But we do need to develop patience. And how shall we do that unless we face delays, even prayers that seem to go unanswered for years on end? It is when the answer seems delayed and the need dire that the fire of endurance solidifies our patience.

*Thanks, **Lord,** for Your workmanship in my life. Help me trust that these trials are strengthening me and not destroying me. In Jesus' name, amen.*

_____

_____

_____

_____

_____

July 29

Ask and Believe

If any of you lacks wisdom, he should ask God, who gives generously to all without finding fault, and it will be given to him. But when he asks, he must believe and not doubt, because he who doubts is like a wave of the sea, blown and tossed by the wind (James 1:5, 6).

Scripture: James 1:5-8

My autistic son struggles with fear and is particularly frightened of bugs. Every day before we go out, he asks me whether the bugs are going to get him. I assure him they will not bother him, and then he runs off to play with an unburdened spirit.

One day he approached a group of little boys who had caught a grasshopper in a jar. "Is the bug going to get me?" he asked.

"Yeah, look, it's *on* you!" they teased. Horrified, my son ran to me, frantically trying to brush the imagined grasshopper off his back. It took me some time to convince him that he was out of danger.

Sometimes I'm like that with God. I come to Him, asking for wisdom and reassurance; later, I easily doubt the word I've received in the face of countless real or imagined crises. In my flurry of emotion, I somehow avoid resting in the good and loving words of my Lord.

*Thank You, **Lord,** for Your wisdom. Help me to remember it, though, and trust it, even when the world seems to contradict Your wise words. I pray this prayer in the name of Jesus, my Savior and Lord. Amen.*

_____

_____

_____

_____

_____

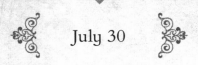

God Honors the Poor

The brother in humble circumstances ought to take pride in his high position. But the one who is rich should take pride in his low position, because he will pass away like a wild flower (James 1:9, 10).

Scripture: James 1:9-11

Our society seems to associate "poor" with "shameful." It wasn't until I became a missionary, though, that I truly began to comprehend this in all its power. We were poor, rarely knowing where our next meal would come from. Yet never did the Lord fail to provide. Relying on Him like that was hardly a thing of shame! In fact, soon dependence upon Him became an exhilarating experience as we saw our needs being met, time after time.

Coming back to America, I realized that it was far too easy to take a regular paycheck for granted. So for me, our Scripture verse contains a gentle challenge: Always look at things through Heaven's eyes. Thus I can see that any level of financial well-being is a gift to be received humbly.

Are you in need at the moment? God honors you and will provide. Are you doing well? You are being humbled by God's great provision.

Dear Father in Heaven, help me never forget to thank You for humbling me by giving me so much. Help me also to remember to thank You for needs that arise, needs that turn my heart back to dependence upon Your daily bread. In the name of Your Son, my Savior, I pray. Amen.

_____

_____

_____

_____

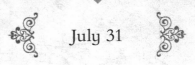

Rules of Engagement

Temptation comes from our own desires which entice us and drag us away (James 1:14, *New Living Translation*).

Scripture: James 1:12-15

One of the first principles you learn in the martial arts is that you should never let the attacker set the rules of engagement. For example, one scientific study looked at women who were attacked by men. The women who shouted "No!"—and fought back—had a much greater chance of survival than those who succumbed to fear and submissively allowed the attacker to have his way.

We could view Satan as a mugger. He throws temptations in our path and convinces us that we must give in, either by bullying us with shame or seducing us with myriad "innocent" justifications. Yet we are called to fight back with an aggressive counterattack, just as Jesus countered Satan's temptations in the wilderness.

What temptation hounds you right now? Are you letting the enemy set the rules of engagement? One effective counterattack is to simply avoid the people and places that make you most vulnerable. As someone once said, it is better to shun the bait than struggle in the snare.

Lord, give me discernment to see temptations coming well before I am thrust into the heat of battle. Help me form good habits of prayer and Bible reading, strengthening my defenses. Most of all, continue to assure me of Your constant presence and love. For it is Your power, ultimately, that wins every spiritual battle. In Jesus' name, amen.

_____

_____

_____

_____

August

Christ is all, and is in all.

—Colossians 3:11

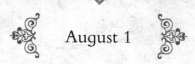

August 1

Loud Tongues, Deaf Ears

My dear brothers, take note of this: Everyone should be quick to listen, slow to speak and slow to become angry (James 1:19).

Scripture: James 1:16-21

A Native American saying goes like this: "Listen, or thy tongue will keep thee deaf." I have found myself struggling with this principle in raising small children, especially when shouting orders seems the best way to go. It's all too easy, when I'm feeling particularly tired, to jump to conclusions and just react without truly listening to what my children have to say. I've often had to apologize for unjust reprimands.

I have realized, too, that sometimes I really don't *want* to hear what my children have to say. Yet a little bit of eye contact and a gentle smile goes so far with them.

God has been reminding me that a listening heart is a humble heart. And the humbler I am before Him, the more I will be able to hear others before contributing my "two-cents' worth." As another saying goes (this one from Arabia): "When you have spoken a word, it reigns over you. When it is unspoken, you reign over it."

*Thank You, **Father,** for being quick to listen to me when I come to You in prayer. Help me develop a listening ear and a humble heart in my interactions with others, that I might witness to Your love. In Christ, amen.*

_____

_____

_____

_____

_____

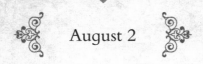

Telltale Tongue

If anyone considers himself religious and yet does not keep a tight rein on his tongue, he deceives himself and his religion is worthless (James 1:26).

Scripture: James 1:22-27

The destructive power of words was vividly demonstrated by how water crystals changed their structure—according to words spoken to them! In an article in *Christian Today*, researcher Masaru Emoto, author of *The Hidden Messages of Water*, showed that water crystals which had positive words like "love" and "thanks" spoken to them changed into the most beautiful snowflake-like shapes. On the other hand, words like "fool" or "stupid" caused the water to break down.

We know that our bodies contain a high percentage of water. Is it possible, then, that words could literally tear a person apart?

No wonder the Lord places such importance on our words, making their quality equal to the quality of our religion. Yet why is it so hard, especially within our own families, to speak consistently with kindness? I'm sobered by the enormous physical and spiritual influence my words can have on the ones I dearly love. Is it your prayer today to make that influence a positive, life-giving one?

God, in light of their power for good or ill, let my words be ordered by You. I know I can speak with kindness, if You will help me recollect all of the good things You have spoken to me in Your Word. In Jesus' name, amen.

_____

_____

_____

_____

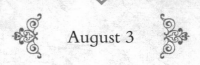

August 3

Blessings for the Day

It is good to proclaim your unfailing love in the morning, your faithfulness in the evening (Psalm 92:2, *New Living Translation*).

Scripture: Psalm 92:1-8

Mornings are hard for me because I work late into the night. So I'm often tired when morning dawns, and my quiet times then become less than inspiring. I can easily begin to feel spiritually depleted.

There is hope for me, though! In fact, the psalmist hit upon an important principle that I began trying in my own quiet times with God. I felt challenged to take a few minutes each morning to "proclaim"—or meditate upon—the divine attribute that I need most during the day: God's unfailing love. As I did this, I pictured a mighty hand holding and sustaining me through the stress of the day. Then at the end of the day before I lay down to sleep, I took a few minutes to reflect on how God had revealed His love for me during the day.

After a few days of this simple spiritual exercise, I felt better able to handle my daily stresses and strains. More importantly, I sensed a closer connection with the indwelling Lord.

We're often called to be more faithful, or to do more for God. But I believe we often just need to stop and remember how much He loves us, no matter what.

*Thank You, **Father,** for Your nurturing hand of love, which is my source of strength today. In the precious name of Jesus, I pray. Amen.*

_____

_____

_____

_____

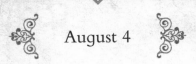
When the Boss Isn't Watching

All the nations will be gathered before him, and he will separate the people one from another as a shepherd separates the sheep from the goats (Matthew 25:32).

Scripture: Matthew 25:31-46

What is really in our hearts shows through when we think no one is watching. At my workplace some employees get busy when the boss walks in, but they put forth less effort when he walks out of sight. Employees like that merely want to look good for the boss.

Christ calls us to go well beyond a concern for mere appearances. He wants our genuine compassion for those in need. It's really the difference between His sheep and the goats ("fake sheep"). Sheep not only have a heart for the Lord, but also for His people and His business—even when they aren't aware that He is watching.

While we are on this earth, we can be transformed from goats into sheep. And we need to let God's Spirit do that work in us, day by day. Because once we step into eternity, the matter will already be settled.

Lord God, help me see where I have the heart of a goat and help me change fully into a sheep. And may my sheep's heart influence others so they may spend eternity in the place You prepared for people, not in the place prepared for the devil and his angels. In the name of the Father, the Son, and the Holy Spirit, I pray. Amen.

_____

_____

_____

_____

_____

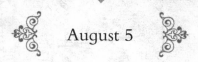

August 5

No Room at the Inn

If you show special attention to the man wearing fine clothes and say, "Here's a good seat for you," but say to the poor man, "You stand there" or "Sit on the floor by my feet," have you not discriminated among yourselves and become judges with evil thoughts? (James 2:3, 4).

Scripture: James 2:1-4

My husband, Hal, and I parked near the motel's office after a long, hard day of riding motorcycles. I was hot and sweaty, and my helmet had matted my hair to my head. I went in to get us a room. "Sorry," the clerk said. "We're full."

We rode to the next motel. This time Hal went in and got us a room. As I waited for him to do business with the clerk, I remembered seeing only two or three cars in the parking lot of that previous motel. And the clerk said they were full! Maybe it's Hal's looks—or the way his helmet doesn't mat his short hair—but since that day Hal has gotten our rooms while I wait outside . . . and we get turned away far less often.

We would have been good customers for the first motel—honest, trustworthy, a blessing as we let the light of Christ shine through us. But we were turned away, and the motel's owners may have lost more than they know.

Lord, help me to see the value in each person You bring across my path. And give me the wisdom to distinguish earthly treasures from eternal treasures in setting my own priorities. Through Christ I pray. Amen.

_____

_____

_____

_____

_____

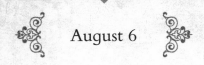

Upside Down

Are they not the ones who are slandering the noble name of him to whom you belong? (James 2:7).

Scripture: James 2:5-7

Several years ago, author Bill Myers wrote a children's book series called Journeys to Fayrah. When the characters in the story found themselves in the land of Fayrah, everything seemed upside down. But the characters soon learned the truth: the world was right side up; *they* were upside down.

Sin can so skew our thinking that we may not know what is right. Because of sin, everything in our word can get turned inside out, down side up, upside down, wrong side out, right side in, backside front, and front side back. Whew! It's tough to tell right from wrong in such a situation. That's why we need God to guide us.

To us, things seem backwards. We think of the rich as possessing kingdoms and the poor as possessing little or nothing. Yet today's verses tell us that those who are poor "in the eyes of the world" are rich in faith and will inherit the kingdom because they sincerely love God. Those who may have riches and power—yet slander Christ's name—truly are the poorest of the poor.

Lord, let me never be counted among the ones who are slandering Your noble name. Instead, help me to live as one who loves You with a sincere and dedicated passion. And may each person I meet today see something of Your nobility in me. In Jesus' precious name, I pray. Amen.

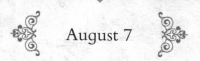

August 7

Short List of Sins?

Whoever keeps the whole law and yet stumbles at just one point is guilty of breaking all of it (James 2:10).

Scripture: James 2:8-11

A prominent attorney in a town where we once lived told my husband, "The Ten Commandments would be pretty good if it weren't for that one about adultery." Within a few years we heard of circumstances that revealed the likely reason for his point of view.

We all tend to gasp at other's sins, yet we quickly excuse our own. Christian comedian Mike Warnke once said that, after describing his former life of sin, some people would say to him, "Well, I never did anything *that* bad!"

He would reply, "Yes, and you were headed to the same hell as I was!"

We often stand amazed at spectacular testimonies and conversion stories. But Mike Warnke also pointed out that it takes little common sense for a drowning person to reach out to grab a floating branch and cling to it for salvation. But what of someone who has lived a basically clean life, someone in no obvious need to escape the deadly clutches of sin? For that person to recognize his need for a Savior . . . Well, perhaps that's the bigger miracle.

Father, when I view my list of sins as much shorter than others', I'm in danger of minimizing the very things that sent Your Son to the cross. Help me to see all sin as devastating and destructive. And help me to love others as if their sin list is as short as I imagine mine to be. In Jesus' name, amen.

_____

_____

_____

_____

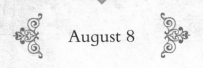

August 8

Twice Blest

Judgment without mercy will be shown to anyone who has not been merciful. Mercy triumphs over judgment! (James 2:13).

Scripture: James 2:12-17

I know of a woman who grew up in a home filled with harshness and anger. Now an adult, she still goes home and cares for her once-abusive parent. When I questioned this, she said she knew that she could hang onto the pain and return hurt for hurt. Some would think she has that right. After all, aren't parents supposed to "bless" their children, to bring good things into their lives?

"But maybe I was placed in this home so I myself could be the blessing," she said. "It's not always about what we get, but what we give."

How could she treat her parent so well after the way she was treated? "I was just as hateful toward God," she said. "But He showed me mercy in forgiving my sins. How can I refuse to show mercy in return? My Lord was so generous in mercy to me, and as a result I am a friend of God. I chose to extend mercy to my parent, and now I have gained a loving friend."

Indeed, mercy triumphs over judgment. And as Shakespeare wrote: "Mercy is twice blest: It blesseth him that gives and him that takes."

Dear Father, thank You so much for the mercy You have shown me, mercy too deep for me to fathom. Give me the courage to extend mercy to others, even when I have been wrongly treated. I pray in Jesus' name. Amen.

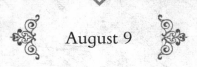

August 9

Fingerprints of Faith

You believe that there is one God. Good! Even the demons believe that—and shudder (James 2:19).

Scripture: James 2:18-20

When a person merely says, "I believe in God," it is not enough to bring salvation. Even the demons can assent to cold, hard facts of reality—while continuing to work evil. But when we who hear the gospel respond in true faith, that faith will show through in what we do.

We can do nothing without leaving evidence behind. Even a burglar sneaking through a house leaves traces of his presence: a footprint in the carpet, a fallen hair with DNA, a fingerprint on a doorknob. Similarly, where faith exists, evidence marks it as genuine.

Satan and his demons have been in the very presence of God and of the pre-incarnate Christ. They know who Christ is and proved it when they screeched at Him, "What do you want with us, Jesus of Nazareth? . . . I know who you are—the Holy One of God!" (Mark 1:24). Yet what does the evidence of their actions say about them?

Good works are the evidence of a genuine faith, the evidence left behind wherever faith has gone. In other words, right action is the fingerprint of faith.

Dear Father in Heaven, as I walk through this life, help me to live in such a way that I leave behind a trail of evidence of my faith in You. And let that evidence be sufficient so that someone might follow the trail to You. I pray in the name of Jesus, my merciful Savior and Lord. Amen.

_____

_____

_____

_____

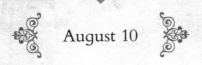

Actions Reveal Belief

You see that a person is justified by what he does and not by faith alone (James 2:24).

Scripture: James 2:21-26

This verse doesn't contradict the truth that salvation comes through faith alone. It simply tells us that talk is cheap. We can say anything, but what we truly believe in our hearts will seep out in our actions. When we say we are followers of Christ, we may mean our words sincerely. But those words are worthless until action backs them up. In other words, *show* me, don't just *tell* me you have faith.

And the kind of "showing" we do should benefit those around us. As J. S. Whale wrote in *Christian Doctrine:* "Faith without ethical consequences is a lie. Good works must necessarily follow faith. God does not need our sacrifices, but he has, nevertheless, appointed a representative to receive them, namely our neighbor. The neighbor always represents the invisible Christ."

We can say anything. But our actions betray what our hearts truly believe. If we speak like a saint but treat others like dirt, how could we ever be justified?

Dear heavenly Father, keep reminding me that my actions will always speak louder than my words. In order to grow in good works, let me focus on the exemplary life of Your Son. The more I get to know Him, the clearer I see the power of good works done in the power of the Spirit. Thank You for giving yourself, through Him, to the world. In His name, amen.

_____

_____

_____

_____

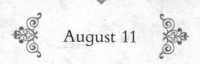

Anonymous Notes

A gentle answer turns away wrath, but a harsh word stirs up anger (Proverbs 15:1).

Scripture: Proverbs 15:1-4

Someone had placed the note in the offering plate in response to an opinion I had voiced in the sermon. I hadn't considered that my view was controversial, but I had obviously touched a nerve with at least one person in the congregation.

The comment piqued my attention because I was not aware of the particular information forwarded to me in the terse note. Unfortunately, I had no method of dialoguing with the writer. The note was unsigned.

It's difficult to exchange ideas or to grow in knowledge if we cannot speak to or listen to one another directly. This applies to criticisms as well as compliments, disagreeable subjects as well as agreeable ones.

Face-to-face conversations can help to clear up misunderstandings and at least give us a chance to apply the proverb above: if we know who is angry with us, we can at least know who it is that needs a gentle answer.

Loving God, make me aware that it is so easy to disagree with one of my brothers or sisters in Christ. Sometimes the difference is petty; sometimes I think it is immense. Help me to ponder my words before I speak (or write) so that I might always disagree in love. In Christ I pray. Amen.

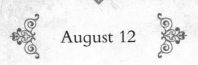

August 12

Stumbling Through Life

We all stumble in many ways. If anyone is never at fault in what he says, he is a perfect man, able to keep his whole body in check (James 3:2).

Scripture: James 3:1-4

I wanted to do something special for the children's sermon that might surprise the kids or show them a fascinating aspect of God's world. I decided to demonstrate, through a science experiment, how acts of love can "lift up" someone's spirits. The experiment was simple—add enough salt to a bowl of water, and the salt will lift to the surface an egg that had sunk in the clear tap water.

On Saturday, I tried this experiment at home, just to be sure it would work. Twice, it went off trouble-free.

But on Sunday morning with the children gathered around me—in front of a packed room of adults—the experiment flopped. (Eventually it did work, but only after I had made a mess on my pulpit robe and spilled water across the carpet—which amused both the children and everyone else.)

Oh well. We all stumble and look foolish occasionally. Once again, I'm reminded that God alone is in control.

*I confess, **Lord,** that there are times when I mess up my life—and sometimes the lives of those around me. Help me always to be aware of Your presence and to let You take control. You, alone, have the right plan for my life if I will remain quiet and listen for Your voice. In the wonderful name of Christ I pray. Amen.*

_____

_____

_____

_____

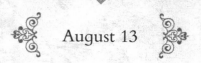

August 13

In Remembrance

With the tongue we praise our Lord and Father, and with it we curse men, who have been made in God's likeness (James 3:9).

Scripture: James 3:5-9

We sang "In Remembrance of Me" as our communion hymn during worship. The song begins with Jesus offering the cup and bread to His disciples. He asks them to eat and drink in remembrance.

As the hymn unfolds, the vision of remembering Christ expands: "In remembrance of me, heal the sick. In remembrance of me, feed the poor. In remembrance of me, open the door, and let your brother in." [rodentregatta. com.article/4560/and-on-the-third-day]

I knew that receiving the cup and bread brought Christ's presence to me on Sunday. Now, the words suggested a special way to know Christ's presence every day: do some tangible act of love in remembrance of Him. Feed a hungry person, open a door, send a card, cry with a friend, hug a child, say a gracious word to a neighbor. But pause and do your act deliberately in Jesus' name.

This approach makes our words, too, particularly powerful. A word of kindness—spoken in remembrance of all that Christ has done for us—becomes an extension of His own heavenly love through our earthly tongue.

O God, I know that You love all of Your creation. Today, show me some person whom I can serve as an act of remembrance of Christ. And let my words, too, convey His goodness to all who hear. In Jesus' name, amen.

_____

_____

_____

_____

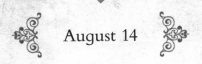

What Spills Out?

Can both fresh water and salt water flow from the same spring? My brothers, can a fig tree bear olives, or a grapevine bear figs? Neither can a salt spring produce fresh water (James 3:11, 12).

Scripture: James 3:10-12

As I drove across the speed bump, the filled-to-the-brim coffee mug that I held in my hand spilled over the side of my cup and slopped coffee on my pants. I was upset at myself for being so careless. Yet I knew that it could have been worse. I might have been drinking grape juice or a raspberry smoothie!

Also, I realized that when I am "bumped" in life, the contents of my inner being often will spill out. What I think and do when I am "bumped" shows whether or not Christ is powerfully present in my life.

So I have to ask myself: When the contents of my inner self spill out, what will others see or hear?

When someone cuts me off in traffic, how do I react? When others scuttle my schedule for the day, am I willing to alter my plans to meet their needs? When I hit the inevitable speed bumps in life, what spills out? Is my cup filled with the love and mercy of Christ?

Dear Lord in Heaven, I know that there are times when I'll encounter difficulties along the road of life. As I meet others on my travels, give me the calmness of Your Spirit that I may bless them in the name of Jesus Christ. It is in His name that I pray. Amen.

_____

_____

_____

_____

_____

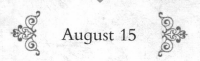

Whom Do You Bless?

Who is wise and understanding among you? Let him show it by his good life, by deeds done in the humility that comes from wisdom (James 3:13).

Scripture: James 3:13-16

I eagerly await December, knowing that I will watch the 1940s film *It's A Wonderful Life* at least once during the month. James Stewart portrays George Bailey, a small business owner, husband, and father, who grew up in Bedford Falls. George comes to think his life is worthless—until the angel Clarence shows him a nightmarish alternative universe. It's the picture of a Bedford Falls as if George had never lived, never touched the lives of so many people, even in the smallest ways.

As a small-town banker, George had selflessly invested in the trials and tribulations of his neighbors. Thus, when George became desperate, those same neighbors, one by one, offer him their money. As each comes forward, George utters their names in loving awe. Those people had been deeply blessed by the life of George Bailey, a life of good deeds done in humility.

Never discount the worth of your smallest deed in the name of our Lord Jesus Christ. You have no idea whom you might bless.

*Make me aware, **O Loving God,** that I have opportunities each day to bless the lives of people who cross my path. May Jesus shine out of my life as You make me a blessing to someone today. In the name of Christ, amen.*

_____

_____

_____

_____

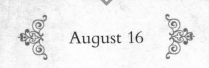

August 16

Quiet Moments

Peacemakers who sow in peace raise a harvest of righteousness (James 3:18).

Scripture: James 3:17, 18

I awoke that morning with a raw, raspy throat. I had laryngitis. Barely did an intelligible sound break forth from my mouth. My children, of course, were delighted. I was unable to bark orders at them to do this or to do that—to wear clothes to school that I deemed suitable, to move faster in order to be at school on time, to eat a solid breakfast that would nourish them. Not today. There was no voice.

It didn't take long to realize just how calmly and peacefully breakfast proceeded that morning. When someone asked something of me, I could respond only in a weak whisper. And everyone else began talking softly too! They responded to me in the same manner in which I spoke—calmly, quietly.

Right there in the midst of eating my oatmeal, I realized what was happening. The tone of my voice had influenced the mood of the whole morning.

Amazing, the lessons we learn in the quiet moments.

*From time to time, **God,** remind me that I can hear You and I can hear others so clearly when the noise and clamor of my inner life are silenced for a few moments. May Your still small voice speak to me and through me each day, as I make some space for You. In the name of the Father, the Son, and the Holy Spirit, I pray. Amen.*

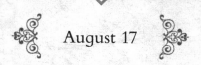

Ripples of Words

The wise in heart are called discerning, and pleasant words promote instruction (Proverbs 16:21).

Scripture: Proverbs 16:21-24

I stand at the edge of the pond and toss a pebble into the water. Ripples spread from the center in an ever-widening circle until they move out of sight.

Recently, I received an e-mail from a minister in Pennsylvania who said he had chanced upon my e-mail address. For some time he had wanted to tell me that the mentoring I had done with him while he was a seminary student was, in large part, the reason he had remained in ministry and was content in his calling. I had been his supervisor nearly a quarter of a century ago. Today, I can't put a face with the name.

The smallest words that we speak are like a pebble dropped into water. They spread far enough away that we can no longer detect them. Yet lives are touched daily by such ripples.

Our lives can send out ripples of faith that affect countless people, known and unknown. It may seem hard to believe, but our ripples can change the face of the world in which we live.

*Help me to remember, **loving God,** that I am Your face, Your hands, and Your voice in this world where I move daily. May others see You and know of Your goodness because they see You in me. In the name of Jesus, Lord and Savior of all, I pray. Amen.*

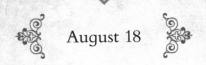

A Wise Choice

She will guide you down delightful paths; all her ways are satisfying (Proverbs 3:17, *New Living Translation*).

Scripture: Proverbs 3:13-18

While I was in college, I thought the wisest thing I could do was pledge to a sorority and get to know all the right people (those who were popular). "Then I'll have it made," I thought.

But Janie, one of the workers for Campus Crusade for Christ, had different advice for me. "Come to our Bible study," she suggested. But what was wise advice seemed foolish to me at the time. I partied while my GPA plummeted. Yet I still was not satisfied.

One night as I stood wondering why a particular frat party didn't seem as fun as parties usually seemed, I remember thinking, "What am I doing? I could be at home studying." I was finally on the path to wisdom.

I took Janie's advice, as well, and reconnected with the source of wisdom himself. That's what the writer of Proverbs suggests. Like a parent or a wise friend, he touts the value of wisdom. What you gain by grasping her is more satisfying than anything you might seek. Have you discovered that yet?

Lord, Your wisdom truly cried out to me and delighted to embrace me. Thank You for seeking me when I didn't seek You. Through Christ, amen.

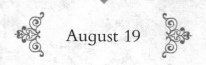

August 19

Fruitless War

You want something but don't get it. You kill and covet, but you cannot have what you want. You quarrel and fight. You do not have, because you do not ask God (James 4:2).

Scripture: James 4:1-3

My roommate and I were at war, because I believed my boyfriend preferred her to me. Actually, I was the one at war. Just the previous week, my boyfriend came to me with the suggestion that we take a break from our relationship. So when I returned home one night and found him in my apartment talking with my roommate, I went ballistic.

Within weeks, I moved out, full of injured pride and accusations. I was angry at them and especially at God. "You knew this would happen when I moved in with her! Why didn't you warn me?" I fired at God in prayer.

"You didn't ask," was His quiet response.

I had to admit that I hadn't asked God about my relationship or living situation—or about much of anything. I did what I wanted and suffered the consequences. Like an explorer who claims a piece of land simply because he stumbled upon it, I tried to claim what I thought was mine. How many battles I've fought over people, possessions, or places without God's guidance!

Dear God, I'm sorry for coveting instead of asking for Your will. But I'm also grateful for Your healing touch when I hurt myself through my own mistakes. In Jesus' name I pray. Amen.

_____

_____

_____

_____

_____

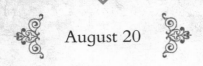

August 20

The Pride Slide

God opposes the proud but favors the humble (James 4:6, *New Living Translation*).

Scripture: James 4:4-7

He leveled his finger at me as I stood ready to hand him a tract on a New Orleans street corner. After berating me for "spoiling his fun," he suddenly stopped. "For many years, I wanted God to speak to me in an audible voice," he said, with an honesty that surprised both of us, seeing as how I hadn't asked him. "But He didn't." He then chose to avoid God, because God didn't respond the way he'd hoped.

I couldn't help thinking of his response years later, when I too was angry with God over a series of financial setbacks, and I demanded that He answer my request for help and direction—*right now*. As I discussed the situation with my younger brother, he quietly said, "You need to humble yourself before God."

I didn't want to hear that. I wanted God to speak in the time and fashion I chose. But once I took my brother's advice, I could accept God's clear response.

It seems I had fallen into the trap of pride. God resisted my demands until I willingly relinquished my "rights" in favor of honoring Him.

Lord of Heaven and earth, I'm beginning to see that I can't have my way and Yours at the same time. Help me choose to honor You, instead of grasping for my own glory. Through Christ I pray. Amen.

_____

_____

_____

_____

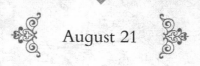

Come Close

Come close to God, and God will come close to you. Wash your hands, you sinners; purify your hearts, for your loyalty is divided between God and the world (James 4:8, *New Living Translation*).

Scripture: James 4:8-10

Near my college dorm lived a squirrel with an odd habit of running up to people instead of shying away from human contact. I found the behavior disconcerting because of rumors that the squirrel was rabid. (Actually, the squirrel was simply used to being fed by students.)

One day as I tried to enter the dorm, the squirrel met me at the front door. The closer to him I moved, the closer to me he moved. So I backed away, immediately feeling foolish for doing so.

I have a tendency to retreat from God, as well, especially in the midst of a struggle. Sometimes the fault lies with my divided loyalties, the kind James talks about in this passage (being torn between wanting success according to the world's standard and wanting to live for God.) But sometimes I directly resist conforming my ways to God's. Yet James assures his readers that drawing close to God will result in His drawing close as well—like a magnet drawing another. And that which draws also purifies. We can't remain the same when a holy God is near.

Loving God, I need Your Spirit to calm me enough to draw close to You. Heal my tendency to resist or run, through Christ my Lord. Amen.

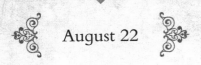

August 22

Quick to Criticize

There is only one Lawgiver and Judge, the one who is able to save and destroy. But you—who are you to judge your neighbor? (James 4:12).

Scripture: James 4:11-14

I gleefully shared with my family the story of a neighbor in my apartment building who claimed to write songs for famous musicians. "She's lost touch with reality," I proclaimed. Another family, I reported, needed therapy because of their habit of fighting in the hallway.

I soon felt guilty. Not only had I speedily passed on information about others, I had shown anything but grace to my neighbors, who were members of the family of God. I was quick to judge them for their foibles, but I couldn't as readily see my own critical spirit. Of course, judging them was far easier than praying for them—or with them—in ways that preserved their dignity.

As James taught, God is the only qualified judge. And judging others is hardly a way to promote peace and good will. Instead, it demotes and devalues. It also shows what we need most: God.

Quick to critically quip? Try being "faster on the draw" to draw nearer to God.

Dear God, when I'm tempted to judge others, remind me of the ways I have failed You. Let me see the log in my own eye before pointing to the speck in another's eye. Then armed with Your forgiveness, help me to accept others as You accept them. Thank You, in Jesus' name. Amen.

_____

_____

_____

_____

_____

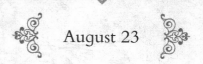

August 23

Making Plans

What you ought to say is, "If the Lord wants us to, we will live and do this or that" (James 4:15, *New Living Translation*).

Scripture: James 4:15-17

Ever been so convinced of the future that you announce it to everyone before you're truly assured of it? I was so certain that two potential writing projects were "a go" that I told everyone about them and even planned my schedule around both. I didn't have a backup plan. So when the "No" came for both projects, I reeled into a tailspin of depression.

During that bleak time, I slowly realized that when I'd prayed about both projects, I never received a clear sense of God's Yes. Instead, I followed my own plans and called them His. I felt foolish as I told the same people I'd boasted to before, "Looks like I was mistaken."

I then asked God, "Well, what can I do now?" I ended up working on two entirely different projects!

Announcing a presumed outcome is a bigger gamble than discerning tomorrow's weather. As an outcome-forecaster, I'm often quite wrong. Maybe that's why James warned so strongly against "boasting about your own plans" (see James 4:16, *NLT*).

Holy One, forgive me for the times when I follow my own path before seeking Your direction. When I fail to discern Your guidance, I lose more than I gain. Thank You for guiding me through Your Word, through circumstances, and through the wise counsel of others. In Christ's name, amen.

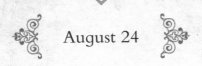

Glow in the Dark

Do not participate in the unfruitful deeds of darkness, but instead even expose them; for it is disgraceful even to speak of the things which are done by them in secret (Ephesians 5:11, 12, *New American Standard Bible*).

Scripture: Ephesians 5:8-11

When I was a kid, I loved anything that promised to glow in the dark. I was fascinated by how exposure to light caused a package or toy to take on an unearthly glow in the darkness. My brothers and I used to spend hours wiggling the items under lamps, then waving them around the darkest closet or the deepest corner of the basement.

Light can work in other ways. The light of God's truth exposes the wrongs we do. Like the time I told one of the ministers of my church how "unfair" God was for taking so long to answer my prayer for employment. He gently rebuked me for resting on my laurels (i.e., waiting on God to act instead of doing something myself). Mostly, I needed to repent of my attitude toward my circumstances.

If we are to live as people of the light, our unfruitful deeds need exposure to the cleansing light of Christ. In that way, we believers will "glow" in a dark world.

My dear heavenly Father, sometimes I fail to reflect Your light. When I require the exposing light of Your truth, give me the humility to submit instead of balking. Then help me to let that light shine out for Your glory in all I do or say. Through Christ's name I pray. Amen.

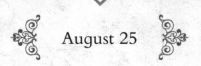

August 25

God's Will for Us

Do not put out the Spirit's fire (1 Thessalonians 5:19).

Scripture: 1 Thessalonians 5:16-22

As I notice the date of this devotional, I'm reminded of my son who celebrates his birthday today. I remember my little "preemie" who is now white-haired, stands six-feet-two, and towers over his three daughters. His role now, like mine of yesteryear, is to care for his family and nurture his children in their development. The hereditary mantle has passed to him.

We know Silas and Timothy were as dear to Paul as sons, and he was preparing them for the mantle of leadership. The earliest of his epistles, Thessalonians, was written by Paul in conjunction with these two young men, his protégés. Paul encouraged sobriety of life, constant watchfulness, respect for church officials, consideration of the needy, and cultivation of spiritual gifts as duties of the Christian life.

Difficulties are natural to a new church, of course. But Paul was building his life into disciples who keep the Spirit's fire burning bright. Like Paul, we too can offer our young people practical and wise advice on maintaining what has been accomplished in our congregations.

*Thank You, **God,** for the words of Paul that spell out our duties as Christians and our responsibilities to You. Amen.*

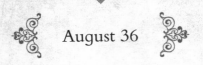

Turn Loose of Things

Your wealth has rotted, and moths have eaten your clothes. Your gold and silver are corroded. . . . You have hoarded wealth in the last days (James 5:2, 3).

Scripture: James 5:1-6

People of my vintage are getting rid of their "stuff." Material things that were so essential and loved in earlier years no longer seem so important. Many of us have had to dismantle the homes of our parents and in-laws, and we've found that some of the treasures saved through the years hold little attraction for us anymore. In fact, most of us have much more stuff than we need, our attics and basements overflowing. And many of our children don't want what we have saved. Their lifestyles, home decors, and tastes are different from ours.

Among the things that I love are my great-grandmother's bed and my grandmother's clock. But will any of my children take the time to tuck linens neatly at the footboard or wind the clock weekly? I doubt it.

Think about James, a fisherman on the Sea of Galilee, who worked in partnership with Peter and Andrew. Can you imagine him having many "things" to hoard and carry around with him?

Dear Father, I live in such a commercial world, where the almighty dollar reigns supreme. Teach me to discern what is important and what is not. And help me convey the values of Your kingdom to my children, day by day. In the name of Your Son, my Savior, I pray. Amen.

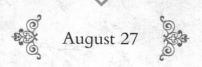

Patience Is a Virtue

You have heard of Job's perseverance and have seen what the Lord finally brought about (James 5:11).

Scripture: James 5:7-12

James exhorted the church at Thessalonica to have patience in their sufferings. He used Job as an example, a man who lost his health, his wealth, his children, and his honor among peers. He was willing to go to the ash heap, to suffer horrible sores that covered his body, to lose his standing in the community, and to separate himself from his friends—all with the result of growing from the experience. His life was transformed, his faith surely strengthened.

James's object in writing this letter to the early Christians was to confront the sins and errors they were committing, while encouraging them in all the trials they faced. He stressed the importance of patience in the Christian life.

We who live in an instant-gratification society would do well to heed James's advice. For many of us, patience seems hard to come by. Yet God is more concerned with our relationship to Him than with our accomplishments for Him. As the great medieval poet John Milton put it, having lost his sight in middle age: "They also serve who only stand and wait."

Father God, we who want things done yesterday need to slow down and wait for Your perfect timing. Teach me patience and perseverance, and help me to accept that it will require times of waiting. In Jesus' name, amen.

_____

_____

_____

_____

_____

Pray with Me

Is any one of you in trouble? He should pray. Is anyone happy? Let him sing songs of praise (James 5:13).

Scripture: James 5:13-15

Miss Ina was my prayer partner. I visited her regularly over the years, in her home, in the hospital, and finally in a nursing facility. "Let's pray," I would begin, and then she would chime in, her words a wonderful complement to mine. It was always a beautiful, synchronized prayer, with each of us praying for different things but communing with God in close harmony.

Miss Ina also loved flowers. One day, I told her of the garden I was growing at our church, in memory of my husband. "Go into my backyard, and dig up the hydrangea," she insisted, "and plant it in your garden." I did as she instructed me.

Years passed. Returning from a trip, I called my church to catch up on happenings.

"Miss Ina died," my minister told me.

I went later that day to water the garden. The hydrangea was a mass of blue blooms. When I saw it, I felt as if Miss Ina were still praying for me.

James told the early church that prayer was the great resource of Christians in need. Could we use it a bit more often?

Father, I know how powerful prayer is. Help me use it often, eagerly seeking Your best for my brothers and sisters in Christ. In His name, amen.

_____

_____

_____

_____

_____

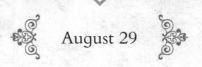

Power in Prayer

The effective prayer of a righteous man can accomplish much (James 5:16, *New American Standard Bible*).

Scripture: James 5:16-18

How can we pray effectively, as James urges? Several years ago someone sent me "The Five-Finger Prayer" in an e-mail. It can help us organize our prayers like this:

Your thumb is nearest to you, so begin by praying for those closest to you—family and friends.

Next comes the pointing finger. Pray for those who teach, instruct, and heal, including teachers, doctors and ministers. They need support and wisdom in pointing others in the right direction.

The longest finger reminds us of our leaders, those who shape our nation and guide public opinion. Pray for our president and other leaders in business and industry.

The ring finger is considered the weakest. It should remind us to pray for those who are weak, in trouble, or in pain.

The smallest of all, the little finger reminds us of how we should think of ourselves in relation to God and others. Your pinkie can remind you to pray for yourself. By the time you have prayed for the other four groups, your own needs will find their proper perspective.

O Lord, help me shed my self-centeredness that I might sincerely and effectively bring before You the needs of others. I believe, with James, that the real power in living comes only from You. In Jesus' name, amen.

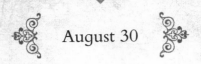

August 30

Such a Great Privilege

Whoever turns a sinner from the error of his way will save him from death and cover over a multitude of sins (James 5:20).

Scripture: James 5:19, 20

At a recent prayer meeting at my church, our minister asked people to share about how they came to Christ. One man answered that he prayed for salvation in a revival meeting when he was 13 years old. Another responded that he was baptized after a youth group meeting when he was 12 years old. Others mentioned Sunday school teachers who had been instrumental in leading them to know Christ. Some named parents and grandparents.

My minister went on to ask us whether we still feel the excitement, the emotion, the joy we felt when we first entered the waters of baptism. I remember crying all the way down the aisle on that Easter Sunday morning, at 12 years old, when I made my profession of faith.

Sometimes we become complacent about the great gift of salvation that God extends to every human being. We forget to show others our faith and use our influence to win them to Christ. Yet it is our Christian responsibility to do so. And James ends his letter by telling us what a great work it is. Can you imagine covering a multitude of sins? What a privilege!

Father, help me frequently to recall today the hour when I first believed. And help me retain my childlike faith so that others may see Your glory through me and turn to You in faith. Through Christ I pray. Amen.

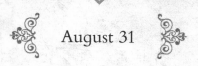

With Paul in Ephesus

I pray that out of his glorious riches he may strengthen you with power through his spirit in your inner being (Ephesians 3:16).

Scripture: Ephesians 3:14-21

I think of Rembrandt's fine portrait of Paul in prison (the place from which Paul wrote his letter to the Ephesians). Light from above falls on Paul's aged face. One shoe is kicked off, perhaps to relieve a tired foot. He is deep in thought with pen in hand, contemplating what he will write next to encourage the Lord's people.

Recently it was my privilege to tour Ephesus, one of the greatest ruined cities in the western world and Turkey's architectural pride. The Grande Theatre looms in awesome splendor, built by the Romans to hold a capacity audience of 24,000. It was here that Paul preached during his stay in Ephesus between AD 53 and 55. Until a year ago it was used for music concerts, but wear and tear on the structure have made this no longer possible.

As I climbed the steps and surveyed the massive, magnificent structure, I could almost hear Paul proclaiming, "I pray that you . . . may have power, together with all the saints, to grasp how wide and long and high and deep is the love of Christ" (Ephesians 3:17, 18).

*Thank You, **God**, for Your saints who have gone before me to teach me of Your love. As You transform my heart, day by day, give me a concern for the spiritual growth of my fellow believers. In Jesus' name, amen.*

September

You are the people of God; . . . you have received mercy.

—Peter 2:10

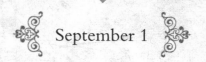

September 1

Surprise Witness

"I will be quick to testify against sorcerers, adulterers and perjurers, against those who defraud laborers of their wages, who oppress the widows and the fatherless, and deprive aliens of justice, but do not fear me," says the L̲ᴏʀᴅ Almighty (Malachi 3:5).

Scripture: Malachi 3:1-5

I love intense courtroom scenes in movies. I particularly enjoy watching the psychological strategies unfold as each attorney attempts to prove the innocence of his or her client. The best part is when it appears the "evil" attorney is about to win, but at the last possible moment, the "good" attorney calls a surprise witness to the stand. Brand new testimony then wins the day!

It often seems as if the evil in our world is going to win, doesn't it? Everywhere we look, sin abounds. And those who flagrantly parade their sin, without any fear of the Lord, sometimes appear to be doing better at life than those who pursue righteousness and honor God. But at the last moment, God will call himself as a surprise witness against all evil, finally bringing justice to His people. Now that's a dramatic conclusion!

Dear Father, remind me that those who appear to be getting away with evil will one day have to answer to You. May I never compare myself with others but only look to You as my standard and guide. In Jesus' name, amen.

_____

_____

_____

_____

_____

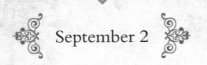

Paid in Full

Speak tenderly to Jerusalem, and proclaim to her . . . that her sin has been paid for (Isaiah 40:2).

Scripture: Isaiah 40:1-5

I'll never forget the day when my parents made their final house payment. Our family had a huge "Paid in Full" party, complete with a mortgage-burning bonfire! This was truly a joyous occasion for my parents. After being indebted to the bank for 30 years, they were finally free.

Since the fall of Adam thousands of years ago, humankind has been in debt. This is not a debt we can pay back with our finances, good deeds, or even our lives. And it won't go away in a mere 30 years! It exists because of our sin nature, and there isn't a thing we can do about it on our own.

Thankfully, though, God didn't leave us on our own. He sent His Son, Jesus, to set us free from our sin debt. He actually *became* sin for us so we could become righteous in God's sight (see 2 Corinthians 5:21). And when He hung on the cross, He declared, "It is finished" (John 19:30). It's time to celebrate, brothers and sisters in Christ. Our debt has been paid in full!

*Thank You, **Dear Father,** for sending Jesus to pay the price for my sin. Because of Your love for me, You have marked my debt "paid in full." Help me never to forget the extent of the debt I owed—and what it cost You to free me from it. Through Christ the Lord, amen.*

_____

_____

_____

_____

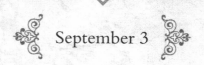

Only One Thing Will Remain

The grass withers and the flowers fall, but the word of our God stands forever (Isaiah 40:8).

Scripture: Isaiah 40:6-11

It's been said that nothing is certain but death and taxes. Yet one day even those will cease. Everything we can see or think of on this earth will be gone. God promises to do away with the earth and Heaven that currently exist in order to replace them with new versions (see Matthew 24:35 and 2 Peter 3:13). The only thing that will remain is God's Word.

Throughout the ages certain persons have tried desperately to snuff out the Word of God. In many countries today, to preach—or even to read the Bible—means putting your very life in danger. And in America there's an increasing effort to remove God's Word from the public eye. But God has declared that His Word will stand "forever." We know that it has and will.

Knowing this, let us place our trust in it. We can't afford to gamble our future on the passing things of this world. Instead, rely on the sure foundation of the Word of our God. It is a piece of Heaven come to us and it can, as well, bring us to Heaven.

> *Dear Lord, help me live my days in light of eternity. Show me where I have placed too much value on things that will one day disappear, and help me to put my trust in You and Your precious Word alone. I pray this prayer in the name of Jesus, my merciful Savior and Lord. Amen.*

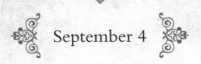

September 4

What Kind of Tree Are You?

Produce fruit in keeping with repentance (Matthew 3:8).

Scripture: Matthew 3:4-10

Several years ago, my husband and I moved into a rental home in California. We had a few trees in our yard, but since we moved in the middle of winter (and because neither of us are tree experts), we had no idea what kind they were. But once spring came and we could see their fruit, we no longer had to wonder; a tree that produces oranges, for instance, is . . . an orange tree.

Every day, the people we live with, work with, and hang out with are watching to see what kind of fruit we produce. They may not listen to our words about Christ, but once they see fruit that offers them a glimpse of genuine spiritual life, they'll no doubt become interested in our Savior. After all, who can resist the true love, peace, and joy that Jesus offers?

When we first came to God, He gave us the fruit of His Spirit. It's now up to us to keep producing the fruit of good works to reflect the greatness of God's saving work in us. Thus others will see our fruit and know what kind of "tree" we are—a tree of life, sent by God.

Father God, thank You for giving me the fruit of Your Spirit that I might be an example of Christ to others. May others be drawn to You by Your work of grace in me. And when I fail, keep me from discouragement while giving me the courage to come to You in repentance and renewed hope. In the name of Jesus, Lord and Savior of all, I pray. Amen.

_____

_____

_____

_____

_____

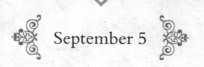

September 5

Can't Buy Love

A voice from heaven said, "This is my Son, whom I love; with him I am well pleased" (Matthew 3:17).

Scripture: Matthew 3:11-19

I vividly remember each of my children as they were in their infancy. I spent my days (and nights) feeding them, cleaning them, and holding them. They couldn't do anything for themselves, let alone serve me! Yet, I loved each one immensely.

Jesus was 30 years old when He began His ministry. Until then, He didn't really "do" anything for God. He simply loved His Father with all His being. Jesus' baptism marked the start of His "official" ministry, but the Father's proclamation of His love for Jesus came *before* Jesus began serving Him. God was well pleased with Jesus just because He was His Son, not because of what He did.

It is true of us, as well. God loves us because of who we are, not because of what we do. You see, we are *creatures who need love;* that is the deepest truth of who we are. So God loves us.

Now that my children are older, they do things for me because they love me, not to earn my love. Let us have the same attitude toward our heavenly Father, whose unconditional regard for us is always free.

Dear Lord, thank You for Your unconditional love toward me. Out of gratitude, may I serve You with all my strength. In Jesus' name, amen.

_____

_____

_____

_____

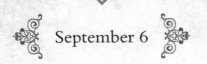

You Belong

Once you were not a people, but now you are the people of God (1 Peter 2:10).

Scripture: 1 Peter 2:1-10

As a youngster, Jeremy spent most of his years in and out of foster homes. He'd stay with a family for a time, then for different reasons, the family would have to give him up. After a while Jeremy felt constantly rejected and abandoned, sensing he had nowhere to belong. Then, when Jeremy was 12, a family adopted him for good. He finally received the love and sense of belonging he'd searched for throughout childhood.

Perhaps you can relate to Jeremy. Maybe you were raised in a broken home and felt as if you never had a "real" family. Or maybe you've been deeply betrayed or hurt as an adult and can't seem to find anywhere to go for help. God wants you to know that He has adopted you into His family.

At one time, we were all like Jeremy: on our own, without a sense of purpose, and nowhere to go for the unconditional love we so desperately needed. But as children of God, we're now His people, called into His family, and given a new destiny. Like Jeremy, we can now say, "I belong here."

*Thank You, **Lord,** that You have chosen me as Your own. Help me to remember that no matter what I may go through or how alone I might feel, You are always there for me. Through Christ I pray. Amen.*

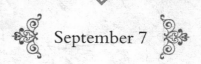

September 7

The Message Is Still the Same

Repent, for the kingdom of heaven is near (Matthew 3:2).

Scripture: Matthew 3:1-3; Mark 1:1-8

As the years come and go and generations pass, things that were once considered wrong by society have become increasingly acceptable. Part of the reason may be that the Bible has largely been written off as "old-fashioned" and "irrelevant" (even among some preachers). But the truth is, God's Word still speaks to us today, and the message is still the same, regardless of any culture's so-called ethical progress.

John the Baptist proclaimed the message of repentance over 2,000 years ago. The message has not changed in all these years; the kingdom of Heaven is still near. John was letting people know that the Messiah would soon make His first appearance, and they needed to be ready for Him. In our time, we must remember that Jesus is preparing to make His second and final appearance.

Will we be ready for Him? Just like John, we must herald the warning that the kingdom of Heaven is near. We must cry out to sinners and believers alike: Repent; get ready to receive your king!

Heavenly Father, thank You that Your Word contains timeless truths, that it does not change just because the world changes. Help me to heed Your warning—which is just as relevant today as it was in John the Baptist's day. In the name of my Savior, Jesus Christ, amen.

_____

_____

_____

_____

_____

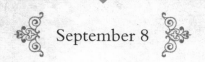

September 8

Save Me from Myself

But the more I called to him, the more he rebelled. . . . I lead Israel along with my ropes of kindness and love (Hosea 11:2, 4, *New Living Translation*).

Scripture: Hosea 11:1-7

Charles's choices were tearing the family apart. Where was the loving husband and father his family once knew? Years of drinking had changed him, and he was deaf to the cries of his wife and children.

His perilous ways led him down the path of self-destruction. Darkness enveloped him. Yet just when he was about to give up on life, he heard the pleadings of his teenage son in an ultimatum: "Pop, we can't live like this any more. Get help, or get out!" Somewhere inside him the man he had been heard these words of tough love. "Lord, help me!" was his soul-deep response.

That very night a call to Alcoholics Anonymous brought John to their home. Over gallons of coffee and hours of conversation, Charles grabbed hold of a thread of hope. And slowly that rope pulled him from his darkness.

I, too, hear God's calls to me. He still offers the ropes of kindness and love. How can I ignore His invitation to be set free from my dark, painful places?

Father, please don't give up on me. I know deep within my heart that I need Your love. Change my rebellion into openness. In Jesus' name, amen.

_____

_____

_____

_____

_____

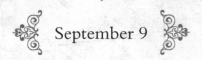

September 9

Unfailing Presence

Although the world was made through him, the world didn't recognize him when he came. . . . But to all who believed him and accepted him, he gave the right to become children of God (John 1:10, 12, *New Living Translation*).

Scripture: John 1:10-14

The doors of the bus opened, and I stepped out into the busy terminal. I searched the waiting crowd for my father, but he wasn't there. I went out to the street to look for him. He wasn't there, either. Soon I was the only person left waiting to be met. Where could he be? He was always on time.

A car was parked across the street, and I noticed the driver waving at someone. He got out of the car and began to walk toward the terminal. The gentleman's stride looked familiar and, as I strained to see the man's face, I realized it was indeed my father. Why didn't I recognize this man whom I had loved my whole life?

He soon told me that his recent eye surgery had transformed his vision, and he'd put aside the glasses he'd worn since childhood. As we hugged he whispered, "Don't worry, I'll still claim you as my daughter."

It is the same with God. He loves us with unfailing love and faithfulness, even when we fail to recognize His presence.

Father God, forgive me for my blindness to Your constant presence. Help me to see You even in the ordinariness of my days. In Jesus' name, amen.

_____

_____

_____

_____

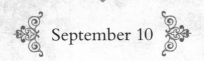

September 10

From the Heart of a Child

God chose the weak things of the world to shame the strong (1 Corinthians 1:27).

Scripture: 1 Corinthians 1:26-31

A last-minute phone call brought our three families together, even though the demands of school, work, and church activities often held us hostage. It was unusual for everyone to be able to pull away from responsibilities for a family meal spanning three generations.

There was excitement in the air as we gathered around a table filled with our favorite foods. We stood holding hands, waiting for a blessing to be said. Finally, one of the children said, "Well, who's going to say grace?" No one answered. Then a little voice began, "Thank You, God, for a happy heart, for rain and sunny weather. Thank You, Lord, for our food," he paused, took a deep breath, then continued in a booming voice, "and that we are together! Amen."

"A little child will lead them" says Isaiah 11:6. And my 6-year-old grandson did just that. Not wise or strong by worldly standards, but by God's Spirit, this little boy enabled us to rejoice in the Lord's bounty and grace. It was a lesson in wisdom and gratitude from the heart of a child.

Dear Lord, I come to You with a grateful heart. Thank You for using those who are open to Your Spirit to teach me lessons in humility. And help me never judge others by their apparent strength or wisdom, for You look at the heart. In the name of Jesus, my merciful Savior and Lord, amen.

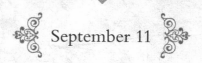

September 11

Different People, Differing Gifts

Now there are different kinds of spiritual gifts, but it is the same Holy Spirit who is the source of them all (1 Corinthians 12:4, *New Living Translation*).

Scripture: 1 Corinthians 12:4-13

As I waited for the worship service to begin, people were still coming into the sanctuary. I offered thanks to God for each one of them, recalling all the lives they've touched with their kindness and love. One woman prepares meals for an ill neighbor. Our young people go to nursing homes to read and sing for the residents. Another group makes quilts for hospitalized children. The women's study group makes and consecrates prayer shawls for those suffering pain and loss. Men and women go to members' homes to do repairs; no job is too small. Still other members work the food bank, stocking shelves and preparing baskets for needy families.

I thought of one woman in a nursing home who was willing to take prayer requests. She spends part of each day talking to God about those in need of His touch. Her neighbor across the hall telephones people who are house-bound, offering encouraging words and a listening ear.

Different people. Differing gifts. Yet, each person is pouring the oils of God's grace over someone's life. Thus God builds His church and transforms the world.

Lord, I want to follow the examples of my fellow church members in service to You. What gift have You given me? In the name of Jesus, amen.

_____

_____

_____

_____

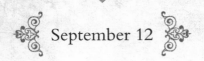

Remembered and Honored

Now all of you together are Christ's body, and each one of you is a separate and necessary part of it (1 Corinthians 12: 27, *New Living Translation*).

Scripture: *1 Corinthians 12:14-27*

Our family perpetuates a unique tradition each time we gather to celebrate a special occasion. We hold hands around the table before offering a blessing, and the same question comes forth each time: "Who isn't here with us today?"

We speak the names of dear ones not present. These include family, friends, teachers, neighbors, and ministers who are missing from our circle. Until we say their names, our family circle isn't complete. Our tradition encourages us to remember those who have touched our lives but are now in the presence of the Lord. It is not unusual for tears of gratitude to flow freely for those who have been a part of our life's journey.

Those present and those named are equally important to our lives. They are all indispensable, as they have each gifted us in their own special way. Each is a separate and necessary part of our family, and we need to claim one another to truly be complete. Church is a lot like that too, isn't it?

God, in the silence of Your presence, I name those in my family and my church whose presence has also gifted my life. I thank You now for the great truth of the communion of the saints. In Christ's name I pray. Amen.

_____

_____

_____

_____

_____

September 13

Wrapped in Prayer

We ask God to give you a complete understanding of what he wants to do in your lives, and we ask him to make you wise with spiritual wisdom. Then the way you live will always honor and please the Lord, and you will continually do good (Colossians 1:9, 10, *New Living Translation*).

Scripture: Colossians 1:9-14

"It's time!" Every school morning my mother's call brought us to the back door. She drew us close to her, asking, "Are you two ready? Do you have any tests or projects due?" Then: "Let's talk to God about your day."

Her prayers asked God to watch over us. She told Him about our tests, projects, and whatever she thought we were worried about that day. She prayed we would please Him, ending by thanking Him for each of her children and the promise their lives held for the future. With the "Amen," my brother and I were out the door and on our way to school.

All my life, Mother's prayers have been with me, wrapping my days in prayer. Through her daily example of faith and prayer, I grew to know God better and better. Now, I pray for my own children and grandchildren. I pray they will learn what God wants them to do with their lives, and that whatever they do will honor and please Him.

> *Dear Heavenly Father, thank You for the prayers of my mother. Help me to pray in the same faith-filled way this day. In Jesus' name, amen.*

_____

_____

_____

_____

_____

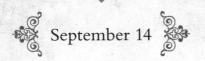

Out of My Darkness

"Joseph, son of David," the angel said, **"do not be afraid to go ahead with your marriage to Mary. For the child within her has been conceived by the Holy Spirit"** (Matthew 1:20, *New Living Translation*).

Scripture: Matthew 1:18-25; 2:13-15

The chief operating officer along with the vice president of human resources knocked on my open door. They sat down at my invitation and then turned my life upside down, nearly crushing me with just five words: "Your position has been eliminated." I couldn't believe my ears. I thought I would never be the same again. I felt adrift, discarded.

I couldn't sleep, I wouldn't eat, I didn't want to face my friends and colleagues. The answering machine picked up my messages. All I could do was cry out to God, "Where are You?"

I wonder if that is how Joseph felt? This apparently wasn't his child, but God told him not to be afraid. He must take Mary as his wife, and the child would be special. Joseph trusted God's Word and obeyed His instructions. The child was called Immanuel, "God with us."

Joseph shows me how to deal with disappointment, loss, and pain in my own life. I am to trust God to rescue me. I will not be crushed; He will carry me through.

God, thank You for Your protective hand as I walk in faith each day. Help me listen for Your instructions—and obey them. In Christ's name, amen.

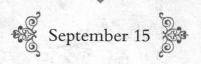

September 15

Shalom!

The LORD turn his face toward you and give you peace (Numbers 6:26).

Scripture: Numbers 6:22-27

Peace: a rare commodity these days. Though there seems little the individual can do to bring peace to our troubled world, the believer can know perfect peace in his or her personal world. It's a needed protection from burnout, a condition some consider almost inevitable in our hectic society. Busyness sweeps across even our church congregations like a mighty wind. Programs multiply, and with them the suggestion that truly dedicated Christians will sign up for every cause.

Whatever happened to the simple things, like toasting marshmallows over a campfire for no reason other than friendship? Having lived well past my three score and ten, I can guarantee that you will remember campfire friendships long after the myriad committees and campaigns have faded from mind. Jesus, you recall, took time for a campfire snack by the sea with a few friends, and good work was done. The point is, those who walk close to the Prince of Peace will never burn out.

> **Lord,** *grant me peace and serenity in a world obsessed with doing. In the most practical ways, teach me the difference between busyness and servanthood. I thank You, in the name of Jesus. Amen.*

_____

_____

_____

_____

_____

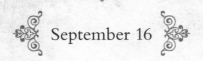

The Least Brother

I tell you the truth, whatever you did for one of the least of these brothers of mine, you did for me (Matthew 25:40).

Scripture: Matthew 25:31-40

Emilio was small and dark-skinned, with black hair and sparkling eyes. He spoke broken English, but he took his custodial duties in our office seriously, grateful for the job. He lived with his wife and six young children in a third-floor walk-up apartment. He taught a Bible class in their storefront church building.

One day I invited Emilio to our home for Sunday dinner. The family arrived packed into a battered old car. Emilio and I romped outdoors with the rascally youngsters while his petite wife helped Elsie in the kitchen. Dinner was an adventure! Emilio told me this was the first time anyone in America had invited his family to their home for a meal. He insisted on returning the favor. That dinner, too, proved adventurous.

Emilio was the poorest member of our office crew. While everyone treated him kindly, inviting a family with six lively kids for Sunday dinner was . . . inconvenient. But I'm glad we did it. Elsie and I cherish the memory of two memorable meals with a poor immigrant family that so richly blessed us.

Heavenly Father, teach me the joy of being inconvenienced by serving others in Your name. In fact, fit me with servant sandals for Jesus' sake! In the name of the Father, the Son, and the Holy Spirit, I pray. Amen.

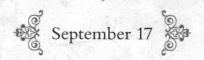

September 17

A Sure Foundation

That house . . . did not fall, because it had its foundation on the rock (Matthew 7:25).

Scripture: Matthew 7:24-29

An oft-told story from family lore taught me the peril of poor foundations. One of our great uncles, an Old Country fisherman, built a low-roofed cabin on the lee side of Encampment Island on Lake Superior's north shore. On November 28, 1905, a fierce northeaster wind swept down the lake, taking a deadly toll on ships and seamen. Lost in darkness and blinding snow, the 454-foot bulk freighter *Lafayette* struck the cliffs opposite the island and sank. Miraculously, there was no loss of life.

Meanwhile, my great uncle and his family slept, secure in the knowledge that their beach cabin had weathered many a northeaster, protected by a rocky ridge running the length of the small, narrow island.

Then, a strange bumping. The cabin moved! Great-uncle stepped from his bed into icy water to find the cabin's only door jammed. Escaping through a small window, the family sought shelter in the root cellar. By first light they saw the beach was bare, their cabin built on the sand washed away. For the first time in history, waves had breached the island.

*Thank You, **Lord,** that I rest secure on the Rock of Your salvation. And amidst the decisions I'll face today, let me focus on the sure foundation of Your Word, that I may obey it in all things. In Jesus' name, amen.*

Brotherly (and Sisterly) Love

Be devoted to one another in brotherly love. Honor one another above yourselves (Romans 12:10).

Scripture: Romans 12:9-13

Two decades ago I had an unlikely friend, Sister Naomi, a godly woman marked by joy and patient faithfulness. She was a teacher, gifted poet, photographer, and naturalist. I found we shared many interests. She came to our home for dinner, and my wife and I dined with her at the priory. During our many conversations, theology never came up.

The dedication of a new addition to our small church building would soon be upon us, and I invited Sister Naomi to display her nature photos throughout the building. She arrived in a sub-compact red car bristling with easels bearing a considerable stack of large, mounted photos. On a whim, I asked her to participate in the dedication program. She told three children's stories, the most memorable part of the program. Following the reception, as we loaded her car, Sister Naomi paused. She embraced me and said, "Lloyd, we meet at the cross."

Thus an aging Benedictine nun blessed a Baptist minister, no longer so young. I found a brotherly love existing between us as we sought to honor one another as we honored our Lord.

*Thank You, **God,** for our unity through Your indwelling Spirit. May I sincerely reach out to all who name Jesus as Savior. Through Him, amen.*

_____

_____

_____

_____

_____

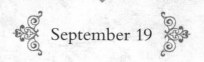

My Friend Al

Be willing to associate with people of low position (Romans 12:16).

Scripture: Romans 12:14-21

Al was an ordinary man who seldom took risks. He held the same job in a button factory for many years. Buttons changed with fashion—wood, glass, metal, ceramic, bone, plastic—but Al's particular function never changed. When seniority brought him in line for a foreman's job, he turned it down. Year after year Al carried the same battered lunch bucket with its Thermos®, sandwiches, and New Testament tucked inside.

Al and his wife, Hazel, never missed church services. They learned about Christians in Europe, displaced by war, who were anxiously seeking sponsors so they could start over in America. Al proposed that the church sponsor a German family, but wary of the cost and problems other churches had experienced, the minister deferred action.

Moved by compassion, Al and Hazel tapped their own savings. Within a few weeks a family with two children arrived. They blessed the church for many years, more than paying their way—and all because a cautious man of a "low position" dared to take a blessed risk.

*Teach me, **dear Father,** that in Your sight we all live on the same level, fully dependent on Your grace. After all, for every human being, the ground is level at the cross. All praise to You, in Christ's name. Amen.*

_____

_____

_____

_____

_____

Gentle Witness

**Always be prepared to give ... the reason for the hope that you have.
But do this with gentleness and respect** (1 Peter 3:15).

Scripture: 1 Peter 3:8-15

I would not suggest that our home models the ideals set forth in some Christian writings. Few religious pictures hang on our walls. Our shelves hold varied kinds of books. But our simple faith in Christ and our commitment to one another have kept us married for 64 years. We hope that our lives bear witness to the master, Christ.

Some years ago, a young teen niece spent a few days with us. She came from a large family where faith was not a factor. We were a typical, empty-nest, somewhat retired couple, busy with many things.

We entertained our niece the best that older folks can, but mainly she had to entertain herself. She observed our sometimes disorderly lifestyle. Apart from habitual pre-meal prayer, we made no attempt to involve her in devotions. We lived as we do, whether or not guests were present.

Feedback came a few weeks later, when our niece's foster father phoned. "Know what she said about you? 'They're always smiling!'" Now why should that seem so remarkable?

Dear Lord, help me speak often of You to others, but let me live always for You, letting the light of Your presence shine through me. I pray this prayer in the name of Jesus, my Savior and Lord. Amen.

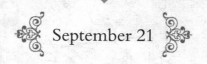

September 21

Let It Shine!

Let your light shine before men, that they may see your good deeds and praise your Father in heaven (Matthew 5:16).

Scripture: Matthew 5:1-16

During college years I worked at a rescue mission. One summer evening we were setting up chairs for the nightly street meeting, when a drunken man staggered down the street toward our mission corner. A new volunteer in a straw hat had joined our set-up crew. He caught sight of the man, who seemed about to fall, and rushed to him with a chair. Easing the delirious man down, the volunteer fanned him with his hat, asking whether we should call a doctor.

Some of us smiled. The man was just another skid-row vagrant, hopelessly lost in booze. The volunteer was obviously new to the streets and naive about mission work. Still, I wondered what was going on in the befogged brain of the vagrant, who rarely saw compassion from mission workers hardened by repeated disappointment.

You see, the con schemes are ingenious, promises endless, failure all but inevitable in this type of mission work. So, how easily we forget that God loves alcoholics too, and that we are not responsible for the response to the light, only that we let the light shine. I hope that volunteer never lost his compassion.

> **Dear Heavenly Father,** *help me see the hurting and helpless with eyes of compassion, just as You see them. In the name of Jesus I pray. Amen.*

_____

_____

_____

_____

_____

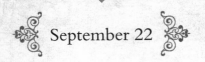

September 22

Wicked Wedges

Fulfil ye my joy, that ye be likeminded, having the same love, being of one accord, of one mind (Philippians 2:2, *King James Version*).

Scripture: Philippians 2:1-11

Franklin D. Roosevelt once wrote to a friend about the issue of foreign-born immigrants: "We must remember that any oppression, any injustice, any hatred, is a wedge designed to attack our civilization." He was right. When citizens turn on each other out of hatred, a wedge is driven deep into that society. Such a rift will eventually lead to a collapse of basic civility.

In Philippians 2, Paul wrote to protect the church from the very thing that destroys nations. The first verse reveals the importance of drawing upon our divine resources. Once that's done, the spiritual attitudes of verses 2 through 4 make wedge-making impossible.

Of course, the ultimate inspiration for these unifying traits comes from Christ himself, as seen in verses 5 through 11. Broad, intimate familiarity with Christ's life is the best protection against the mindset that leads to wicked wedges. And that's when the old acronym for JOY is fulfilled: Jesus first, Others second, Yourself last.

Dear Father, may Your love permeate my heart and heal every division, for Jesus' sake. In His precious name I pray. Amen.

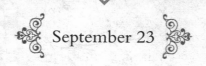

Back to Basics

Verily I say unto you, Except ye be converted, and become as little children, ye shall not enter into the kingdom of heaven (Matthew 18:3, *King James Version*).

Scripture: Matthew 18:1-5

Vince Lombardi, legendary football coach of the Green Bay Packers, was reprimanding his team for an embarrassing loss. He held the pigskin high and began his remarks with, "Gentlemen, this is a football." The players had apparently forgotten the basics of the game, and Lombardi knew that you never grow beyond certain fundamentals. They form the foundation of success on the field.

It's no different in the Christian life. When the disciples asked Jesus who was the greatest in the kingdom of Heaven, he set a little child before them. Our Lord coached His team to spiritual victory by delivering a "back to basics" message. The qualities of a child, especially a humble, teachable, trusting spirit, form the very foundation of kingdom greatness.

Most football players dream of a Super Bowl victory, or of achieving the ultimate honor—induction into the Football Hall of Fame. But such greatness is reserved only for those who never forgot the basics. Likewise, any disciple of the master must maintain the basic qualities of a little child if he wants to be a champion for Christ.

*Thank You, **Lord,** for making me a part of Your team. Help me maintain those qualities fundamental to lifelong success. In Jesus' name, amen.*

_____

_____

_____

_____

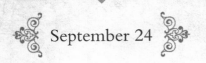

September 24

Good, or Best?

There were certain Greeks among them that came up to worship at the feast: the same came therefore to Philip, which was of Bethsaida of Galilee, and desired him, saying, Sir, we would see Jesus (John 12:21, *King James Version*).

Scripture: John 12:20-26

One evening after a church service, revivalist Vance Havner told the song leader, "We had a good service."

This perceptive young man replied, "Too good."

Havner was puzzled. "What do you mean?"

"I know this crowd," the song leader answered bluntly. "They should have been on their faces before God, but everybody settled for a nice, good service."

What a mistake! Sometimes the good is the enemy of the best.

When certain devout Greeks visiting Jerusalem saw the public acclaim Jesus was receiving (see v 19), they asked Philip if they could see the Lord. There were many religious festivities in progress, all good in themselves. But seeing the Messiah himself was deemed far better! And as Jesus indicated in verses 23-26, enjoying a *celebrated* Christ is good, but serving a *rejected* Christ is best of all.

What did those Gentile seekers learn? Attending public worship is good, but seeing Jesus is better. And a commitment to Christ that is worth dying for . . . is best of all.

Lord, as I spend time with You, help me never to settle for second best. In the name of the Father, the Son, and the Holy Spirit, I pray. Amen.

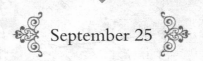

Crawling with Fear

Fear not them which kill the body, but are not able to kill the soul; but rather fear him which is able to destroy both soul and body in hell (Matthew 10:28, *King James Version*).

Scripture: Matthew 10:24-33

Olga stood quietly against a wooden background in a popular vaudeville show while her partner threw knives and hatchets into the wood around her. All at once, during the act, she let out a scream and promptly fainted. The audience feared the worst. But when she was revived in her dressing room, Olga explained: "I suddenly felt something crawling on my leg and discovered a spider. Oh, I'm *so* afraid of spiders!"

As ridiculous as this performer's phobia in the face of a far greater danger, fearing human beings more than God is even more absurd. That was precisely Jesus' point in today's passage. Without the wrong perspective, we all tend to overreact to persecution.

Jesus reminded His followers to expect ill-treatment (see vv. 24, 25). When it happened, and it would, He told them to remember God's perfect knowledge of the minutest details and His complete control over everything. Finally, Jesus made loyal witness the "make-or-break test" of discipleship (vv. 31, 32). When we remember these things, we will stand firm with nerves of steel.

Heavenly Father, let me behold You with the eyes of faith until all my fears melt away in Your presence. In Jesus' name I pray. Amen.

_____

_____

_____

_____

_____

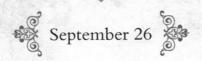

September 26

No Time Like the Present

The end of all things is at hand: be ye therefore sober, and watch unto prayer (1 Peter 4:7, *King James Version*).

Scripture: 1 Peter 4:7-11

"This time, like all times, is a very good one, if we but know what to do with it," said Ralph Waldo Emerson. I think the apostle Peter would have agreed. Certainly a bad time is a good time to live for the Lord. To do any less would only make a bad time worse. And if that *bad* time is also the *last* time, then there is even more reason to have a God-focused life.

With the prophetic clock nearing the midnight hour, Peter offers clear instruction regarding the use of time. First, a sober mind and a prayerful heart will preserve our integrity in an evil world (v. 7). Second, we need a fervent love that forgives all wrongs (v. 8). Third, a mutual hospitality and a gracious sharing of God's gifts—be they spiritual or material—will promote healthy relationships (vv. 8-10). And fourth, we need a truth-centered, Spirit-empowered ministry that brings glory to God (v. 11).

Emerson was right. This is a very good time, if we know what to do with it.

Dear Father in Heaven, help me to live by Your agenda, today and always. May my life be the summary of what I have learned in Your Word, whether I face joyful prospects or painful trials. In the name of Your Son, my Savior, I pray. Amen.

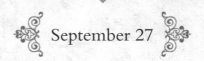

September 27

Your Cash Advance

So when even was come, the lord of the vineyard saith unto his steward, Call the laborers, and give them their hire, beginning from the last unto the first (Matthew 20:8, *King James Version*).

Scripture: Matthew 20:1-16

Christian F. Gellert (1715-1769), a German philosopher and author, died at Leipzig where he had been professor of theology at the university. In his final moments, he made this simple request: "Only repeat to me the name of Jesus. Whenever I hear it, or pronounce it myself, I feel myself refreshed with fresh joy. God be praised, only one hour more." All who have served our kind master with a sincere and grateful heart have made similar statements.

Today's parable teaches the prospect of heavenly rewards. And though some will receive more than others, we all have more than we deserve. To be hired at all, that is, chosen to salvation (v. 16), is itself no small compensation. The day we got on His payroll, whether at sunrise or near midnight—or anywhere in between—was the day our lives obtained real value and purpose.

As Gellert learned, just thinking of Jesus is like receiving a generous cash advance before the big payday.

Lord, when I finally stand before You, face to face, I long to hear "Well done, thou good and faithful servant." Thank You for making my life useful in an aimless world. And thank You, as well, for the prospect of the perfect world to come. In Your holy name I pray. Amen.

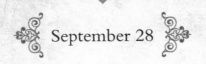

September 28

Back to Work!

Whosoever will be great among you, let him be your minister; and whosoever will be chief among you, let him be your servant (Matthew 20:26, 27, *King James Version*).

Scripture: Matthew 20:17-28

Shortly after Jesus told the disciples of His approaching death, the mother of James and John appeared with a special request. She asked the Lord if her two sons could sit on each side of Him in the kingdom. Jesus answered in two parts.

First, He asked whether they could endure the bitter cup of suffering that would precede such an honor. They answered, "We are able." Jesus affirmed their painful destiny, but that alone would not guarantee this position.

The second qualification rested solely with Jesus' heavenly Father (see v. 23). The will of God determines all.

This ambitious mother reminds all parents to beware of wanting more for their children than God intends. To overshoot God's plan is as disastrous as undershooting it. In fact, even attempting to secure an unfair advantage will create a backlash, as it did for James and John (see v. 24) real path to greatness—humble service.

Seeking personal glory just wastes time. Let's get back to work.

Lord, *forgive me when I think more of status than service. The only favor I ask is Your blessing on my humble work. In Jesus' name, amen.*

_____

_____

_____

_____

_____

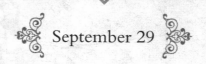

Who Was Jesus?

The life appeared; we have seen it and testify to it, and we proclaim to you the eternal life, which was with the Father and has appeared to us (1 John 1:2).

Scripture: 1 John 1:1-4

Is Jesus really God? Was He simply a teacher, a "good man," or an impostor? Movies like *The DaVinci Code* spur heated conversations around the watercooler, in the break room, and the coffeehouse. Who was Jesus?

The search for answers arises in each generation. When the apostle John wrote 1 John around AD 85–90, he was addressing this question. He penned this letter to reassure Christians in their faith and to expose false teachings.

A main problem in the church at this time was conformity to the world's standards and a lack of commitment, much like the challenges we face today. John wanted to put the church back on track as he recapped what he'd witnessed. His eyewitness account is as much a reminder to us as it was to several Gentile congregations in his own day. God, who was from the beginning, came to earth. John heard Him, saw Him, and touched Him. This man Jesus forgave sins, healed the sick, raised the dead. Who else but God in the flesh could do that?

Lord, may I never forget the depth of Your sacrifice or water down the intensity of Your message. Thank You, in Your precious name. Amen.

_____

_____

_____

_____

_____

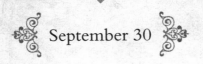

September 30

Victory in Jesus

God raised him from the dead, freeing him from the agony of death, because it was impossible for death to keep its hold on him (Acts 2:24).

Scripture: Acts 2:22-35

One of the last things my Nan said before she died was: "We may not see each other again on earth, but I will be waiting for you in Heaven. Because you believe, our good-bye is not forever."

I find great comfort in that statement. I will see Nan again, because, as she did, I believe in the power of the resurrection and the power in the blood of Christ. There is nothing stronger than it or more important than what you believe regarding it. The power of Jesus' blood has washed me clean and secured my home in Heaven. The resurrection confirms Christ's victory and His control over everything. That belief has changed my life.

In verse 24, Peter began with a statement about the resurrection because it could not be denied. The crowd teemed with people who would verify the event. This enabled Peter to base his message on an unshakable foundation. His audience was witness. They saw it happen. He challenged them to allow it to change their lives. And that is the challenge to all of us to this present hour.

Father, may I live each day assured of Your victory over death. May I remember that my old life is dead and buried, and I have been resurrected into a new life with Your Son, Jesus. In His name I pray. Amen.

_____

_____

_____

_____

My Prayer Notes

October

In him you . . . are being built together to become
a dwelling in which God lives by his Spirit.
—Ephesians 2:22

The Purpose of Church

They devoted themselves to the apostles' teaching and to the fellowship, to the breaking of bread and to prayer (Acts 2:42).

Scripture: Acts 2:37-47

I have a friend who is disillusioned by the church. He believes that the cruelest criticism, the juiciest gossip, and the most smug superiority take place on Sunday mornings. He chooses not to follow a God who seemingly prompts this type of response in His children.

It saddens me that this has been his church experience. And it raises a serious question in my mind: What kind of church does God want us to be? According to the apostle Peter, a church gathering should be a place where we are devoted to teaching, fellowship, communion, and prayer. God should be completely free to work within the church, resulting in deep devotion to Him. It should be a gathering where people can find help and comfort. It should be a place where we can worship God without shame.

What a wonderful testimony when seekers see us praising God and enjoying each other's fellowship—and having a good time doing it. When we are truly devoted to God's teaching, we are fulfilling His purposes for the church: reaching the lost, to bring glory to His name.

> **Lord,** *help me take the first steps in personal renewal so that my whole church family can return to Your purposes for us. In Jesus' name, amen.*

_____

_____

_____

_____

_____

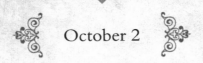

October 2

The Family Business

Again Jesus said, "Peace be with you! As the Father has sent me, I am sending you" (John 20:21).

Scripture: John 20:19-23

I have a friend who owns a chain of veterinarian clinics. His eldest daughter has chosen the field of animal medicine, like her father. She has two sons, and one day she will pass her love and compassion for God's creatures down to them, should they choose to follow in her footsteps. It's a family business.

My husband's uncle is a schoolteacher. His daughter and son are also schoolteachers. He has passed his love of learning and teaching down to his children. It's a family business.

All Christians are part of the family of God, and that family, too, has a business. Jesus says in verse 21, "As the father sent me, I am sending you." The legacy has been passed down to us to fulfill the Spirit-minded mission of our Father.

Just as my friends received special training to learn their family trades, Jesus gives us the Holy Spirit to empower us to reach the lost. We are to preach the good news about Jesus, teach our children to follow in the footsteps of their heavenly Father, and embrace the family business.

Father, thank You for reminding me that I have a great legacy to pass on to my children. Grant me the boldness, courage, and compassion needed to carry out Your family business. Through Christ I pray. Amen.

_____

_____

_____

_____

_____

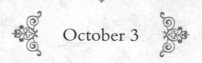

October 3

The Buzz Around Town

So in Christ we who are many form one body, and each member belongs to all the others (Romans 12:5).

Scripture: Romans 12:3-8

While I watch a busy bee colony hum, I am awestruck with how God designs nature to speak to us. In a bee colony, the queen bee is in charge of reproducing; she keeps the hive buzzing. Drone bees are companions to the queen. Worker bees collect pollen and nectar and keep the hive cool by fanning their wings.

What would happen if one bee felt superior? The structure of the hive would collapse. Without the queen there is no colony. Without the drones there is no growth in the population. Without the workers, the bees would starve to death. Each function is essential to the health of the whole.

In some ways, the Christian life is like a busy hive. We are all gifted differently, but we need each other for the whole family to function effectively. We should not "think of [ourselves] more highly than [we] ought" (v. 3). We are one body of believers, with individual members, blessed with various gifts. If a bee colony can function as a healthy unit despite vast individual differences, then so can we.

Father, help me to be excited about the gifts with which You have blessed me—and not be jealous of another's. I have something to offer, and I do not need to be ashamed. Keep me faithful, then, in my particular ministry, focusing only on pleasing You. In the name of Christ, amen.

October 4

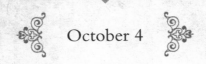

The Interpreter

All of them were filled with the Holy Spirit and began to speak in other tongues (Acts 2:4).

Scripture: Acts 2:1-13

Raymond G. Gordon, Jr., is the editor of *Ethnologue: Languages of the World, 15th Edition*. This reference book lists 6,912 of the world's known languages. I imagine it is impossible to be fluent in them all! To fill this void, interpreters are employed in multicultural conference situations to translate questions or speeches into the mother tongue of the listening audience.

In the film *The Interpreter,* Nicole Kidman is employed to translate at a United Nations meeting. Imagine her surprise if, when the keynote presenter began to speak, he could miraculously talk in the native tongue of each represented country.

You might think "only in the movies," but you would be wrong. It happened years ago and is recorded in the book of Acts. Amazingly, individuals in an international crowd could recognize their own languages from the mouths of Galilean apostles declaring the wonder of God.

Historically, God has used the spoken word to reach people of all nationalities. In fact, He is speaking to you today. If your heart is open, You will hear the most wonderful things.

*Open my ears, **Lord**. I want to hear Your declarations of love, Your gentle corrections, and Your wise guidance in my life. In Jesus' name, amen.*

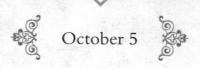

October 5

Not Reformed, Reborn

Then Peter stood up with the Eleven, raised his voice and addressed the crowd (Acts 2:14).

Scripture: Acts 2:14-21

Peter's audacity while following Jesus could have discredited his entire ministry. He spoke without thinking, he was brazen and hasty, and he denied Jesus three times. What transforms such an impetuous man into one of the pillars of the church?

Peter became a natural leader of the disciples after Jesus ascended into Heaven. He was the first to stand up to the mocking crowd on the Day of Pentecost. This new Peter was forgiven and restored, no longer arrogant and cowardly, but humble and bold. The Holy Spirit gave him a powerful confidence to speak up. He was reborn.

Despite the sins that once entangled us, we too can be reborn. God can take the personality traits that led to our fall and use them to bring Him glory.

God didn't give Peter a personality transplant. He was still bold, daring, and spontaneous. But through the new birth Peter received the indwelling Holy Spirit. Now Peter could use his traits to draw people closer to God, rather than fulfill his own self-centered plans.

> *Lord, help me to recognize the personality traits in me that can become either a blessing or a curse. Then, transform these traits into qualities that will bless Your name and draw others closer to You. I pray this prayer in the name of Jesus, my merciful Savior and Lord. Amen.*

_____

_____

_____

_____

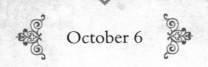

October 6

Secret Weapon

Then Peter, filled with the Holy Spirit, said to them, "Honorable leaders and elders of our nation" (Acts 4:8, *The Living Bible*).

Scripture: Acts 4:1-12

When has someone rained on your parade? We all occasionally face those times when our best efforts seem unappreciated or misunderstood. It happens at home, school, and church—and it happened to the disciples.

It had been an intense time in Jerusalem. The wild series of events following Pentecost were anything but business-as-usual. Healings of body and spirit created joy in some but skepticism, and even hostility, in others.

Peter and John found themselves right in the middle of all the uproar. But notice Peter's attitude. He had been frozen by fear until the fire of God's Spirit transformed him. He and John prayed, and healing happened. How could anyone have a problem with that?

But they did. No matter how sincere our service for the Lord, sooner or later someone or something will try to discourage us. The next time it happens to you, don't try to hang in there by your own strength. The "secret weapon" of the Holy Spirit, so available to Peter and John, is also yours for the asking.

Gracious Father, when I care too much about what others say or think, lift my focus higher, all the way to Your face. In Jesus' name, amen.

_____

_____

_____

_____

_____

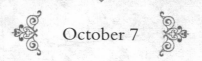

October 7

Attitude Adjustment

When the Council saw the boldness of Peter and John, and could see that they were obviously uneducated non-professionals, they were amazed and realized what being with Jesus had done for them! (Acts 4:13, *The Living Bible*).

Scripture: Acts 4:13-22

In 1965, a shy girl from a dairy farm in New York was trying to fit in as a freshman at Lycoming College in Williamsport, Pennsylvania. Everybody else seemed more self-confident. How could she ever feel as if she belonged?

I was that girl, and the only way I pulled it off was by staying close to Linda, a friend from home. She was as bubbly and friendly as I was reserved and quiet. Being with her, I dared to smile and relax.

In the face of the unfair accusations of the Sanhedrin, Peter and John could have reacted with either violent anger or cowering fear. They did neither. Peter spoke with respect and confidence. John wasn't cowering, but bold. The Council was impressed. Being with Jesus had made them noticeably different.

Is there an area in your life in which you feel inept and inadequate? Spend some time right now with Jesus and let Him do an attitude adjustment.

Lord, I am too often fearful in my witness to You. Forgive me and transform me. Send your Holy Spirit to perform an extreme makeover in the musty corners of my mind and heart. Through Christ, amen.

_____

_____

_____

_____

_____

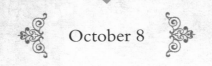

October 8

To Boldly Go

After this prayer, the building where they were meeting shook and they were all filled with the Holy Spirit and boldly preached God's message (Acts 4:31, *The Living Bible*).

Scripture: Acts 4:23-31

Cuddled together on the couch in front of our television set, my husband and I eagerly awaited the opening line from *Star Trek: Next Generation*. Captain Jean-Luc Picard's deep voice said the words we never tired of hearing regarding the mission of the starship *Enterprise* "to boldly go where no one has gone before." We couldn't wait to see what happened next.

Released from prison, Peter and John joined the rest of the disciples and a crowd of believers in a prayer service. Ho hum? Not on your life! If you look seriously at this passage, you'll find a scene more exciting than any sci-fi fantasy. This was real, and it was full of power. The prayer takes up only a single paragraph, but it changed everything in that situation. Drawing an analogy between current events from Rome to Jerusalem, they invited God to send boldness and healing power to Christ's followers. The answer came in a literal shaking of the building—and a spiritual shaking that would change countless lives.

O Lord God, I am so grateful for Your Holy Spirit. Thank You for the sweeping difference He makes in my life, replacing confidence for cowardice. Equip me to boldly go where I have seldom been—into lives that need the radical shaking of Your matchless love. In Jesus' name, amen.

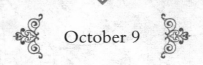

October 9

Radical Righteousness

The property was yours to sell or not, as you wished. And after selling it, it was yours to decide how much to give. How could you do a thing like this? You weren't lying to us, but to God (Acts 5:4, *The Living Bible*)

Scripture: Acts 5:1-11

I wish I could just skip over certain passages in the Bible—and this is one of them. A husband and wife sell property but give just part of the money to the early church, claiming it's the full price. Each of them dies instantly after telling that lie.

I try to push away an awful idea. Isn't God overreacting? But I know, way down deep, that God's holiness is as perfect as His justice. I may never really understand this passage, but it teaches me something I need to learn. Ananias and Sapphira wanted to look more pious and generous than they were willing to actually be. The Father who created them and loved them saw right through their phoniness. And clearly, at the very beginning of the church, God's serious intentions must be established—for the good of all the believers at that time and for all who would follow down through the centuries.

Ouch. He sees through my own phoniness! Leaning on His mercy, I dare not underestimate His righteousness.

*Search me, **Father,** and shine light on the hidden places in my heart. Forgive me the times I so easily make excuses for my sin. Teach me to walk in holiness, knowing You alone are holy. In Jesus' name, amen.*

_____

_____

_____

_____

_____

Get a Grip

My advice is, leave these men alone. If what they teach and do is merely on their own, it will soon be overthrown (Acts 5:38, *The Living Bible*).

Scripture: Acts 5:27-39

Today a local high school outlawed "hoodies." Those cozy sweatshirts have become a staple in many wardrobes, but it seems they've also become places to hide everything from music to weapons.

"What's the world coming to?" We hear people say that, and we think it ourselves. Reading the daily paper or watching the TV news can be detrimental to our mental health! And sometimes national and world events cause even people of deep faith to get nervous. School violence, political scandals, terrorist threats—it's enough to make you want to crawl back under the covers and hide.

The situation in the early church wasn't much rosier. Danger awaited from the Romans, and sometimes from the Jewish authorities, for any who dared to disagree with them. And yet, here are the disciples, stubbornly refusing to stop speaking about Jesus. Their lives had been so fundamentally changed by the Messiah that they could hardly go about living without sharing what they had experienced of Him. They had been gripped by a force more powerful than fear.

> **Lord,** *many things drain my courage and attack my faith. I long to grip Your reality so firmly that all fear must fall away. Through Christ, amen.*

_____

_____

_____

_____

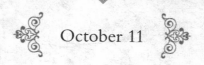

October 11

Gossiping the Gospel

But the believers who had fled Jerusalem went everywhere preaching the Good News about Jesus! (Acts 8:4, *The Living Bible*).

Scripture: Acts 8:1-8

In study hall, my friend Linda and I passed notes to each other written in French. We had two reasons. We needed the practice and somehow, we thought, if we were caught, the teachers on duty wouldn't know what we were saying. It never occurred to us that even the shop or drivers' ed teachers might have taken French at some point in their academic careers. And the threat of detention couldn't squelch our need to share our lives with each other.

After Stephen's murder, the believers scattered in many directions. So would they keep quiet about their beliefs after seeing what happened to him? Talking about the Nazarene could be hazardous to their health, so why borrow trouble?

But the Bible paints a vivid picture of men whose need to tell the Christ story was stronger than their fear. Like Linda and me, they were compelled to share their journey. As teenagers, we wrote about our parents, our boyfriends, and our dreams. The disciples talked about a person who had changed their souls. No comparison.

Lord, it is all too tempting to gossip about trivial things. Help me to talk instead about what matters—to talk about You. In Christ's name, amen.

_____

_____

_____

_____

_____

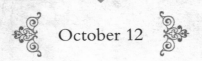

Ripples of Redemption

God's message was preached in ever-widening circles, and the number of disciples increased vastly in Jerusalem; and many of the Jewish priests were converted too (Acts 6:7, *The Living Bible*).

Scripture: Acts 6

From the warm security of the dining room window, I watched the breeze kick up ripples on the pond. The movement was beautiful, as if God were creating a unique choreography for the falling leaves, a performance just for me. My spirits lifted out of the doldrums I'd been experiencing. I nestled in His presence, soaking up the wonder of the scene.

A phone call jarred me back to earth. When I returned to the window, the wind had died down, and the glorious dance was over. Then came the splash. A frog had jumped into the water, creating a series of ripples that spread halfway across the pond. The frog wasn't very big, but the effects were far-reaching.

The persecution of the early believers could have ended the work of Christ. Logically, it should have. But in God's economy, the subtraction of freedom resulted in the multiplication of ministry. Like ripples in a pond, the glory spread in expanding circles—reaching down through time, even to you and to me.

God, I am grateful for those who've gone before me, spreading Your truth. Help me carry on their work in some way today. In Jesus' name, amen.

_____

_____

_____

_____

_____

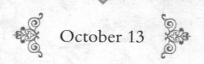

I Didn't Make It Up

The gospel I preached is not something that man made up (Galatians 1:11).

Scripture: Galatians 1:11-17

In Bible college I learned that some time back in the AD 300s, when a church council met in Carthage to discuss which books had been received as genuine Scripture, they applied four tests to each document considered. Those tests involved analyzing apostolicity, universality, content, and inspiration.

Each document had to come from an apostle or a close associate of an apostle. It had to have been widely accepted and used by the churches down through the years. The subject matter had to conform with the established *regula fidei* (the "rule of faith") and finally, the document would show evidence of divine inspiration.

Paul had once been a persecutor of Christians, thinking he was doing God's work by ridding the world of people who believed in Jesus. However, as he turned his life over to the Lord, he recognized that, without a doubt, men did not make up the gospel of Jesus Christ. For him, truth rang out as the gospel came straight from the throne of God. We can be sure of that too. We can trust our Bible.

> **Father,** *I'm so grateful for the written Word of God, the Bible, that You have given us. Keep me reading it every day! In Jesus' name, amen.*

_____

_____

_____

_____

_____

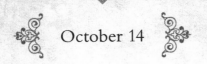

October 14

Its Not a Lie!

I assure you before God that what I am writing you is no lie . . . . "The man who formerly persecuted us is now preaching the faith he once tried to destroy" (Galatians 1:20, 23).

Scripture: Galatians 1:18-24

When Dale applied for ministerial credentials, those in charge requested that he write out his testimony. Dale's strong relationship with God may have been evident to those closest to him, but church leaders needed to examine the evidence of his life before they presented him with those important credentials. Dale wrote several pages that began, "I was saved by faith, through the blood of Jesus Christ." He wrote about attending college and seminary, and about various retreats he'd attended.

In our Bible reading today, Paul longed for his associates to be assured that he was telling the truth. He wanted all around him to know of his relationship with the Lord. People knew he was the one who had persecuted the church, but they began to see him in a new light. Their previous enemy had suddenly met Jesus on the road to Damascus. As Paul told his skeptics these truths, their hearts opened to him. In fact, they began to praise God heartily because of him.

Dear Heavenly Father, I long to be an asset to the church and not a hindrance. Thank You for helping me to maintain the truth in my relationships with others. I can be that asset only as I share, honestly and fairly, with others. In the name of Jesus, my Savior, I pray. Amen.

_____

_____

_____

_____

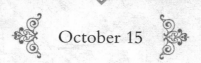

October 15

You Want Me to Give Up What?

Whatever was to my profit I now consider loss for the sake of Christ (Philippians 3:7).

Scripture: Philippians 3:2-11

My husband and I decided to downsize. We held a yard sale and took some items to a charity thrift store. When we moved into a one-bedroom cottage, I needed to downsize a bit more. Yet we found that we spent more time traveling from place to place in our little travel trailer then we did in our cottage.

Still, I clung to some of the things I had accumulated over the years. I especially wanted to keep my grandmother's gravy boat, the doll house my husband and I built during our first year as a married couple, and a trunk full of photo slides. I wasn't so willing to give those things up.

Paul talked about things he *willingly* gave up for Christ. As I read today's passage in the Bible, I found myself becoming more willing to let "things" go. I took grandma's gravy boat to the antique store. The church nursery could use that sturdy doll house. And my daughters are dividing the slides among them. I can see now that none of those things are as important as serving the Lord.

Dear Heavenly Father, because of Your provision over the years, I have all that I need. Thank You. Keep me in Your will as I seek to serve You. And may I always hold my belongings with open hands, knowing they are "on loan" from You. In the name of Your Son, my Savior, I pray. Amen.

_____

_____

_____

_____

_____

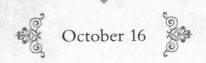

October 16

Wild Woman for God

The church . . . was strengthened; and encouraged by the Holy Spirit, it grew in numbers, living in the fear of the Lord (Acts 9:31).

Scripture: Acts 9:22-31

Linda was such a wild woman that I wondered how she ended up attending our conservative church. She had no concept of church manners. She hugged people and kissed them on the mouth. In the middle of the sermon, she'd call out a question. Our minister would respond to her questions and go on teaching.

Not long after she began attending church, Linda had a stroke. She could hardly talk, and her right side was completely paralyzed. As she began to recover, she learned to write with her left hand so she could fill in the blanks in a women's Bible study workbook.

Linda was baptized that spring. Two more strokes followed, but her infirmity never dampened her enthusiasm for life or for the Lord. She volunteered to help with Vacation Bible School and made pizza for the youth group. This wild woman for God passed away in September. Her encouragement and enthusiasm for life continues to spur us on.

Dear Heavenly Father, it is with people like Linda on my mind that I come to You today. They may not know all the rules, yet they encourage and bless me as vessels of the Holy Spirit. I lift a thankful heart for them. In the holy name of Jesus, my Lord and Savior, I pray. Amen.

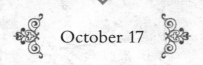

October 17

Grape Bubble Gum

My God will meet all your needs according to his glorious riches in Christ Jesus (Philippians 4:19).

Scripture: Philippians 4:10-20

Jobless and near the end of his savings, Brad prayed for his family's needs. One day, in the grocery store, his 6-year-old begged for grape bubble gum. Brad hated to refuse, but even that small purchase wasn't in the budget. Brad could hardly see through his tears as he drove home. When he pulled into the driveway, he noticed brown bags sitting beside the front door. Inside, he found groceries and . . . grape bubble gum! That small gift encouraged him to remember that God meets needs—and even throws in extra blessings from time to time.

Paul poured out his heart concerning the Philippians' spiritual need before expressing his gratitude for the gifts the church had sent with Epaphroditus. When he used the words "God will meet all your needs according to his glorious riches in Christ Jesus," he was making sure his readers understood that it was not to them, or to himself, but to God that their gratitude belonged. It is a joy to know that God meets our needs. And He meets them far beyond our expectations.

Almighty and everlasting Father, thank You for meeting my needs, and thank You for the abundance with which You meet them. Like Paul, I recognize that You supply all things according to Your riches in Christ Jesus. In His precious name I pray. Amen.

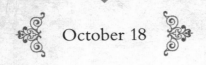

October 18

Drums? O, No!

"Who are you, Lord?" Saul asked. "I am Jesus whom you are persecuting" (Acts 9:5, 6).

Scripture: Acts 9:1-9

Saul thought he was doing a good work for God. Instead, it was the Lord himself he was persecuting.

On Wednesday nights our church music is upbeat and joyful. So, one night a 15-year-old brought his drums and set them up on the platform so he could participate with the worship team.

The following Sunday morning, a church member insisted that the drums be removed. I explained that the boy wasn't planning to play drums on Sunday morning. And I also shared my concern that if the church rejected the boy's music he might himself feel rejected by the church. As the worship team sang that morning, the complainer sat with folded arms and an angry face.

Sometime during the service, though, the Lord spoke to her heart. Afterwards, she apologized to the minister and to the worship team. The woman thought she was upholding the integrity of the church. Instead, her attitude was hurtful. Like Saul, she had it wrong. But also like Saul, she set it right.

Heavenly Father, help me not to look down on those who are new to the faith. Help me to recognize that I might discourage and defeat others with negative words and actions. May I always remain positive and encouraging. Through Christ I pray. Amen.

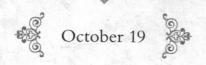

Just As I Am

The Lord said to Ananias, "Go! This man is my chosen instrument to carry my name before the Gentiles and their kings and before the people of Israel" (Acts 9:15).

Scripture: Acts 9:10-21

New in town, I went to the bank to set up an account. A teller with tattoos and a nose ring waited on me. In my desire to witness my faith to her, I asked if she'd lived in town long. "Only a few months," she said. "My husband is the minister of one of the town's churches."

I hoped my face didn't register my thorough surprise. As I walked away, I thought of an old song we used to sing, "Just as I Am." I wondered how often I looked at a person and failed to see the heart.

Saul was a man who wanted to do God's bidding. He thought those who believed in Jesus were a cult that needed to be destroyed. He sought out believers to throw them in jail and beat them.

And I imagine Ananias may have felt a bit like I did when I first met that tattooed bank teller. But I learned that because of her background and interests, the teller-minister's wife could reach people I might never even have the opportunity to meet. That was their ministry in town, and it was a good one.

Heavenly Father, thank You for loving me just as I am. With a transparent heart I come to You and I ask that You look inside and change anything that does not line up with Your purposes. Through Christ my Lord, amen.

_____

_____

_____

_____

_____

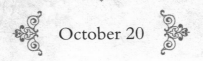

October 20

Seeing With Jesus' Eyes

Lord, you know everyone's heart (Acts 1:24).

Scripture: Acts 1:15-26

This month I've been challenged repeatedly to serve as a minister of reconciliation. It's been difficult to be a peacemaker among those unwilling to forgive or admit mistakes. The hardest part has been trying to decipher the truth amidst so many differing versions of the same event. It's been an impossible task for me, but God's Word has been a lamp unto my feet.

As I sought direction in Scripture, my role became clear. Only God knows the heart. Only God knows the wounds and motivations behind people's perceptions and actions in life. My task was not to reconstruct every detail of what happened, but to love those who had been hurt while holding everyone accountable for their behaviors. As I focused on each individual involved, I resolved to help them come closer to God *through* their hurt rather than *around* it. It worked.

In 2 Corinthians 5:16, Paul exhorts us to "regard no one from a worldly point of view." When we view each other's weaknesses through the mind of Christ, we are better able to edify, to strengthen, to love.

Lord, thank You for cleansing my heart with Christ's precious blood. Help me to see others through His eyes, with compassion. In His name, amen.

_____

_____

_____

_____

_____

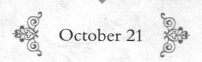

October 21

Blessed Through Giving

Freely you have received, freely give (Matthew 10:8).

Scripture: Matthew 10:1-15

Giving and receiving are kingdom concepts. "We love because he first loved us" (1 John 4:19), and "God loves a cheerful giver" (2 Corinthians 9:7). All good things come from God and return to Him, from the very love that led to the whole creation, to our particular material possessions. God is maker, keeper, sustainer. In fact, Colossians 1:17 tells us that in Jesus "all things hold together." Indeed, "by him all things were created" (Colossians 1:16).

I have learned much about receiving and giving in the past two years. After working full-time for 10 years as a medical doctor, God called me to leave the exam room and follow my husband to seminary. We have received financial gifts and prayer support through many people who believe in our calling. At times, God's provision has been overwhelming, moving me to tears. As a result of the generosity showered upon us, I have become a more cheerful giver. I now live each day actively looking for opportunities to give.

By sharing with thankful hearts, we bless the giver from whom all blessings flow. Thanks be to God!

Father, as I seek Your kingdom and Your righteousness, You faithfully meet all my needs. You are a God of blessing who sustains, who gives, who loves. Help me to give out of love as well. Through Christ, amen.

_____

_____

_____

_____

All for His Sake

On my account you will be brought before governors and kings as witnesses to them and to the Gentiles (Matthew 10:18).

Scripture: Matthew 10:16-25

This passage reminds me of the reality and prominence of God's plan. When we interpret our earthly circumstances through worldly eyes, it is easy to despair. Sometimes things don't look so good for believers, do they? But when we perceive through the Spirit, we remember God's sovereignty and can trust that He is still in control.

After Saul's conversion, he was persecuted every day of his life. Jesus' words recorded by Matthew came true for Paul and for all the disciples. They were sent out "like sheep among wolves" (v. 16), but their persecution served to spread the gospel message throughout the world. There was a purpose in everything that the disciples had to endure, and the same is true for us.

God's rules have not changed, and "Jesus Christ is the same yesterday and today and forever" (Hebrews 13:8). In all things, God still "works for the good of those who love him, who have been called according to his purpose" (Romans 8:28).

Beloved, that includes you and me. He holds us in the palm of His hand. Hallelujah!

Lord, thank You that my suffering is not in vain when I suffer with You and for You. Your grace is sufficient for me. In Jesus' name, amen.

_____

_____

_____

_____

_____

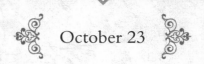

October 23

Sharpening Our Sword

I did not come to bring peace, but a sword (Matthew 10:34).

Scripture: Matthew 10:32–39

Three years ago I had a dream of Heaven. As I climbed up a ladder along with countless angels, my surroundings became progressively more colorful. There were rainbows, bubbles, waterfalls, and a blinding brilliance that filled me with joy.

Suddenly, I was taken to a place of despair and darkness. There were shrieks and gnashing of teeth, and I was desperate to leave. Then God's Word came to me, and I started repeating, "Greater is He who is in me than he who is in the world" (see 1 John 4:4). With each uttered word, I was moved farther from Hell and closer to glory. Finally, I was back in Heaven, and I woke up.

God's Word is powerful. When Jesus was tempted in the desert, He defeated the devil through the Word, the sword of the Spirit. God's Word is "living and active" (Hebrews 4:12). As we sharpen our Sword through use, we are rescued, healed, restored, renewed. The Word gives us victory.

The fact is, Jesus brought us a sword. He wants us to use it that we might live victoriously, just like Him.

Lord, the words You speak are spirit and they are life. Stir up a hunger in my heart for the Word, that I may be transformed in my mind, having victory over all my foes. In the name of the Father, the Son, and the Holy Spirit, I pray. Amen.

_____

_____

_____

_____

_____

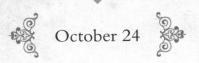

Running After the Mystery

Have nothing to do with godless myths and old wives' tales; rather, train yourself to be godly (1 Timothy 4:7).

Scripture: *1 Timothy 4:6-16*

Today's passage warns us against distractions, especially verbal debates about doctrinal differences that lead nowhere. Rather than waste our time on such discussions, we should train ourselves in godliness. So what should this training look like?

In 1 Timothy 3:16, Paul says, "Beyond all question, the mystery of godliness is great: He appeared in a body, was vindicated by the Spirit, was seen by angels, was preached among the nations, was believed on in the world, was taken up in glory." Paul defines the mystery of godliness as the life, death, and resurrection of Jesus. As we train ourselves to be godly, we enter into the very life of Christ. Growing in godliness is all about becoming like Him by the power of the Spirit.

My intense training program in godliness took off when I started meditating on Scripture and applying its truth in my daily life. In Romans 12:1, 2, Paul exhorts us: "to offer your bodies as living sacrifices," choosing to be "transformed by the renewing of your mind."

God's Word is the treadmill of the spiritual life.

Father, as Your spoken Word brought forth the whole creation, speak life into me through Your written Word. Renew my mind, that I may be fully equipped for every good work. Through Christ I pray. Amen.

_____

_____

_____

_____

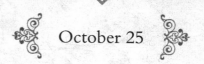

How's Your Heart?

For this people's heart has become calloused; they hardly hear with their ears, and they have closed their eyes (Acts 28:27).

Scripture: Acts 28:25–31

A hard heart is far from God. It is unyielding, judgmental, uncaring, self-centered, and stubborn. A hard heart hates; it is unforgiving and exudes death. Conversely, a soft heart yields. It gives the benefit of the doubt. It considers the needs of others. It cares. It loves. A soft heart provides rich soil for a fruitful walk with God and one another.

Once God's love was poured into his heart, Paul lived yielded to the Holy Spirit. God's love transformed him. He received a new heart that was soft and eager to share Christ "boldly and without hindrance" (v. 31).

We, too, were given new hearts when we were baptized. Still, do you agree that our tendency to develop a hard heart is not completely gone? I am so thankful for the Holy Spirit's conviction; because He lives in me, I cannot keep a calloused heart for very long. Hardness of heart is uncomfortable within me now. Praise God!

The more we yield to the Holy Spirit, the softer our hearts become, open to receive and give the love of Christ, who is our life.

Lord, I cannot live abundantly apart from You. Help me to yield to the Holy Spirit daily, that I may live in love each day. I pray this prayer in the precious name of Jesus my Savior. Amen.

_____

_____

_____

_____

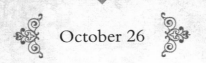

October 26

Feeding on Him

While they were worshiping the Lord and fasting, the Holy Spirit said, . . . (Acts 13:2).

Scripture: Acts 13:1-12

The more I yield to the Holy Spirit, the more I hear God's voice. I remember one of the first times this happened. It was 1998, shortly after I attended a retreat that changed my life. During the second night there, Jesus' love overwhelmed me; He ministered to the depths of my being.

Soon I started reading the Bible regularly. I was working as a family doctor at Hurlburt Field Air Force Base in Fort Walton Beach, Florida. I read the Bible during lunch and between patients. I learned to live in God's presence by abiding in His Word.

One afternoon, after several challenging patients, I needed a break. I headed to the snack bar when suddenly God spoke to my heart, saying, "Why not feed on Me instead?" Without missing a beat I headed back to my office, where the Lord fed my soul through His Word.

Jesus said, "My sheep listen to my voice; I know them, and they follow me" (John 10:27). Yes, Lord, You are my shepherd. I know Your voice, and I want to follow You.

> **Lord,** *You said to Your disciples, "I have food to eat that you know nothing about" (John 4:32). Yes, Lord, I know. I've tasted it. There is no food like the sound of Your voice. Speak to me, Lord; open my ears to hear You and my heart to obey You. In Your name I pray. Amen.*

_____

_____

_____

_____

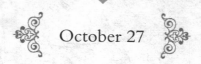

October 27

Following in the Dark

Simon himself believed and was baptized. And he followed Philip everywhere, astonished by the great signs and miracles he saw (Acts 8:13).

Scripture: Acts 8:12-25

"Pastor, I think he exited here," I said attempting to keep our mini-mission team together as our two vans zoomed down the super highway. Following someone at night challenged everyone to stay alert. It took us about two minutes to realize I was wrong.

Although we started out following a trustworthy friend, the further we traveled the more difficult it was to distinguish his van from the rest. Our minister noted the frame around the license plate and focused on that. But I inadvertently misled him because I had no focal point.

Similarly, Simon started the Christian walk following his trustworthy friend, Philip. But Simon had his eyes on the wrong focal point. Even though Scripture says he believed, he continued traveling in spiritual darkness because he had not repented of his sins.

Often we wander off the straight and narrow path due to ignored sins. Repentance turns us around and steers us safely to our eternal destination.

Father, thank You for the light of the world. I ask for Your guidance and strength to overcome the temptations of darkness. In Christ's name, amen.

_____

_____

_____

_____

_____

October 28

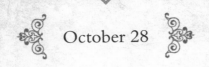

Desert Drive

Now an angel of the Lord said to Philip, "Go south to the road—the desert road—that goes down from Jerusalem to Gaza" (Acts 8:26).

Scripture: Acts 8:26-38

"Why now? I thought my job was secure," Joyce cried when God redirected her course. Going back to school after the age of 50 shook her from her comfort zone and threw her onto a "desert road." On graduation day, every one of her classmates told her they never would have made it through the course without her friendship and encouragement. After Joyce's "desert" experience, God rewarded her with a job far better than she'd imagined.

When God redirected his course, Philip obeyed without complaint and traveled the designated desert road. Before long, he met a man sincerely searching for the truth. Philip then realized God's purpose in taking him from a successful ministry in Jerusalem. Placing him on the desert road involved encouraging others along the way.

Life is unpredictable. Jobs are terminated. Plans change. However, God is in control of all things and has a purpose for sending us out on the next desert road. When we are obedient, He opens Heaven's gates and pours blessings on us—and on each person we meet in Christ's name.

Omniscient Father, You know the plans You hold for me, which may include a "desert road." Grant me wisdom cheerfully to encourage others along the way. In Jesus' name I pray. Amen.

_____

_____

_____

_____

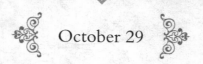

Zealous for God

I was thoroughly trained in the law of our fathers and was just as zealous for God as any of you are today (Acts 22:3).

Scripture: Acts 22:3-16

On August 14, 2003, a glitch in the nation's power grid stranded commuters in New York City, Detroit, and Toronto. Hordes of people groped their way in the darkness to surface from subways and swarmed around docks waiting for ferries to take them home.

Thousands of people, who lived within walking distance, plodded through the streets on that hot and muggy afternoon. Amazingly, most remained calm and eager to show the world they could persevere until they arrived home. Some walked over eight miles to their destinations—only to find that they couldn't enter the buildings. Although their zeal carried them to the door, they lacked the power that their electronic keys demanded for entry.

Before his conversion, Paul was much like those walkers. He knew where he wanted to go. He was willing to go the distance. However, had he continued on the course, he would have been extremely disappointed when he reached Heaven's gates. All the zeal he could muster would have lacked the power to gain entry.

There is only one source of power that unlocks the gates of Heaven: the blood of Jesus Christ.

O God, *ignite in me the zeal to do good*

_____

_____

_____

_____

_____

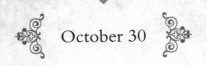

October 30

Unlikely Recipients

Some of them . . . began to speak to Greeks also, telling them the good news about the Lord Jesus. . . . and a great number of people believed and turned to the Lord (Acts 11:20, 21).

Scripture: Acts 11:19-26

Equipped with coupons for frozen treats redeemable at a local restaurant, I distributed goodwill to the obvious—parents with small children. Broadening my mission, I shared the coupons with department store cashiers and bank tellers. Sour faces softened into pleasant smiles. Wrinkles seemed to vanish from elderly faces as they thanked me for an unexpected favor. However, handing coupons to burly men seemed ridiculous because the coupon awarded a meager four-ounce serving of ice cream. Amazingly, even they received it with as much enthusiasm as the children.

Equipped with the good news of a risen Savior, first-century Christians traveled into distant cities sharing with the obvious—other Jews searching for the Messiah. Courageously, they broadened their mission by opening the gospel to unlikely recipients. Through God's mercy and grace, Greeks believed with as much enthusiasm as the children of Israel.

Sovereign God, You know the ones who need to hear the good news of Jesus Christ. Equip me with enthusiasm and courage that I might share the hope that is in me with someone today. I pray this prayer in the name of Jesus, my merciful Savior and Lord. Amen.

_____

_____

_____

_____

_____

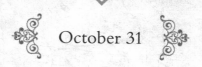

October 31

Entrapment

God did this so that men would seek him and perhaps reach out for him and find him, though he is not far from each one of us (Acts 17:27).

Scripture: Acts 17:22-28

A scrawny, odd-looking creature staggered onto the road in front of us. At second glance, we realized it was a tiny kitten with its head stuck in a bag. Parking the car, my husband picked up the pathetic creature, removed the bag, and sat it on the path that led home. When Gene returned to the car, he said the bag was a single-serving, cat-food pouch. In an effort to consume every last morsel of food, the kitten trapped herself in darkness.

With an earnest desire to delve into religion, the Athenians surrounded themselves with as much philosophy and religious myth as available, trapping themselves in spiritual darkness. God sent Paul to "pull the bag of deceit" off their heads and expose them to the light of Jesus Christ.

Many false doctrines infiltrate the church in the guise of tolerance. God gave us His written Word to help us seek Him and find Him through the sacrifice of Jesus Christ. He beckons us to expose others to the Light and set their feet on the only path that leads to Heaven.

Creator and sustainer of my soul, thank You for setting my feet on the path that leads to Your door. Help me to expose others to the light of Jesus Christ. In His name, I pray. Amen.

November

*You are the body of Christ, and each one of you
is a part of it.*

—1 Corinthians 12:27

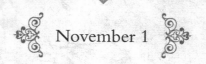

November 1

Bind Us Together, Lord

There is one body and one Spirit—just as you were called to one hope when you were called—one Lord, one faith, one baptism; one God and Father of all (Ephesians 4:4-6).

Scripture: Ephesians 4:1-6

After assembling a 1500-piece puzzle, I felt it was a shame to dismantle it and stuff it back into the box with the intent of some day reassembling it. The picture of the lighthouse was too beautiful—and the task too tedious—to start all over again another day. However, moving the puzzle proved impossible. No matter how tightly joined those pieces appeared to be, the picture crumbled at the slightest movement. The perfect solution—apply adhesive in order to bind the pieces together permanently. Glued to a snack stand, that puzzle continues to showcase our diligence with its beauty.

In assembling the body of Christ, God designed each believer with a specific purpose and placement within the church. Even though we seem intricately connected, God realized how easily we would crumble under the shifting currents of worldly pressures. His perfect solution?—the gift of the Holy Spirit applied to the hearts of all believers. He permanently binds us in the bond of unity and love.

Father, I'm thankful that You've placed us in the world to show forth one hope, one Lord, one faith, one baptism, and one God. Amen.

_____

_____

_____

_____

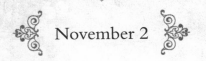

November 2

Making a Memorial

Until we all reach unity in the faith and in the knowledge of the Son of God and become mature, attaining to the whole measure of the fullness of Christ (Ephesians 4:13).

Scripture: Ephesians 4:7-16

Already 60 years in the making, a monument honoring the Native American hero, Crazy Horse, stands high in the mountains of South Dakota. But only the face is completed. Since the death of the original sculptor, Korczak Ziolkowski, in 1982, the work continues under the talented hands of seven of his ten children. Considering the meticulous procedure, it is doubtful that Ziolkowski's children will live to complete the project. In that event, the organization will assign others the task.

God assigns prophets, evangelists, ministers, and teachers to sculpt Christians into memorials honoring Jesus. The procedure takes a lifetime of meticulous work. When necessary, others pick up the project where the first had to leave off. Even this devotional was designed by our Lord to chisel a little here or polish a bit there. The author is honored to be used by Him to impart His truths to fellow believers. Through the discipline it took to write this devotion, she too has been chiseled and polished. In this way, we, His precious monuments, build up one another to reflect the fullness of Christ.

__Divine Creator,__ bless those You have chosen to sculpt me into the likeness of Your Son, Jesus Christ. In His name I pray. Amen.

_____

_____

_____

_____

_____

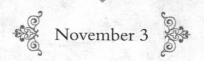

What's the Big Deal?

[They] argued forcefully and at length. Finally, Paul and Barnabas were sent to Jerusalem, accompanied by some local believers, to talk to the apostles and elders about this question (Acts 15:2, *New Living Translation*).

Scripture: Acts 15:1–5

When I was a teen, I asked my friend, Sarah, if she wanted to come to church with me. Her father looked at me, puzzled, and said, "But she can't go. She doesn't have a hat and gloves." Such accessories were common when he was growing up; he assumed it was still a requirement. (Apparently, he hadn't been to church recently.)

We all have certain preconcieved notions about worship, don't we? Often, these ideas have little scriptural basis. In the early church, some Pharisees became Christians and brought their religious traditions with them. They insisted that Gentiles must first become converts to Judaism if they were to be eligible for salvation through Christ. It became a blistering dispute in the early church.

Paul knew that the very essence of the gospel message hinged on this debate: What did Jesus Christ do for me on the cross? This was the crux of the dispute. It is still the most important question you will ever answer.

Heavenly Father, when You sent Your Son to the cross, He did all that was necessary to win my salvation. Thank You, in Jesus' name. Amen.

_____

_____

_____

_____

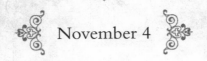

November 4

Adding Layers?

We believe that we shall be saved through the grace of the Lord Jesus, just as they will (Acts 15:11, *Revised Standard Version*).

Scripture: Acts 15:6-11

In our day and age, it's hard to believe that the early church was divided over an issue like circumcision. More specifically, church leaders argued about whether Gentiles needed to be circumcised before they could receive salvation through Christ. To modern sensibilities, circumcision is just an elective medical procedure. But to the early church in the first century, it represented much more. It symbolized the covenant God had made with Abraham. It meant obedience to the Law.

And now Paul traveled all the way to Jerusalem to meet with the church elders and apostles about this question. He insisted that newly converted Gentiles did not require circumcision to be in right relationship with God. Jesus Christ's death and resurrection was the fulfilled promise. The law could still act as a moral guide for believers, but salvation could only come through grace alone. No further layer need be added to this plan from God.

Are you struggling with a divisive issue in your church? If so, consider: Does Scripture clearly and consistently support your own position? It's important to know.

Father, thank You that I don't need to add layers to the "system" to be accepted by You. Your system is grace, freely bestowed. So reshape my thinking about any legalism I may still cherish. Through Christ, amen.

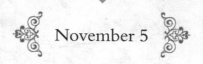

November 5

Listen!

That the remnant of men may seek the Lord, and all the Gentiles who bear my name, says the Lord (Acts 15:17).

Scripture: Acts 15:12-21

While at the Jerusalem conference, Paul and Barnabas spoke to a hushed crowd, sharing the signs and wonders God had performed for the believing Gentiles. Then James, a prominent leader of the church in Jerusalem, affirmed Paul's assertion that Gentiles should not be put under the Mosaic system. No circumcision required! With keen awareness, James quoted from the book of Amos, confirming God's intent to save all who are lost.

Many believe that Gentile Christians outnumbered Jewish Christians at this critical juncture in the early church's history. What might have happened had this fledgling church split apart? Thankfully, we don't have to wonder. The assembly listened to the guiding wisdom of God, transmitted through the mouth of Paul, and ended up protecting and preserving the early movement. The conference ended with the apostles, the elders, and all of the church in agreement about this important debate. The question was settled once and for all: All believers were saved by grace alone. And God was glorified through this powerful display of unity.

Heavenly Father, help me to learn from Paul's crisis-management skills. He listened to You and sought Your wisdom. May Your truth become so much a part of me, too, that I can't be led astray. In Jesus' name, amen.

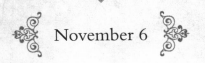

The Offending Cross

If you confess with your mouth, "Jesus is Lord," and believe in your heart that God raised him from the dead, you will be saved (Romans 10:9).

Scripture: Romans 10:5-9

A friend of mine often objects to what he calls the narrow-mindedness of Christianity. "There are many paths leading up the mountain of faith," he insists. "Who is to say that Jesus is the only way?" Well, Jesus said it, for one: "I am the way and the truth and the life. No one comes to the Father except through me" (John 14:6).

Paul affirmed it too: "If you confess with your mouth, 'Jesus is Lord,' and believe in your heart that God raised him from the dead, you will be saved" (Romans 10:9). It sounds so gracious and loving, doesn't it? Confess and believe, and you will be saved. Yet it's a statement that leaves many, like my friend, offended.

The cross does offend people. It leads to that thorny and unpopular premise that *there is only one way to God*. Yet if it were possible that humans could be saved any other way, the cross would not have been necessary. It really is simple. God has established a way to salvation through His own self-sacrifice by His Son, Jesus. Do I accept His offer? Do I confess and believe?

My Redeemer, thank You for providing a way back to You so that I will spend eternity in Your Holy presence. Teach me to revel in Your presence, even now, until the day I see You, face to face. In Your name, amen.

_____

_____

_____

_____

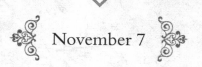

How Else Will They Hear?

How, then, can they call on the one they have not believed in? And how can they believe in the one of whom they have not heard? And how can they hear without someone preaching to them? And how they can preach unless they are sent? (Romans 10:14, 15).

Scripture: Romans 10:10-17

A brilliant debater, Paul used a sequence of rhetorical questions with his audience to stress the importance of preaching the gospel. He was building up to his main point: the need to send preachers to the mission field.

God could have chosen another means, rather than humans, to spread the message, of course. Angels would have been quite convincing, for example. But perhaps human beings are the best at reaching other humans.

God doesn't want anyone to miss the opportunity to be saved. Christ's very last words, right before He ascended, were: "Therefore go and make disciples of all nations, baptizing them in the name of the Father and of the Son and of the Holy Spirit, and teaching them to obey everything I have commanded you" (Matthew 28:19, 20). We Christians must share the message of salvation. How wrong it would be to keep others from enjoying the love and forgiveness of our heavenly Father!

Dear Lord, open my eyes to those in my own mission field who haven't heard of You. Help me to overcome any shyness or reluctance as I seek to share my faith. I pray in Jesus' holy name. Amen.

_____

_____

_____

_____

_____

Holy and Wholly

They saw that I had been entrusted with the task of preaching the gospel to the Gentiles, just as Peter had been to the Jews (Galatians 2:7).

Scripture: Galatians 2:1-10

For the last six years, I have been raising puppies for Guide Dogs for the Blind in San Rafael, California. An eight-week-old puppy is entrusted to me from the GDB kennels, and for the next 16 months I will love, train, and socialize that puppy. After formal training from instructors, the dog will be partnered with a blind individual. Together, they will become a team.

But not all of the puppies become guides. A Guide Dog is one that seems to take to its entrusted task with a natural intuition.

It was clear to the leaders of the early church that God had entrusted Peter with the task of preaching the gospel to the Jews, and Paul to the Gentiles. Not exclusively, of course. When Paul entered a town, he went first to the temple. And we know Peter ate with Gentiles. But each man knew his principal calling. God had entrusted them according to their passions.

Do you know what your calling is? Where are your passions? God has given you that interest for a purpose.

Lord, You made me with a purpose, but what did You have in mind? Lead me clearly to uncover and develop those interests and abilities. Make the work of my hands today count for eternity. I pray in Jesus' name. Amen.

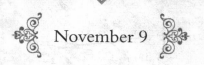

November 9

Gravity's Pull

When Peter came to Antioch, I opposed him to his face, because he was clearly in the wrong (Galatians 2:11).

Scripture: Galatians 2:11-21

Those were strong words from Paul. He called Peter a hypocrite! What had he done? Peter had come up to visit Paul in Antioch and had comfortably eaten with the Gentiles. Then certain Jewish legalists arrived to join him, and he buckled—he went back to his old, legalistic eating pattern. He even influenced Barnabas—Paul's faithful sidekick—to follow his lead!

This wasn't just about food preferences, of course. It came back to the question, settled long ago, of whether circumcision (or any other legalism) was necessary for salvation. With characteristic bluster, Peter acted first and thought about it later. He turned from liberty in Christ back to bondage under law.

I have a little bit of Peter's personality in me, and I suspect that most of us can relate to him to some degree. Our old habits can be like gravity, pulling us back to a rather sad but comfortable way of living. Peter had spent three years shadowing Christ, yet he still battled with his sinful nature. Thankfully, Paul's divinely inspired guidance pulled him back.

Dear God, I know that unless I stay in steady communication with Your Spirit within me, sin will pull me down. Give me the eyes to see my sins, confess them to You—and turn away from them! In Christ's name, amen.

_____

_____

_____

_____

_____

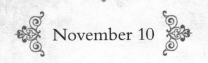

Who's Afraid?

God is within her, she will not fall; God will help her at break of day (Psalm 46:5).

Scripture: Psalm 46

The girl's breath came in frightened gasps. Night after night, she faced the gloomy gauntlet. Trees loomed like bony witches as she hurried along between deep roadside ditches, sure that some toothy thing would clamber out and chase her down. She chastised herself for entertaining such silly fears. But every night she arrived home in a cold sweat, heart racing with the effort it took not to run.

One day, she came across a tattered bookmark that she'd been given long ago in Sunday school. The shepherd pictured on the bookmark seemed wise and kind, but the stout staff in his hand made it clear that He knew how to deal with bandits and wolves. She held the picture in mind as she headed home that night. And she whispered the psalm that went with it: "The Lord is my Shepherd."

She could almost feel Him beside her, strong and fearless, the moment she called. Years later, after she'd met the shepherd personally, she realized that He really had been there. Now she knew His promise, too, never to leave.

Lord, help me to remember that You are my powerful and loving Shepherd. Thanks for Your promise never to leave me alone. In Jesus' name, amen.

_____

_____

_____

_____

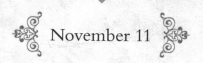

Diabolical Distraction

He who began a good work in you will carry it on to completion until the day of Christ Jesus (Philippians 1:6).

Scripture: Philippians 1:3-11

Our setting: the unseen world surrounding human activity. A demonic professor instructs a student in the art of distraction. "So, encouraging him to focus on how wonderfully he's serving the Enemy wasn't effective, eh?"

"No, your nastiness."

"Then try offering him wormy thoughts about what a disappointment he must be to that One he serves. You can grind him into the dust by making him think only of himself. Don't let him think about other humans at all. And make sure his thoughts of his God produce guilt; this will entice him to avoid that miserable idea of . . . *grace.*"

Both demons shudder. "The really beautiful thing is, he'll mistake these thoughts for humility and think he's doing a good thing to reflect upon his wickedness. Really, he's simply enjoying self-centeredness at its opposite extreme! 'It's all about me' is the thing to remember—good me or bad me makes no difference. Just keep the focus on 'me,' and you will successfully distract him from accomplishing the Enemy's purposes."

***Good Master,** You knew what You were getting when You chose me. I make mistakes, but please don't let me spend too much time thinking about either my accomplishments or my failures. It's all about You, Lord, and what You began in me You will complete. Thanks, in Jesus' name. Amen.*

_____

_____

_____

_____

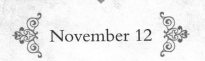

November 12

The Mess Becomes Beautiful

Now I want you to know, brothers, that what has happened to me has really served to advance the gospel (Philippians 1:12).

Scripture: Philippians 1:12-18

Her world has been smashed, her dreams cruelly shattered. There is someone to blame, the one who performed the offending deed. She could choose hatred. She could snarl bitterly every time someone spoke his name. She might even spend the rest of her life indulging in a continuous tirade against that perpetrator. And she knows people who live that way. They're ugly in spirit, and when she's around them, she feels as though their poison might seep into her skin through their breath.

There is another choice, but she knows it will not be easy. She can choose to obey God—the more difficult path because it means forgiving and letting go of the anger. But then comes the fun part, where she will stand back and watch Him turn the devil's plan on its head. She'll have her sweet "revenge" by choosing purposeful, obedient action rather than allowing another's actions to dictate her response. She will choose peace, which is more valuable than everything she lost. She will trust her Lord to fashion the mess into a beautiful, holy thing.

O Lord, help me to remember that my real enemy is the evil one and that my salvation comes in loving You. Help me to trust and obey, even when I can't see how You might possibly use it for good. Waste nothing, Lord. Use every crumb of my pain to advance Your work! In Jesus' name, amen.

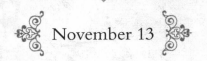

November 13

I Have Decided

I eagerly expect and hope that I will in no way be ashamed, but will have sufficient courage so that now as always Christ will be exalted in my body, whether by life or by death (Philippians 1:20).

Scripture: Philippians 1:19-26

Those who hate the gospel have killed the young minister. His wife is left alone amidst a village full of hostile and dangerous people. The government will not help her. There are no other believers nearby, but she is strengthened, knowing that many brothers and sisters around the world are praying for her.

She remembers the day she confided in her husband, "I am not certain that I will have sufficient courage, if death should be required of me."

Her husband had comforted her, wiping away her tears of shame. "None of us has that faith in ourselves. We must have that faith in God. He will provide the strength when we need it. Whatever happens, Dear, He will give us the courage that we need to be faithful. Only decide in your heart that you will never turn back, and the most difficult question has been answered." The young widow looks out her window and considers a village full of helpless, imprisoned souls. She straightens, brushes the wrinkles from her gown, and goes out to minister among them.

Lord, You know how often I am afraid of the things You ask me to do—and the things You might ask of me! Help me, in Christ's name. Amen.

_____

_____

_____

_____

_____

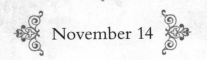

Royalty in Disguise

Whatever happens, conduct yourselves in a manner worthy of the gospel of Christ (Philippians 1:27).

Scripture: Philippians 1:27-30

An exiled king wanders his domain in disguise. Unknown and unappreciated, he guards his people against terrors that would overwhelm and destroy them if he should abandon his charge. Rather than appreciate his work, however, the people regard him with suspicion.

And yet, there is something about this man that makes them shrink into themselves should he look their way. They seem to well up with unaccountable guilt when he regards them with a loving glance, as he so often does. He possesses a certain regality that cannot be veiled by the travel-worn clothing. He stands erect; his stride is confidant, his voice kind or stern as needed.

People get the disturbing feeling that he knows exactly who he is and what he is meant to be doing. Some are jealous and hate him because of it. But every so often, one will edge closer, cloaked by darkness, and ask this strange man what it is that makes him so different. Soon they are conducting themselves in the same worthy manner as their ever-so-worthy mentor.

O God, strengthen my inner person so that, no matter what my circumstances may be, I will conduct myself in a way that reveals my true identity. Whether I have support from others or find myself abandoned and alone, I ask one thing: Let me be faithful to You. In Jesus' name, amen.

Aliens and Strangers

Our citizenship is in heaven (Philippians 3:20).

Scripture: Philippians 3:17—4:1

"Man, do you ever feel as if being in this world just hurts too much—like you can't stand it anymore?" The second young man glanced at his friend and then back to the gang of kids clustered outside the school. "Yeah. I mean, look at them! I try to tell them they're headed for real trouble. I want to point them in the right direction, but they look at me like I'm nuts. It's like being in a lifeboat watching the *Titanic* go down, and the people on board won't believe the ship's sinking. I feel so helpless sometimes, not to mention feeling like the biggest misfit in the universe!"

His friend smiled. "Why does it surprise us that we don't fit in? Hey, this isn't our permanent address."

The young man thought for a moment. "Yeah, you're right. It's not our home. We're just here on assignment for awhile, right?"

"You know, we can't save the whole world, buddy. But we have an assignment while we're here. And we're not supposed to let it drag us down."

"How?"

"Come on, let's pray. It'll help them and us."

Abba Father, this world is not my home. Show me what You want me to do here, and strengthen me to obey. When it seems like too much, remind me of that beautiful, restful place ahead. Through Christ I pray. Amen.

_____

_____

_____

_____

_____

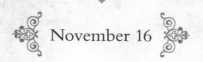

November 16

Crazy Peace

The peace of God, which transcends all understanding, will guard your hearts and your minds in Christ Jesus (Philippians 4:7).

Scripture: Philippians 4:2-9

"Pam, I just heard what's happened. You must be so upset! Is there anything I can do?"

"Thanks, Judy, but there's really nothing anyone can do."

"It's weird; you look so calm."

Pam laughed. "I can't say I'm completely calm, at least not inside, but I'm working on it. What I do have is a peace that I can't explain, except to say that it's supernatural. It's not coming from me, that's for sure."

"How can you possibly have peace at a time like this?"

"It's because I know the one who's in charge of all things. He's promised not to give me more than I can bear. I know He's got everything under control, even though it sure doesn't look that way for now. And I believe He'll use all of this somehow for the good, if I trust Him with it. I just keep asking Him to help me to believe and be faithful."

"You are nuts." Judy looked wistful. "But I kind of wish I was your kind of crazy."

Jehovah Shalom, You are the God of peace. I give You my heart. Help me feel and believe that You love me in all situations. Through Christ, amen.

_____

_____

_____

_____

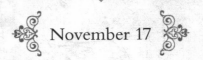

November 17

A Time to Go Forth

God did not give us a spirit of timidity, but a spirit of power, of love and of self-discipline (2 Timothy 1:7).

Scripture: 2 Timothy 1:3-7

"O Lord, what have I done? Why didn't you stop me?" I had assisted in planning Christian events with established groups before. This time I was sponsoring my first, all on my own. It was a dinner theater for single Christians. Tickets were dispersed to their locations for sales. Newspapers, TV and radio announcements were airing promising skits, comedy, door prizes and more. Paralyzed with fear, I knew there was no turning back. I fretted about everything. "What if nobody comes? What if everyone hates it? What if . . . ?"

In due season the dormant potential in our lives demands to flow, while circumstances conspire to build dams of fear. Armed with a team of prayerful people, who were generous with encouragement, I saw this dam demolished. We enjoyed success, thanks be to God.

God has given each of us spiritual gifts to use in His service. The great challenge is to venture forth and use them in His power. Fear must flee in the face of His marvelous power.

Dear God, help me to proceed with the plans You've laid on my heart, in spite of my fears. In Christ's precious name I pray. Amen.

_____

_____

_____

_____

_____

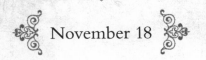

November 18

A Real Friend

I am not ashamed, because I know whom I have believed, and am convinced that he is able to guard what I have entrusted to him for that day (2 Timothy 1:12).

Scripture: 2 Timothy 1:8-14

"Who are you talking to?" I'd ask, with a questioning frown.

"My friend," my 4-year-old daughter would answer emphatically. Only no one was there. Yet, lively conversation streamed from her bedroom, and she insisted her "friend" was real.

I became a bit concerned, but I soon learned that young children often entertain imaginary friends. (Who knows, I probably had one as a child.)

Do skeptics view Christians like this—as we continue to insist that Jesus is our companion and friend, that we walk and talk with Him daily? I can't *see* His presence, yet I *know* His presence; He is no imaginary friend. All who are indwelt by His Spirit know a real and abiding fellowship with this Savior.

Thankfully, as we continue to nurture our friendship with Jesus and boldly proclaim Him Lord, onlookers will glimpse His reality in the way we live. In fact, our lives can be the bridge for others to connect with a real friend.

Dear God, help me to experience deeper realities of Your presence, day by day. And let that presence shape my life into a glowing witness to Your reality. In the holy name of Jesus, my Lord and Savior, I pray. Amen.

_____

_____

_____

_____

_____

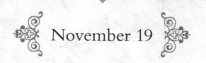

November 19

You're Included

I am obligated both to Greeks and non-Greeks, both to the wise and the foolish (Romans 1:14).

Scripture: Romans 1:8-17

"I was on the summit with a Muslim, a Jew, and an atheist," the speaker said, sharing a story from his recent mountain-climbing venture. "While there, God gave me a special love for those people," she continued, going on to describe the special bond that formed among them.

Paul, steeped in Judaism, paved the way for salvation among the Gentiles. Like him, we are called to minister to the nations.

Thankfully, living in the United States makes it possible for us to meet and befriend folks from all over the world—without ever treading foreign soil. What a broad representation of diverse cultures exists in almost every neighborhood!

I'm thankful that when Jesus surrendered to the cross, He did so for *all* humanity. The blessings and promises of the Bible are inclusive: "Whosoever will, may come." Regardless of ethnicity, intelligence, financial status—Jesus died for everyone. So, to each lovely and unique heart, let us be ready with the invitation to eternal life.

Father, give me the wisdom to witness to cultures different from mine. Like the great apostle Paul, fill me with a genuine eagerness to share the good news with every person I meet, manifesting Your love in the most practical ways. In the name of Jesus, Lord and Savior of all, I pray. Amen.

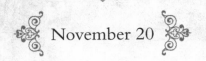

November 20

Let's Not Forget

Remember Jesus Christ, raised from the dead, descended from David. This is my gospel (2 Timothy 2:8).

Scripture: 2 Timothy 2:8-13

Stress had numbed my mind, and I was barely able to function from day to day. What a situation I faced! I could choose to walk forward in faith or in fear. Actually, I mostly teetered between the two. Internalizing my pain, I felt as if my head would implode, and I could barely manage to utter a prayer.

Then God began to draw my focus back to the Scriptures. Today's Scripture begins, "Remember Jesus Christ." My sufferings in this life shrink down to size when placed alongside what Jesus endured on the cross for me.

When life bombards us with tough situations that seem unfair and unmanageable, let us simply remember our beloved Savior. God's power was sufficient to raise Jesus from the dead, and this same power is able to resurrect courage, determination, and strength within us. In Him, we can overcome every challenge. As a wise and experienced missionary once told a group of young people: "The hand that *points* the way is the same hand that *provides* the way."

Father, thank You that as I recall the cross, I am reminded of Your sacrifice of love and of Your resurrecting power. Help me to remember, too, that You are always with me, supplying abundant grace and power for all that confronts me, today and always. In Jesus' name I pray. Amen.

Friendly Reminders

Keep reminding them of these things. Warn them before God against quarreling about words; it is of no value, and only ruins those who listen (2 Timothy 2:14).

Scripture: 2 Timothy 2:14-19

I distinctly remember telling my son to wash his face, comb his hair, and change his shirt before we leave. "Are you ready?" I yell before getting into the car.

"Yeah, Mom." He climbs into the passenger seat as I gawk in disbelief. "You haven't done one thing I asked!"

I impatiently insist he go back and try again. "Why didn't you . . . ?" my questions follow behind him as he re-enters the house. ("Oh, I forgot," is his usual response.)

Weary with the repeated scenario, I threaten to make him a cassette recording titled, "My Instructions before Leaving Home." He could review it before ever getting into the car.

God quickly jolts my memory with how often I "forget" to live in ways that honor Him. And I instantly feel more compassion for my son.

Have you noticed that God's Word abounds in repetitious reminders? No doubt He knows how easily we can forget His goodness, and that all of His reminders have only our best at heart.

Father, forgive me when I hear Your wise guidance but so quickly forget. Bring Your Word once again to the forefront of my mind when I allow myself to become preoccupied with my own agenda. In Jesus' name, amen.

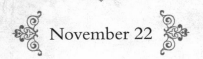

November 22

Time to Stop the Tape?

Continue in what you have learned and have become convinced of, because you know those from whom you learned it (2 Timothy 3:14).

Scripture: 2 Timothy 3:14-17

I love listening to nonfiction books on tape. But I try to be careful about what I choose. Recently I checked out an audio book at the library and found that the author had some excellent insights about the spiritual life. As I continued listening, though, she began veering down the path of New Age reasoning. Time to stop the tape!

We live in exciting times when new information can circle the globe with little effort—whether it be fact or fiction. The subtleties here are myriad, and so often dubious teachings can come wrapped in seemingly scriptural principles. Beware!

God wants us to continue to grow in the knowledge of Him. We are to learn and teach others the unsullied doctrines that have stood the test of time down through the ages in the church. In other words, healthy spiritual growth depends upon our ability to avoid heretical innovations. Straying down paths that merely mimic the Bible can only lead us into spiritual deception.

Father, there are so many teachings becoming popular and being embraced by many these days. Illuminate my mind only by the truth of Your Word that I will not be misled. And as I learn from You, give me the will and wisdom to teach others. Through Christ my Lord, amen.

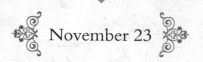

November 23

Endure the Hardship

But you, keep your head in all situations, endure hardship, do the work of an evangelist, discharge all the duties of your ministry (2 Timothy 4:5).

Scripture: 2 Timothy 2:1-3; 4:1-5

Picking it up from the pay phone, one of the security guards said in disgust, "Someone must have just left it here! Let's see if they are doing it outside." The two guards scanned the halls frantically and then darted out the doors.

I was strolling through the mall, but the urgency of their actions caused me concern. "Someone must have done something dangerous," I surmised. Later, I learned the officers were in hot pursuit of . . . a Christian who was passing out tracts explaining the gospel.

Society sometimes puzzles me. During this time of my life, I was struggling with difficulties and had wandered away from the church. I felt alienated from God and could have used any reminder of His faithfulness. Yet these Christians were being pursued by well-meaning citizens as if they were vicious criminals. True, the mall likely had some guidelines about distributing literature. But my point is simply this: However we seek to share the gospel, we will no doubt face some stiff opposition. Don't be surprised by it; determine to endure in God's strength.

Lord, You commanded me to "go." Give me courage to open up the gospel in a world that tries so hard to shut it out. In Jesus' name, amen.

_____

_____

_____

_____

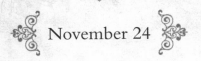

November 24

Lost

I came from the Father and entered the world; now I am leaving the world and going back to the Father (John 16:28).

Scripture: John 16:25-33

I'd entered unfamiliar territory. The further I drove, the more uneasy I grew. Finally, I had to admit I was lost. When I stopped at a gas station to ask for directions, the clerk was thoroughly unclear about how I ought to proceed.

A person standing at the counter overheard my dilemma, however, and interrupted: "Oh, I know where that is. In fact, I'm going that way myself. Just follow me."

When we drew near to my destination, he honked and pointed to the parking lot I needed. I was so grateful, and having a guide to direct me, I enjoyed the trip.

I don't know the literal "route" to Heaven, but I do know that my Lord Jesus Christ dwelled there from eternity, came to earth, and then went back again. I can trust Him to take me to Heaven, and I can trust Him to be my guide today and every day along all the pathways I'll travel while on this earth. All I have to do is ask for His wise and clear direction.

Father, thank You for Your most excellent guide in Your Son, Jesus. Thank You for making the way to You so clear: through the cross of Christ, I have forgiveness of sins and adoption into Your family. In His name, amen.

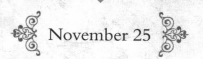

No Garbled Message Here!

We also thank God continually because, when you received the word of God, which you heard from us, you accepted it not as the word of men, but as it actually is, the word of God, which is at work in you who believe (1 Thessalonians 2:13).

Scripture: 1 Thessalonians 2:13-16

As children, we played a game called "Telephone." All players sat in a circle. The first person whispered a phrase to the one on her right. The next person whispered the same phrase to the next. Around the circle it went until the last person spoke it aloud. Then the first person verbalized the original phrase—which was usually entirely different from the final version!

It's not so different now, over 50 years later. Usually, by the time a story goes around a few times, it's nothing like the original. The "facts" tend to become distorted.

There is something very comforting in knowing that the good news Paul preached about Jesus is the same message now as it was in the first century. The essential facts of His eternal deity, blessed incarnation, atoning death, glorious resurrection, ascension, and second advent remain at the heart of our faith, unchanged.

And the message hasn't lost any of its original power, either. It still changes lives today, just as it did when Paul first preached it.

Father, thank You that Your Word is clear and trustworthy, no matter how many times it is told and retold. In the name of Jesus, amen.

_____

_____

_____

_____

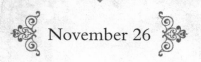

November 26

Many Adoptions

Not only so, but we ourselves, who have the firstfruits of the Spirit, groan inwardly as we wait eagerly for our adoption as sons, the redemption of our bodies (Romans 8:23).

Scripture: Romans 8:18-25

One of our sons-in-law has been adopted four times so far in his 34 years. No, he's not an incorrigible youth that had to be handed off repeatedly to new families. His first adoption occurred when his birth-mother gave him to his adoptive parents. Scott's adoptive father died when he was only a year and a half old. In the years following, his adoptive mother remarried. His new stepfather adopted him when Scott was three years old.

His third adoption occurred when Scott, as a young man, was baptized and adopted as a son into God's own family. Several years later, when he married our daughter, we "adopted" him as our own son.

Even though he's been adopted these many times, he still looks forward to the manifestation of his ultimate adoption: when he will receive his glorified body as God has promised. Until that day, all of us believers "groan inwardly," as Paul says. As we await our full redemption, let us face our daily tasks with joy—and a powerful witness to the one who makes every aspect of our glorious future possible, our Lord Jesus Christ.

Father God, thanks for my heavenly destination, which is far beyond anything I could ever imagine. In Christ's name, amen.

_____

_____

_____

_____

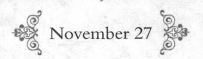

In the Hard Places

Paul and Barnabas appointed elders for them in each church and with prayer and fasting, committed them to the Lord, in whom the had put their trust (Acts 14:23).

Scripture: Acts 14:21-23

"What seems to be the problem?" I asked.

"He's just impossible," she said. "Sneaks out of the house in the nigh Skips school. Poor grades. Just don't know what I'm going to do with him."

"Do you think you've worried enough to change him?"

"What do you mean?"

"Well, obviously, all your worry hasn't changed his behavior, has it?"

"No. Probably won't either," she said, as she dabbed at her eyes with tissue.

"Then let's do what God's Word says to do. Suppose we pray togethe and fast, and commit him to the Lord?"

"Think it will work?"

"It sure beats worrying. I used to fret and stew over everything, until realized that when I let God be in charge, He takes care of things better tha I ever could."

"My worry is telling God I don't trust Him enough to let Him handl it, isn't it?"

And that was the day Millie let Jesus begin to operate in her son's life.

Lord, help me to trust You a little bit more in every situation I face. It's a growth process for me; help me along! In Jesus' name, amen.

_____

_____

_____

_____

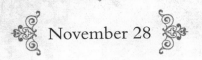
Crises for the "Christ Ones"

If you suffer as a Christian, do not be ashamed, but praise God that you bear that name (1 Peter 4:16).

Scripture: 1 Peter 4:12-19

In one of those terrible times in my life when the walls were caving in around me—and everything I perceived to be solid, shook and trembled—I sat in prayer with my journal on my lap and wrote this:

> My Child,
> I do no permit trials to strangle
> but to strengthen.
> I do not allow heartache to hurt
> but to heal.
> I do not send pain to punish
> but to increase perseverance.
> Receive all I have to give
> that you may become all I see you to be.

Pausing to look at things from God's perspective will give us a whole new clarity in our lives. He sees our struggles in the context of the whole journey, our destination being the moment we stand face to face in His presence. Until then, we can be thankful to bear the name, "Christ one."

Father God, help me to get Your take on a situation before I go into a tailspin that leads nowhere. In the name of Christ my Lord, amen.

_____

_____

_____

_____

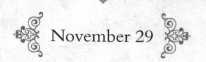

November 29

Already Loved!

Rise up and help us; redeem us because of your unfailing love (Psalm 44:26).

Scripture: Psalm 44:17-26

While taking a class in world religions, I was struck with a wonderful insight. Nowhere in any religion in the world, with the exception of Christianity, is God revealed as a loving Father who redeems us by grace alone.

I was stumped by the word *redeem* for a long time. Then one day I stumbled across an explanation of the Bible's original Greek word: It means to "buy back" a slave from the market. I suddenly saw the implication: I was a slave held by Satan. When I accepted Christ and entered the waters of baptism, I was released from that bondage. No longer Satan's property, I didn't have to do his bidding. I received a new master.

Let's face it. There is no reason in the world God would purchase me (I'm not that cute). The only reason He bought me back from the slave market is because of His unconditional love. And His offer isn't just extended to me but to everyone. All are invited to receive His priceless gift of salvation, purchased with His Son's blood.

Religions tell us to earn God's love by serving Him. Christianity calls us to show our gratitude, in loving service, for the love we already have.

God, thank You for Your love that is greater than I can know. But help me to grasp it a little more deeply with each new day. In Jesus' name, amen.

_____

_____

_____

_____

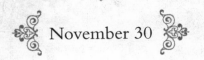

November 30

Strength in Weakness

For Christ's sake, I delight in weaknesses, in insults, in hardships, in persecutions, in difficulties. For when I am weak, then I am strong (2 Corinthians 12:10).

Scripture: 2 Corinthians 11:16-18. 21-30; 12:9, 10

Recently, while struggling through a "down day," I read an account of Fannie Crosby, the famous hymn writer who wrote over 8,000 gospel song texts. She authored songs like "Blessed Assurance" and "I Am Thine, O Lord." She was born in 1820 and lost her eyesight when she was only six weeks old.

Once a well-intentioned minister remarked to her, "I think it is a great pity that the master, when He showered so many gifts upon you, did not give you sight."

She replied, "Do you know that if at birth I had been able to make one petition to my creator, it would have been that I should be born blind?"

"Why?" asked the surprised minister.

"Because when I get to Heaven, the first face that shall ever gladden my sight will be that of my Savior."

Oh, that I might be delivered from distractions and hunger for Heaven as Fannie did! Her weaknesses could have made her bitter; instead, they made her better-fit for her glorious home.

Lord God, hone me for Heaven through each day, in every way. May the ultimate goal—to see You face to face—remain in the center of my vision through every circumstance, trial, and heartache. In Christ's name, amen.

_____

_____

_____

_____

My Prayer Notes

December

There is no Rock like our God.

—1 Samuel 2:2c

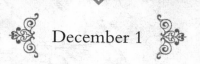

December 1

The Waiting Rock

There is no one holy like the LORD; there is no one besides you; there is no Rock like our God (1 Samuel 2:2).

Scripture: 1 Samuel 2:1-10

A dozen yards up from the road, a heart-shaped rock is embedded in our dirt and stone driveway. Dubbed "the waiting rock," it's the perfect size and shape for little feet to stand upon and wait.

You see, when our eldest granddaughter was 4, she caught the preschool bus at our home. At 8:15 each weekday morning, Grampy and Bailey walked hand-in-hand down the driveway to await the big yellow bus. As Bailey stood with her feet planted firmly on the rock, she and Grampy talked, sang, or told stories.

In Hannah's story, we learn about the rewards of waiting patiently. While longing for her prayer for a child to be fulfilled, Hannah planted her future firmly on God, the solid Rock. Her confidence lay in God's ability to bring her painful wait to a happy conclusion. And when He did, her heart overflowed with thanksgiving and praise.

At times when God seems unresponsive, I too plant my feet on the "waiting rock"—trusting the Rock of Ages to hear my prayer and do what He knows is best for me.

Father, teach me to wait patiently on the Solid Rock until Your answer comes. In Jesus' precious name I pray. Amen.

_____

_____

_____

_____

The Family Tree

In the sixth month, God sent the angel Gabriel to Nazareth, a town in Galilee, to a virgin pledged to be married to a man named Joseph, a descendant of David (Luke 1:26, 27).

Scripture: Luke 1:26-33

When I said "Yes" to my future husband's proposal, I didn't know he had famous ancestors. How exciting to learn that his relatives were descendants of a U.S. President, Ulysses S. Grant! I apparently had at least some claim to an impressive historical figure.

After we wed, Don gave me two heirlooms that had been in his family for years: Grandmother Ruth's 1898 Singer sewing machine cabinet and Aunt Mabel's Larkin secretary desk. One day, we'll pass them to our children.

When Mary agreed to marry Joseph, I wonder whether she was aware that King David's bloodline ran through the young carpenter's family tree? Perhaps she was excited to become part of a respected family. Then, what a blessing to be chosen as the mother of God's Son—through whom would come salvation for all. How that news must have sent Mary's heart soaring! The angel certainly promised an awesome legacy for the newborn: The babe would inherit the throne of King David as His birthright. He would reign over the house of Jacob forever.

O Lord, thank You that, through Your Son, I am counted among the branches of Your family tree—and have become heir to all the riches of Heaven. In Christ's blessed name I pray. Amen.

_____

_____

_____

_____

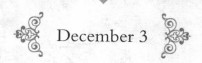

December 3

Momentous Moment

The Holy Spirit will come upon you, and the power of the Most High will overshadow you. So the holy one to be born will be called the Son of God (Luke 1:35).

Scripture: Luke 1:34-38

I vividly recall my husband's reaction when I announced he was going to be a first-time father. Getting home from work a few minutes before he did, I stuffed a small, round pillow under my blouse. When he came in the door, instead of rushing to greet him, I kept my back to him. Immediately sensing something askew, Don came behind me and encircled my waist with his arms. He jumped when he felt the bump in my middle. I whirled around and exclaimed, "You're going to be a father!" My method, though corny, was effective. "Hooray!" he shouted, jumping for joy.

The virgin Mary may have lacked confidence in telling Joseph of her impending motherhood. Since they were not yet married, she no doubt feared his reaction. Yet, despite her fears, Mary said, "May it be to me as you have said," (v. 38). Unreservedly, she submitted herself to God as His chosen vessel, placing herself, her baby, and their future in God's hands. In the end, Joseph—just like my husband—accepted the joyous news as a gift from God.

Heavenly Father, when the future seems uncertain, help me confidently place my life—and the lives of my loved ones—in Your capable, loving hands. In the name of Jesus I pray. Amen.

_____

_____

_____

_____

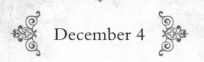

December 4

A Godly Heritage

Moved by the Spirit, he went into the temple courts. When the parents brought in the child Jesus to do for him what the custom of the Law required, Simeon took him in his arms. (Luke 2:27).

Scripture: Luke 2:25-35

We presented each of our daughters at a very young age to be dedicated to God and to receive His blessing. The ceremony offered us time to draw aside from the immediate demands of parenting and look forward to their future. As we held each girl in our arms, we knew that the dedication ceremony gave no guarantee of future joy, nor was it a guarantee against future heartache. (As they grew from childhood to adulthood, we experienced equal measures of both.)

Yet, we reminded ourselves that our children were in the Lord's hands. We trusted Him to fulfill His purpose for each of their lives, and we endeavored to live in ways worthy to be imitated. Now that our girls have children of their own, we continue to trust Him to work in their lives and help them to be good parents.

Joseph and Mary brought Jesus to the temple that day to fulfill the Law. Their act, too, was a way of offering His life into the hands of the Father. And how excellently Jesus would please His parents—the earthly ones and the heavenly one!

Lord, as I influence the children around me, help me to submit to Your transforming influence in my own life. Through Christ my Lord, amen.

_____

_____

_____

_____

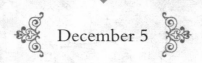

A Glimpse of Glory

On the third day a wedding took place at Cana in Galilee. Jesus' mother was there (John 2:1).

Scripture: John 2:1-11

Weddings vary as much as the brides who plan them. Our eldest daughter chose a traditional church wedding with a pianist, candles, aisle-runner, cushioned pews, and florist bouquets. The bride posed confidently in a beautiful gown, the groom in a tuxedo. A professional photographer captured each moment.

Our youngest daughter was married in a tree-lined park nestled on the shores of a lake. Balloons, streamers, and wildflowers fluttered in the breeze. The casually-dressed bride walked down a grassy "aisle" to join her khaki-dressed groom. Guests, with their own cameras, captured the day on film. If there had been a problem at either wedding, I'm sure, as the mother of the bride, I would have been called upon to "fix it."

Mary, a hands-on mom, became aware of a problem at the wedding she and her Son were attending. She turned to Jesus to "fix" the beverage shortage, and Jesus granted her request. After all, He cared about weddings. His future ministry would demonstrate how the love of a man for a woman so aptly symbolizes God's love for His bride, the church.

Heavenly Father, may each wedding or anniversary celebration remind me of Your precious love for Your Church. In Jesus' name I pray. Amen.

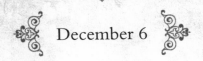

When Appearances Deceive

So when they met together, they asked him, "Lord, are you at this time going to restore the kingdom to Israel?" (Acts 1:6).

Scripture: Acts 1:6-14

Daddy took his 3-year-old daughter fishing. Wanting to shield her from the unpleasantness of baiting the hook, he did it out of her sight. Then . . . *plunk!* He dropped the line in the water and handed Kaylee the pole.

At the slightest movement of the bobber, Kaylee begged, "I wanna see the fish!" Her impatience grew each time she drew in the line and found only a wiggly worm. Finally, exasperated, she scolded her father: "Daddy! Stop catching *worms!*"

Kaylee's confusion came from her misinterpretation of the facts. "Confused" may describe how the disciples felt as they watched Jesus ascend into the clouds. Through-out Jesus' ministry, the disciples thought they knew how His story would end. They had seen Jesus honored and scorned, crucified and resurrected. Now, perhaps, He would claim His kingdom on earth. Their shortsightedness caused them to jump to the wrong conclusion.

Jesus worked behind the scenes to fulfill His Father's plan. Only after the disciples spent time praying and growing in the Spirit would they understand—Jesus' kingdom was not of this world.

God, forgive me when I jump to the wrong conclusions about Your plans. Help me trust You, even when I don't understand. Through Christ, amen.

The Promise to Come

Mary said: "My soul glorifies the Lord and my spirit rejoices in God my Savior" (Luke 1:46, 47).

Scripture: Luke 1:46-55

In the middle of a typical 1950s December, my mother's due date approached. I would be born any day! Winters then were what we now call "old-fashioned." Snow fell thick and deep early in the season and lingered until late spring. Not an ideal time to live in an isolated farmhouse, on an unpaved road, with a baby due!

With my birth imminent, my 9- and 10-year-old sisters bundled up in heavy coats and trudged a mile to use the neighbor's phone. From there they could summon the country doctor. Thankfully, the doctor arrived before I did. My mother praised the Lord for the safe, home delivery of her early Christmas gift.

Growing up, I was teased about having a birthday so close to Christmas. Did I feel shortchanged because my presents came wrapped in Christmas paper? Not at all. There were songs and celebrations, star-filled skies, and miracles waiting to unfold at each birthday. It is an honor to celebrate my birthday so close to that of my Lord's. With Mary, my soul rejoices in the promised gift of God.

My Lord God, thank You for the gift of Your Son and for a mother who taught me how much You love me. May I be faithful in passing on what I have learned of Your goodness and grace. In the name of the Father, the Son, and the Holy Spirit, I pray. Amen.

Heavenly Visitors

Abraham hurried into the tent (Genesis 18:6).

Scripture: Genesis 18:1-8

While Abraham meditated on the Lord, he realized that heavenly visitors had arrived. He asked his wife, Sarah, to make cakes. Then he ran to fetch a calf for a meal, since he was anxious to extend generous hospitality.

In my younger years, I thought I had to make a homemade dessert and serve several dishes when we had friends over for a visit. But after working outside the home for several years, I've learned to prepare more simple dishes. We can still offer wonderful hospitality to a few friends. But there are limits to how often we can entertain—and the amount of preparation I can do. Yet the fellowship is always worth the effort.

Abraham's visitors had a message for him that would change his life. As we have opened our home to missionaries, ministers, and other visitors, my perspective on life has broadened too. My life is richer because of these friends who have shared a cup of coffee or a meal. In fact, we've sometimes wondered if a few of them weren't also heavenly visitors.

Lord, as I spend time before You in prayer, remind me that I can bless and be blessed by my fellowship with other believers. And may our fellowship always take precedence over the details of the meal! In Jesus' name, amen.

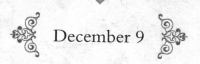

December 9

At the Appointed Time

Is anything too hard for the LORD? I will return to you at the appointed time next year (Genesis 18:14).

Scripture: Genesis 18:9-14

The Lord said He would return "at the appointed time." And the Lord did visit Sarah as He said, and He did unto Sarah as He had spoken: she had a son, Isaac. God fulfills His promises at His pre-appointed time.

My sister, Dot, says that God sometimes waits until her prayer seems beyond the hope of an answer. Then He so often brings an *unexpected* answer. She also taught me about God's perfect timing when she shared her concept of how God sees our circumstances. Dot calls it His "panoramic vision." From a panoramic X-ray, a dentist can determine whether wisdom teeth are forming and if any of them will need to be extracted. He can also see decay that might be hidden from the natural eye.

We usually trust the dentist's wisdom regarding the timing of any needed dental surgery. So perhaps I could learn to trust God's evaluation of what He sees coming my way. Then I could more fully trust His timing for the answer to each prayer—whether it's "yes," "no," or "wait"—instead of clinging so tightly to my own expectations.

All-seeing God, help me trust Your timing for bringing Your promises to pass. You know best when I need something, because You have a good plan for my entire life! Thank You, in Jesus' name. Amen.

_____

_____

_____

_____

_____

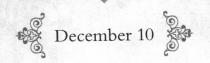

December 10

While We Obey

And it came to pass, that, while he executed the priest's office before God . . . (Luke 1:8, *King James Version*).

Scripture: Luke 1:5-11

Everyone knew about, but no one mentioned, the large round lump on Mrs. Robbin's cheek. It was slightly smaller than a tennis ball, but her doctors would not try to remove it because the tumor's roots spread into her ear.

For years she asked for prayer that God would heal this condition, but nothing happened. So she went about raising her large family, teaching Sunday school, and being a faithful Christian.

One Wednesday night we noticed a large, flat patch over the place where Robbie's lump had been. Robbie said that two days before, she saw a bit of fluid leaking from the site. Then, for days, the place seeped what appeared to be tissue and the roots of the tumor.

Her children had never seen their mom without the lump on her cheek. Everyone rejoiced because of the change. We also noted that this miracle didn't happen because Robbie did, or did not do, a certain thing. It didn't seem to happen as a result of a certain person's faith. But as Robbie continued to be faithful, God was at work in her life.

Gracious Heavenly Father, when I wonder whether You have heard my prayers, remind me that You are constantly working in me. As I stay faithful in my own calling, You are faithful as well. In Jesus' name, amen.

_____

_____

_____

_____

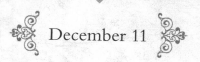

December 11

Expectation of Joy

Thou shalt have joy and gladness; and many shall rejoice at his birth (Luke 1:14, *King James Version*).

Scripture: Luke 1:12-20

When we first moved to Ohio, my husband (who grew up in Minnesota) routinely watched the weather forecast in the wintertime. We were at the home of friends one evening when he looked out and saw it snowing. He grew very serious and said, "We'd better head for home."

I was raised in Michigan—familiar with driving in snow and ice—so I did not understand his constant expectation that the weather would make the roads impassable. His experience with Minnesota blizzards and snow drifts six feet high caused him to expect and prepare for the worst.

Our expectations often flow from our past experiences. Perhaps this is why some people have difficulty expecting blessings from God; they just aren't used to seeing things turn out for the good.

We, who know the promises of God's Word, can choose to believe for the best and blessed outcome. Why? Because God is faithful. He loves to bring joy and gladness to us. His plan for us is a good plan. Look for, and expect, joy.

Faithful God in Heaven, forgive me for anticipating less than You desire for me. Raise the level of my expectations. And help me to know Your joy, in the good times and in the times of trial. I pray this prayer in the name of Jesus, my merciful Savior and Lord. Amen.

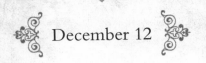

December 12

He Looks upon Me

He looked on me, to take away my reproach among men (Luke 1:25, *King James Version*).

Scripture: Luke 1:21-25

A mother brought her 14-year-old daughter before a TV "judge," stating that the daughter intentionally dressed in a way that would cause men to lust for her. The judge wisely sent the girl to a couple of women who would serve as role models. They'd show her how she could dress more modestly (and thus become more truly attractive as a young lady). After this encounter, the teenager actually changed her attitude. And she instantly began to enjoy more self-respect.

I grew up in a day when dressing modestly was highly valued. Yet, I have come to realize that even though my outer appearance does reflect my inner person to some degree, God looks deeper. He sees my heart.

God sees me individually, viewing even my stresses and temptations, my dreams and longings. Yes, He sees my faults and failures, but the Holy One delights in giving me a deeper measure of abundant life. If only I will open my heart to Him, day by day, I need never suffer any form of reproach.

All-seeing God, help me to live my life in a way that brings You pleasure when You see me. Then help me to keep the intent of my heart pure so that others can see beyond my weaknesses and failures to the glory of Your presence within me. In the name of Your Son, my Savior, I pray. Amen.

_____

_____

_____

_____

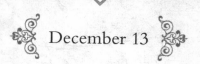

December 13

Believing the Unexplainable

Blessed is she that believed: for there shall be a performance of those things which were told her from the Lord (Luke 1:45, *King James Version*).

Scripture: Luke 1:39-45

Did Mary fully comprehend the prophesy Elisabeth proclaimed? She may not have understood it with her mind; however, she believed it in her heart.

As we neared retirement, my husband and I knew we couldn't continue to maintain the home we enjoyed. Then our older son shared with us that he and his wife wanted us to live near them; thus, they could help whenever we needed some assistance. We thought they'd get a larger home with property where we might put a small trailer-home for us. But God had a bigger idea.

The beginning of a new chapter in our lives started as we moved into a large home with a suite of two rooms and bath just for the two of us. We share the rest of the house with my son's family, and I even share an upstairs office with my grandson, Joshua.

We know there's a purpose here. Far beyond our comfort and enjoyment, we feel that God has more in mind than we imagined. Already God is bringing in visitors whose lives need to be touched by His love through us.

__God of abundance,__ thank You for provision that seemed unbelievable. Help me continually believe You for blessings—that we might pass on the overflow to those whose lives need refreshing. In Jesus' name, amen.

_____

_____

_____

_____

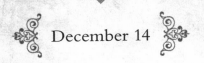

December 14

Rejoice with Your Neighbor

And her neighbors and her cousins heard how the Lord had showed great mercy upon her; and they rejoiced with her (Luke 1:58, *King James Version*).

Scripture: Luke 1:57-63

My little puppy, Poco, had to do a lot of adjusting when we moved in with my son's family and his two cats. Poco handled it all fairly well, but every time she began to eat from her dog dish, Mattie Cat would pounce at her. Even though there were different food dishes and plenty of food, Mattie seemed to begrudge any intruder in her home.

Sometimes people are like that. Though God's mercies and blessings are abundant, some want it all for themselves. Don't we know there is plenty for everyone?

I once felt jealous about a great blessing someone else received. But the Lord seemed to remind me: maybe that person *needed* the small miracle—and the Lord had trusted me to be faithful *without* a miracle. I think about it often and am humbled by God's goodness toward me.

Can we rejoice when our brothers and sisters are blessed? Can we enjoy watching others receive good things? God has allowed the blessings. Let us rejoice with those who receive such goodness from His hand.

God, when You abundantly bless another, help me enjoy Your generosity to them. Whether or not I receive the same good thing, grow me into a maturity that allows heartfelt celebration with them. In Jesus' name, amen.

_____

_____

_____

_____

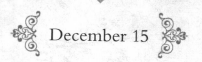

What Lies Ahead?

Declaring the end from the beginning, And from ancient times things which have not been done, Saying, "My purpose will be established, And I will accomplish all My good pleasure" (Isaiah 46:10, *New American Standard Bible*).

Scripture: Isaiah 46:8-13

My wife and I have lived in eight states since we were married in 1950, and even lived twice in Minnesota. Why did we move so much? I changed jobs, even careers, and attended three different universities in three states, earning graduate degrees in two of them.

Yes, we moved constantly, and enjoyed every place where we landed. Yet I believe the Lord has orchestrated all of our life experiences ultimately for *His* pleasure. For example, in our last move we left jobs in Missouri in order to attend a church in Oklahoma, where we have lived for over 20 years.

God knows the end from the beginning, but can we depend on Him to lead us in the most practical daily decisions of our lives? He directs us for His pleasure; therefore, let us enjoy bringing a smile to His face through all our words and deeds. And as we consider our next move, may we ask first how it might bring Him glory.

Heavenly Father, I thank You that You have led me in paths for Your pleasure. In the name of Christ I pray. Amen.

_____

_____

_____

_____

_____

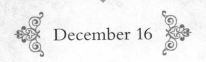

December 16

The Lord's Beauty

The earth is the LORD's, and all its fullness, The world and those who dwell therein. For He has founded it upon the seas, And established it upon the waters (Psalm 24:1, 2, *New King James Version*).

Scripture: Psalm 24

In July of 1963 my wife and I traveled to Wisconsin to visit relatives. Even though I had lived there several years before, this time I especially noticed the beauty of the strip cropping in southwest Wisconsin. I saw the golden yellow of the oats, alternating with the corn and alfalfa, each revealing its own distinctive shade of green.

Yes, when we farmed in Wisconsin, we planted the crops but the Lord, through His provision of rain, sun, seasons, and soil made them grow. And the earth, the crops, livestock, trees, and grass—all proclaim His power and glory. Looking at His works we can discern, at least to some degree, the character of our Almighty Lord.

But in order to appreciate the handiwork of God, we often need to step back from our own busyness. To appreciate the beauty of the earth, it's time to look around a bit! And to appreciate the beauty of the persons whom the Lord has placed in our world—"those who dwell therein"—we may well need to stop and make a friend.

> *Great God of Creation, I thank You that You have made a beautiful earth for me to enjoy—and for my eyes to behold. When I look, let me truly see! In the holy name of Jesus, my Lord and Savior, I pray. Amen.*

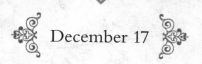

December 17

From Rags to Riches

He raises the poor out of the dust, And lifts the needy out of the ash heap (Psalm 113:7, *New King James Version*).

Scripture: Psalm 113

I was born and raised on a dairy and hog farm in southern Wisconsin during the depression. As a family, by many standards, we were poor. But we never considered ourselves in that light.

The depression of the 1930s forced my dad and other farmers to hang on tightly to their farms. So we always had milk, eggs, chicken, pork, and a big garden to sustain us. And on Saturday nights we went to town to "trade" our eggs for many of our groceries.

For seven years, I attended a one-room country school. Then because of my father's poor health, we moved to a small city. I was too young to even dream of getting a graduate degree. But years later I was blessed with the opportunity to attend college, eventually earning a PhD.

Who would guess a product of a country school would earn a doctorate from Michigan State? Yet it all unfolded, step by step, by God's gracious, lifting hand. And isn't that the way it is with all things in our lives, even our salvation? As an old offertory sentence says: "All things come of thee, O Lord, and of Thine own have we given thee."

God who lifts me up, I praise You that by Your grace I can look forward to daily blessings under Your care. In the precious name of Jesus, amen.

_____

_____

_____

_____

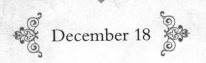

December 18

Let It Rain

Fire and hail, snow and clouds; Stormy wind, fulfilling His word (Psalm 148:8, *New American Standard Bible*).

Scripture: Psalm 148

Oh, those rainy days of June in Wisconsin! Why did it seem to rain so often when we finally had our hay cut and raked? Could we discern the coming weather to time our haying between the rains? Well, sometimes. Yet all the crops needed the rain. The snow, hail, and clouds with rain all came at the appointed time under the sovereignty of God.

I have gardened most of the years of my life, even planted gardens in seven states. And sometimes, just when I planned to work in the garden, God would send His rain.

But let us praise the Lord for rain to water the gardens and the grass. It falls according to the great cycles of weather that He set in motion from the beginning of creation. The rain and snow fall under His watchful eye.

Of course, He knows what we need better than we do, in order for us to live lives pleasing to Him. He looks for an open-hearted servant, in all kinds of weather, who will drink in His blessings and go forth to do His will.

Lord, I have grown in my appreciation for Your creation, with its weather patterns that work for my good. Help me also to grow in my desire to serve You. You have sprinkled into my life the spiritual gifts to carry out Your work; give me the will to follow through! In Jesus' name, amen.

_____

_____

_____

_____

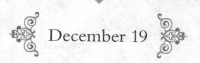

December 19

Dwell in This Reality!

Now is manifested, and by the Scriptures of the prophets, according to the commandment of the eternal God, has been made known to all the nations, leading to obedience of faith (Romans 16:26, *New American Standard Bible*).

Scripture: Romans 16:25-27

The well-known hymn "He Lives" ends with the words, "You ask me how I know He Lives—He lives within my heart."

We'd sung it many times in the churches we had attended up to this point in our lives. We had again sung this song in our local church in Minnesota. Then, in 1974, my wife and I came to Christ in this church.

In a few weeks, we sang the song again. But this time the old hymn came alive to me as it never had before. It no longer meant just a pretty song but a reality in my heart. I now knew Jesus did, indeed, live in my heart. Moreover, the Bible now came alive to me.

Before Jesus' earthly ministry, many believed in a coming Messiah— but to them it meant waiting for a time well into the future. After Pentecost, though, He became a constant reality in the hearts of the believers. Moreover, the apostle Paul wrote of that mystery now manifested, "Christ in you, the hope of glory" (Colossians 1:27). Don't we all seek to dwell in that reality?

__Dear Lord,__ thank You for sending Your Holy Spirit to dwell within me. May He lead me into fruitful service today! In Christ I pray. Amen.

_____

_____

_____

_____

The Miracle of Birth

She brought forth her firstborn son, and wrapped him in swaddling clothes, and laid him in a manger; because there was no room for them in the inn (Luke 2:7, *King James Version*).

Scripture: Luke 2:1-7

While operating our livestock farm in Wisconsin, I helped with the births of dairy calves, pigs, and lambs. I also witnessed the miracle of birth with foals, puppies, chicks, and goslings. I often marveled at the providence of God in all these births. The mammals brought forth their newborn in similar ways, but with the chicks and goslings, God appointed them to peck their ways to life out of their shells.

The Bible tells us of no midwife or relative or other people present at the birth of Jesus, except for the shepherds who visited after His birth. But Jesus was born at the appointed time, the appointed place, the appointed way, of the appointed person.

No birth has ever compared to the Incarnation—the awesome miracle of God himself taking on human flesh to save the world from sin. There wasn't quite room for Him in the local hotels of Bethlehem. But I am so thankful that we can make room for Him in our hearts at a moment's notice. It is as simple as turning our eyes to meet His loving gaze upon us.

Father, the birth of Your Son transformed the cosmos. May it also powerfully affect my words and deeds this day. Through Christ my Lord, amen.

_____

_____

_____

_____

_____

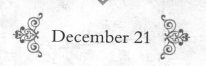

God's Peace

Glory to God in the highest, and on earth peace, good will toward men (Luke 2:14, *King James Version*).

Scripture: Luke 2:8-20

Living in Farmington, Minnesota, and seeking employment, I sent my résumé to a company in Cedar Falls, Iowa. Soon they asked me to come for an interview.

When I arrived in the city, I stopped in a convenience store to ask directions. The lady at the counter told me the company was in the exporting business. I wondered, "What could I do at such a company? Would it even interest me?"

But the Lord gave me peace during the daylong interview. And the job prospect excited me. Furthermore, the Lord gave me peace about accepting the position.

That work as an agricultural commodity market analyst turned out to be the most interesting and rewarding job of my career. I could fully integrate my farm background with my education to accomplish important work.

God's peace comes to our earth, our very being, in the midst of our everyday living. Through it, we can extend good will to all with whom we work and live. It is a commodity in short supply these days—yet God offers it in abundance.

Dear Father in Heaven, help me actively pursue Your peace for my life as You make it available. Help me to pass Your peace on to my family and friends. In the name of Jesus, Lord and Savior of all, I pray. Amen.

_____

_____

_____

December 22

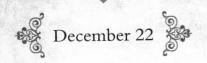

Dressed the Part

What did you go out to see? A man dressed in fine clothes? (Luke 7:25).

Scripture: Luke 7:24-29

Of all the people who stepped off the small plane onto the tarmac, he was the last man I thought to be our guest. With his face half-covered by a shaggy beard and dressed in jeans, T-shirt, a worn cowboy hat, and boots, he walked forward with an extended hand and a big smile. This was our church's missionary speaker for the week? (And did I mention his earring?)

When John the Baptist came as a herald announcing the ministry of the Lord Jesus Christ, he didn't look anything like people expected. He showed up dressed in "clothing made of camel's hair" (Mark 1:6). He didn't *act* in accord with their expectations either. He wasn't a "reed swayed by the wind" (v. 24), but a man who spoke the truth plainly. And Jesus commended him for it.

Will the Lord someday commend me as one who fulfilled His expectations? Will He joyfully declare I lived in accord with His will? Will He one day say to me, "Well done, good and faithful servant" (Matthew 25:21)?

Lord, help me to act, dress, and speak as one who lives in daily obedience to You. I pray that I'll not do or say anything today that brings shame to Your name or pain to Your heart. In Jesus' name, amen.

_____

_____

_____

_____

_____

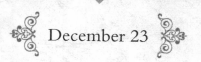

December 23

Simulated Sunlight

He himself was not the light; he came only as a witness to the light (John 1:8).

Scripture: John 1:6-9

When Doug built a room-within-a-room in his basement, he didn't want the finished product to feel or look like a windowless dungeon. So he constructed "windows" of opaque acrylic on one wall. He hung attractive window shades and suspended lights behind the faux windows. Now, with the flick of a switch, he has the illusion of sunlight blazing through from just outside his below-ground sanctuary.

John the Baptist didn't appear haphazardly on the scene before Jesus began His earthly ministry. He "was sent from God" (v. 6) and came as a witness to the true light. John the Baptist and the apostle John, who wrote this Gospel, both affirmed that only Jesus is "the true light that gives light to every man" (v. 9). This was no illusion or simulation. As predicted, the "sun of righteousness" (Malachi 4:2) had come at last.

For those days when we're in the dark—when we don't understand what's happening around us—we can still know that our source of light and love is with us. Our shining, everlasting Savior is the real thing.

God of light, thank You for sending Jesus, my greatest source of light, love, and life. Let me be a clear window through which He shines brightly. In His name I pray. Amen.

_____

_____

_____

_____

_____

Humble Pie

He is the one who comes after me, the thongs of whose sandals I am not worthy to untie (John 1:27).

Scripture: John 1:19-28

As a self-assured young man, Dick lived his life recklessly. Then he lost his left arm in a car accident.

Recovering in the hospital, he told his doctor, "I'll be OK; I'll manage." His doctor barely looked up from his chart. "Is that so? Wait until you try to tie your shoes for the first time."

Dick quickly learned humility. He wears slip-on shoes or shoes with self-adhesive straps. Because of his humbling accident, Dick isn't able to tie his—or anyone else's—shoes.

In humble honesty, John the Baptist said he would never presume to even untie the sandals of Jesus. He recognized Jesus as the one and only God-man. And the Baptist admitted he was only "the voice"; Jesus was the Lord of all (v. 23).

I've not had a humbling experience as painful and life-changing as Dick has suffered—nor do I want one. When I read about John the Baptist, I realize I wouldn't be worthy to untie *his* sandals! But I want to learn from John's example and live a life of humble service.

Lord over all, teach me to live a life of service and humility. To regard others as better than myself. To be honest about who I am and who You are. In the powerful name of Jesus I pray. Amen.

_____

_____

_____

_____

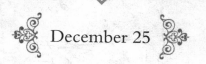

December 25

He's Here

The next day John saw Jesus coming toward him and said, "Look, the Lamb of God, who takes away the sin of the world!" (John 1:29).

Scripture: John 1:29-34

Their daughter, an Air Force nurse, wouldn't be home for Christmas. At first she couldn't get leave. When she did, there were no flights.

But the nurse's sister had a plan. "See if you can get a flight into Detroit. It would only be an hour's drive for us—and a great surprise for Mom and Dad." When nurse Nancy surprised her parents on Christmas, their happy cry rang out: "She's here!"

To the shepherds, the angel announced the arrival of "a Savior . . . Christ the Lord" (Luke 2:11). Some 30 years later, John the Baptist declared this Savior had come and was starting His ministry. Jesus was "the Lamb of God" and "the Son of God" (vv. 29, 34). Just as the angels had proclaimed to the shepherds, so John announced to his hearers: "He's here!"

We too may anticipate our Savior's coming. We can look forward to the day when "the Lord himself will come down from heaven" (1 Thessalonians 4:16). That will be a coming like no other.

Almighty and everlasting Father, I praise You for coming to earth on that first Christmas in the person of Jesus. Thank You that someday He will return as promised. Come, Lord Jesus, I pray! Amen.

_____

_____

_____

_____

_____

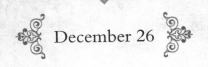

December 26

Tell the Truth

You have sent to John and he has testified to the truth (John 5:33).

Scripture: John 5:30-35

Not long ago a woman in our community called 9-1-1. She told the police she had been kidnapped, but escaped. She was now alone in the park. Could the police come and rescue her?

The police rescued her . . . but they also investigated her story. No one could validate the alleged victim's account, because it never happened. She made up the story.

Jesus always told the truth. He claimed to *be* the Truth (John 14:6), and He said there were two others to testify to the truth of what He said. One was His Father; the other was John the Baptist (see John 5:37 and the verse above).

Christ knew that the people He spoke to esteemed John. So He cited John's truthful testimony about Him.

When others look at my life, I want it to give testimony to the truth of who Jesus is. I don't need to make up stories for attention. Jesus Christ has given me a life worth living, and I am happy to share about it. Like the old hymn says, this is my story—and I want to praise my Savior all day long.

God of all truth, help me be a person who always tells the truth. Help me to be honest in my work and in my relationships. Let my life be a reflection of the truth that is in your Son, the one who loves me and lives within me. I pray in His precious name, amen.

_____

_____

_____

_____

_____

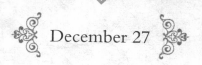
Friend of the Groom

The friend who attends the bridegroom waits and listens for him, and is full of joy when he hears the bridegroom's voice. That joy is mine, and it is now complete (John 3:29).

Scripture: John 3:22-30

Their friendship began when they were both cadets at the US Naval Academy. Now the best man raised his soda bottle to toast his friend and his new bride. He was obviously proud and happy for the newlyweds at the table with him.

"To the happy couple," he began, "on this day I thought would never come!" (And the parents of the beautiful, 30-something bride couldn't have agreed more!)

In today's Scripture reading, the ministry of John the Baptist is coming to a close. His disciples whine that Jesus is baptizing and seems to be drawing everyone over to Him. Yet John shows no regret or sorrow. He tells his disciples that his joy was now complete. He'll now be content to fade into obscurity while the Christ rises to prominence.

We too can be like John. Others can see our lives, our encouraging words and good works, and rejoice in our Savior. It's a privilege like no other to witness to Christ's excellence with our own lives. Just like being the best man at a long-awaited wedding.

Dearest Lord, thank You for my special relationship with You. I praise Your Son, Jesus, because He's both bridegroom and friend. Thank You that I can share all my joys with Him. I pray in His precious name, amen.

_____

_____

_____

_____

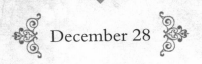

December 28

Does the Walk Match the Talk?

Produce fruit in keeping with repentance. And do not begin to say to yourselves, "We have Abraham as our father." For I tell you that out of these stones God can raise up children for Abraham (Luke 3:8).

Scripture: Luke 3:7-18

When Mark was a boy, he got together with his friends for some destructive "fun." With rocks in hand, they broke a number of windows in their school building. They never got caught and never "ratted" on each other. But when Mark became a Christian years later, he knew he should make amends.

Imagine the surprise when he went to the board of education, confessed to his boyhood vandalism, and insisted on paying for the windows he had broken! The board accepted payment 20 years after the fact.

God cares that we show the genuineness of our repentance in measurable, observable acts of restitution. He cares little if we're royals or commoners. The Lord says we can't rest on our bloodline or ancestry to impress Him. If He wants, He can make people from stones.

If we have plenty, we're to be generous. If we're soldiers, we're to be content with our pay. If we're CPAs, we're to be honest in business. And if we've broken windows, we're to pay for them.

Father, I've not always done right. Help me demonstrate the genuineness of my faith by righting my wrongs when I can. In Christ's name, amen.

_____

_____

_____

_____

_____

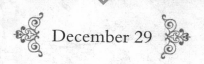

Mistaken Blame

He that backbiteth not with his tongue, . . . nor taketh up a reproach against his neighbor (Psalm 15:3, *King James Version*).

Scripture: Psalm 15

"I think she's guilty," I said, with an emphases on *guilty*. She was the new girl in the dorm, and now we were missing various small items. To me, all evidence pointed to Beth. We didn't have a problem before she moved in, so I concluded it must be her. I slandered Beth with harsh words and spoke against her reputation.

I was wrong, of course, but it was too late to take back my accusations. Beth eventually forgave me, but the damage caused many tears.

Jesus said we are to love our neighbors as ourselves. We are not to speak evil or defame them. God wants us to think the best of our fellow Christians and encourage, uplift, and enlighten with our words.

We are not perfect, nor can we be. Thankfully, God sent His Son to the cross to pay for our imperfections. However, should we not examine ourselves to see whether we truly love our neighbor as Jesus commanded?

Heavenly Father, thank You for loving and forgiving me. As You have loved me, teach me to love others. I love You, Lord, and want others to see You through me. Give me grace to love my neighbor, to understand, and not be judgmental of others. In His holy name. Amen.

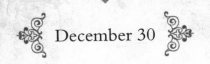

December 30

I Can Do This

The LORD is my light and my salvation; whom shall I fear? The LORD is the strength of my life; of whom shall I be afraid? (Psalm 27:1, *King James Version*).

Scripture: Psalm 27:1-6

Aunt Neil smiled at me. "Don't worry. God and I can do this." Because of a childhood accident, my aunt was blind. Since the age of 9, she had depended heavily on others. Now, she wanted a guide dog and independence. But she would have to fly to Columbus, Ohio, without family, to train with her dog for six weeks.

When she returned with her dog, she said: "See, I told you God and I could do this." Her faith demonstrated that God was in control of her life.

Doubt comes to all Christians at one time or another. I worried about Aunt Neil traveling, but she knew she would not be alone. God would be with her. He heard her prayer, and she was certain she was in His care. Her trust was complete.

Paul learned to be content in whatever circumstance he faced. He was stoned, shipwrecked, imprisoned, and starved; still, he trusted in the Lord.

I would love to follow his example. Wouldn't you?

Dear Lord, I pray that the eyes of my heart may see as clearly as Aunt Neil's could see. Let me not be blinded by the things I see, but let me see by faith. Thank You that I can always trust Your promises. I pray this prayer in the name of Jesus, my merciful Savior and Lord. Amen.

_____

_____

_____

_____

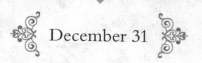

December 31

The Shepherd's Care

He maketh me to lie down in green pastures: he leadeth me beside the still waters (Psalm 23:2, *King James Version*).

Scripture: Psalm 23

Did you know that sheep fear swiftly moving waters? They require quiet waters or streams, because if their wool becomes wet it will pull them under—and they can't swim! Also, they must change pastures often because they eat the grass so close to the root that it needs a chance to grow again.

And sheep require constant care relying heavily on the shepherd. As long as the sheep follow their shepherd, they will have their needs met. He is an expert and knows the best places for food and water. The shepherd carries olive oil as a remedy for the injured or scratched lambs.

The Lord, our Shepherd, cares for us in the way a shepherd cares for his sheep. He sees that we have our basic needs met and often blesses abundantly above them.

Sometimes we focus only on our wants instead of our needs. Our Shepherd isn't holding things back from us. But just as sheep can overeat and suffer illnesses or death, so we often desire things that will hurt us.

The Shepherd gave His life for His sheep; we can trust Him for our needs.

Father God, thank You for the green pastures and still waters in my life. I trust You for my care and protection. Please, help me always recognize the difference between my wants and my needs. In Jesus' name, amen.

_____

_____

_____

_____